# ARCHETYPAL PATTERNS
# IN WOMEN'S FICTION

# ARCHETYPAL PATTERNS IN WOMEN'S FICTION

## ANNIS PRATT

WITH

*Barbara White*
*Andrea Loewenstein*
*Mary Wyer*

INDIANA UNIVERSITY PRESS

BLOOMINGTON

*Frontispiece by Edouard Sandoz from* Greek Myths *by Olivia Coolidge.
Copyright 1949 and © renewed 1977 by Olivia E. Coolidge. Reprinted by
permission of Houghton Mifflin Company. Quotations from* To the Lighthouse *by Virginia Woolf, copyright 1927 by Harcourt Brace Jovanovich,
Inc., renewed 1955 by Leonard Woolf, are reprinted by permission of the
publisher, the Author's Literary Estate, and The Hogarth Press.*

Manufactured in the United States of America

Library of Congress Cataloging in Publication Data
Pratt, Annis.
  Archetypal patterns in women's fiction.

  Bibliography: p.
  Includes index.
  1. English fiction—Women authors—History and
criticism.   2. American fiction—Women authors—History
and criticism.   3. Myth in literature.   4. Women and
literature.   5. Sex role in literature.   I. Title.
PR830.W62P7        823'.009'9287        81-47167
ISBN 0-253-10252-9                      AACR2
ISBN 0-253-20272-8 pbk.     2 3 4 5 85 84 83 82

Our best-remembered teachers are the tough ones,
who discipline our intellects for the longest journeys.

*Bring me my Bow of burning gold,*
*Bring me my Arrows of desire,*
*Bring me my Spear! O clouds unfold!*
*Bring me my Chariot of fire!*

*I will not cease from Mental Fight,*
*Nor shall my Sword sleep in my hand,*
*Till we have built Jerusalem*
*In England's green & pleasant land.*
—WILLIAM BLAKE

# Contents

# Preface and Acknowledgments

During the nearly three hundred years that women have been writing works of fiction, they have constructed a body of material that manifests a considerable degree of continuity, a uniformity of concern, and an abundance of analogue in both subject and method. At the outset of this study I decided to look closely at a significant number of novels by women and determine if these works constituted a field that could be investigated as a self-contained entity following its own organic principles. As I wrote the book, it became clear that the material yielded patterns derived both from the world shared with men and with male writers and from a core of feminine self-expression and assertion very often at odds with that world. The ways that the heroes of the woman's novel came into contact and conflict with the roles proffered them, even when they internalized those roles into their own self-expectations, seemed to determine distinctive elements of plot, characterization, image, and tone that are of interest in delineating the world of women's fiction.

The principles by which I selected the novels that constitute my material were neither wholly scientific nor wholly random but consisted quite simply in reading the widest possible range of novels that my students, coauthors, and I could absorb and analyze. First, I consulted what women's literary histories I could find and looked into both major and minor figures described, in most cases going back to read the novels afresh. Second, I consulted general literary histories and bibliographies of fiction by periods and themes, reading as many of the women's novels mentioned as I could locate. Third, I collected recommendations of lost or forgotten women authors from fellow scholars in the workshops, forums, and seminars of the professional conventions that I attended, as well as from scholars and students with whom I was in correspondence. Finally, I haunted the shelves of the University of Wisconsin—Madison Memorial Library, the Wayne State University Purdy Library, and the Detroit Public Library, hoping to fill in any significant gaps with a shelf-to-shelf survey. Not all of the novels that we read are mentioned in this study since to do so would have involved far too many pages; my intention here is not to describe the field as a whole after the manner of a literary historian but to analyze the patterns that the field suggests as common to women's fiction in the two countries in question. I was able to compress my analyses further because, during the period of composition of this volume, a number of literary histories of women's writings appeared, dealing principally with major writers. Since Elaine Showalter's *A Literature of Their Own*, Ellen Moers's *Literary Women*, and Patricia Meyer Spacks's *The Female Imagination* demonstrate many of the same patterns that I found, I decided in my final draft to condense my treatment of major women novelists and to focus on the minor ones whose works yield patterns interestingly parallel to those better known.

The question of whether women's fiction is of a nature distinct from men's cannot be fully answered, of course, without a systematic novel-by-novel comparison of samples from each. Should I have attempted such a comparison in this study, however, I would have become involved in an endless "Key to All Mythologies," so it was for purposes of brevity as well as out of a desire to examine women's fiction totally in relationship to itself that I have turned away from the intriguing subject of its relationship to the male genre. As is appropriate to both literary histories and archetypal analysis, moreover, I have left the question of taste out of this study in the interests of making the field as a whole available to the reader. To this same end, I have chosen at times to summarize less familiar works of fiction in considerable detail so that the reader may become sufficiently familiar with the texture of the material to test out my conclusions.

I was fortunate at the very outset of this study, in 1970, to come into contact with Florence Howe and to receive the encouragement of the Commission on the Status of Women of the Modern Language Association and of the Women's Caucus of the Midwest Modern Language Association. These two groups have provided many workshops and forums where I have been able to present my hypotheses and exchange both theoretical and bibliographical data with stimulating scholars in the field of feminist criticism. Since a great deal of activity was going on in this new field during the composition of this volume, I have tried as broadly as possible to reflect the findings of other critics and literary historians insofar as they elucidate the nature and history of women's fiction.

The writing of such a book could not have been undertaken without the continued support of the Department of English of the University of Wisconsin—Madison, which enabled me, through a series of grants from the Graduate School, to spend two summers and an entire semester working on the project free of classwork. My co-authors, Barbara White and Andrea Loewenstein, and my editorial assistant, Mary Wyer, contributed above and beyond the call of their duties as research assistants. Other assistants, Andrea Musher and Kris Anderson, brought many details to my attention and were able to help me with the verification and bibliography. The typing of the manuscript was ably undertaken by Barbara Hornick, Jan Wilson, Jane Renneberg, Kathy Reynolds, Karen Wick, and Cindy Townsend.

During the composition of this volume I was stimulated by discussions of women's fiction with many undergraduate classes at the University of Wisconsin—Madison, and I made use of papers and notes given to me by Leslie Ingmanson, Mark Anderson, Janine Struve, Mary Goebel, Meg Seiler, Lindsay Sutherland, Robbie Grossman, Cheryl Dieringer, Laurie Dubrow, Jerry Wilson, and Erica Fishman. In addition, feminist scholars from all over the country, including Mary Anne Ferguson, Elaine Hedges, Florence Howe, Ellen Morgan, Mari Vlastos, Jean Pickering, Roberta Rubenstein, Carolyn Heilbrun, Gloria Kaufman, Grave Ann Hovet, and Margaret McDowell, provided suggestions and ongoing support. Invitations to the campuses of the University of Northern Iowa, Iowa State University, Indiana University at South Bend, Wayne State University, and Eastern Michigan University enabled me to try out my ideas with others in the midwestern region. I owe a debt of gratitude to Audrey Roberts, who took the trouble to read and comment upon early chapters in the book, and an especial thanks to Patricia Jewell McAlexander, Dion Kempthorne, Paula Vadeboncoeur, Agate Krouse, Ellen Langhill, Serafina Bathrick, and Jim Bittner, who allowed me to draw upon their doctoral dissertations for valuable insights and material.

Finally, I have benefited all during my work on *Archetypal Patterns in Women's Fiction* from the magnificently androgynous contribution that my husband, Henry Pratt, has made to that rare flower, an equal marriage, and from the delightful growing up of my daughters, Lórien and Faith Pratt, during the book's completion.

# PART I

# THE ROOTS OF SELF

*The new space, then, has a kind of invisibility to those who have not entered it. It is therefore inviolable. At the same time it communicates power which, paradoxically, is experienced both as power of presence and power of absence. It is not political power in the usual sense but rather a flow of healing energy which is participation in the power of being. . . . Instead of settling for being a warped half of a person, which is the equivalent to a self-destructive non-person, the emerging woman is casting off role definitions and moving toward androgynous being.*

MARY DALY, *Beyond God the Father*

# CHAPTER I

# INTRODUCTION

IN THE BOOK OF CLASSICAL MYTHS THAT WE USED IN THE SEVENTH GRADE, there was an illustration that fascinated me: a very handsome, curly-haired man was accosting an apprehensive woman, bending her over backwards with one muscle-bound arm while encircling her waist with the other. Looking closely, I could see that her kneecaps were less smooth than knotted, that below the knees her legs were tree trunks, and that roots were growing out of her toes. Slender branches sprouted at her elbows, and bark encroached on her waistline. Our teacher informed us that the woman was a river nymph named Daphne who was resisting Apollo's advances by turning into a laurel tree. The text explained that Apollo was "in love" with Daphne but that she had sworn to the goddess Artemis that she would remain "unmarried." Since this narrative is similar to the stories of Alpheus and Arethusa, Pan and Syrinx, Zeus and Leda/Io/Europa/Danae and also recurs in a wide variety of folk stories and songs, art, and sculpture, it constitutes one example of a recurrent form, an archetype.

The term *archetype* derives from the Greek *archi*, a beginning or first instance, and *typos*, a stamp, and denotes the primordial form, the original, of a series of variations. This etymology contributes to a confusion between *archetype* and *stereotype*, a printing term designating the original plate from which subsequent imprints are made and connoting an excessively rigid set of generalizations. Carl Gustaf Jung defines archetypes as primordial forms in that they spring from the preverbal realm of the unconscious, where they exist inchoate and indescribable until given form in consciousness. In Jung's definition the recurrent patterns that I consider in this study are archetypal *images*, literary forms that derive from unconscious originals. In cataloguing the patterns that such images assume Jung and his followers have sometimes been accused of stereotyping, of clamping down excessively rigid simplifications upon complex phenomena. Although this certainly occurs with regard to "masculine" and "feminine" qualities,

Jung does not intend his archetypal categories as fixed absolutes. He recognizes that fluidity is a basic characteristic and that a single archetype can be subject to a variety of perceptions, not only from culture to culture but even within a given culture or the mind of a single individual. Archetypes thus constitute images, symbols, and narrative patterns that differ from stereotypes in being complex variables, subject to variations in perception.

Although archetypal narratives endure through the centuries because of the perennial dilemmas they express, the exact nature of these dilemmas can be lost sight of through the process of retelling and transmission. The links between episodes that render them true plots —motivation and causality, for example—are often eroded during the long process of honing and simplification. My textbook's explanation of Apollo's "love" probably owes more to recent concepts of being "in love" or "romantic love" than to the classical concept of this emotion, which reserved it for homoerotic relationships. Additional information, similarly, would help us understand the concepts of "virginity" and "vows to a goddess" informing Daphne's reaction. We can determine that Apollo was worshipped by the Achaeans, a branch of the Indo-Europeans who invaded much of the world during the second millennium B.C. With a highly militarized, patriarchally structured culture, the Achaeans worshipped a pantheon of gods led by Zeus, a thunder divinity, and were convinced of their right to take over the cultures they conquered and impose their way of seeing things upon them. A frequent narrative form that their accounts of invasion assumed was the story of the rape of some local female divinity by a member of their pantheon of gods. Artemis, we learn, is a pre-Achaean sun goddess revered in both the Middle East and pre-Indo-European Greece for her refusal to submit to monogamous union and whose solar powers were usurped by her "twin brother," Apollo. Daphne is a nature deity like many nymphs, Naiads, and numina of forest, stream, and dale, a goddess worshipped by the original inhabitants. Since Daphne means laurel and laurel leaves were chewed by pre-Achaean priestesses to induce oracular powers, our archetype may explain Apollo's usurpation of the sacred mysteries of a goddess, much as he usurped the powers of Gaea after slaying her python at Delphi. True to the ethic of Indo-European gods and heroes, Apollo conquers a territory by raping its goddess, assimilating her magic, and setting himself up in her place.[1] Daphne wishes to protect her body and her sacred places from forced entry and thus turns herself into a tree. Because of her natural magic she remains forever unravished, Apollo forever in the process of ravishing.

We shall see in this study how the narrative represented by Apollo and Daphne, which I have called the rape-trauma archetype, recurs as one of the most frequent plot structures in women's fiction. The presentation of an archetype in subsequent tellings depends upon the cultural bias of the storyteller and varies with the teller's role in her or his culture. A medieval Christian would make Apollo an embodiment of sin and canonize Daphne for purity or, conversely, blame her for tempting him to his downfall. Norman Mailer would be more likely to color the scene with Achaean heroics, cheering Apollo on and hinting that Daphne should relax and enjoy his assault. Doris Lessing, on the other hand, would be more interested in Daphne's state of mind and more likely to savage Apollo for his crassness. This tendency of archetypes to vary in interpretation from culture to culture and author to author makes the archetypal critic's task complex. She must also be very careful to avoid letting her own situation and biases distort her interpretations.

Since I have been accused once or twice of "believing in archetypes," as if this method derived from some freak of religious conversion, I want to reiterate the pragmatic basis of my approach. Archetypal patterns, as I understand them, represent categories of particulars, which can be described in their interrelationships within a given text or within a larger body of literature. A dogmatic insistence upon preordained, invariable sets of archetypal patterns would distort literary analysis: one must not deduce categories down *into* a body of material but induce them *from* images, symbols, and narrative patterns observed in a significantly various selection of literary works. I conceive of archetypal criticism, thus, as inductive rather than deductive, Aristotelian in its concern with things as they are rather than Platonic in suggesting them as derivatives from absolute, universal concepts. The necessity for inductive, rather than deductive, critical reasoning became clear to me when, quite early in this undertaking, I realized that women's fiction was challenging some of my own most cherished presumptions. I had become entangled in an a priori belief that men and women are created equal: considering men's and women's experience essentially similar, I expected to find definite analogues between patterns in women's novels and configurations described by previous archetypal thinkers as typical of human beings in general. When I compared quest patterns described by Jung, Campbell, and Frye to plot structures of women's novels, however, I found more than surface variations in image and plot. After close readings of more than three hundred women's novels I discovered, quite contrary to what I had expected, that even the most conservative women authors create narratives manifesting an acute tension between what any normal human being might desire and what a woman must become. Women's fiction reflects an experience radically different from men's because our drive towards growth as persons is thwarted by our society's prescriptions concerning gender. Whether women authors are conscious of this feminism or force pro femina in their novels or not, or whether they are overtly concerned with being and writing about women, the tension between what Apollo intends and Daphne is willing to accept, between forces demanding our submissions and our rebellious assertions of personhood, characterize far too much of our fiction to be incidental.

I was thus compelled to accept the "otherness" of women within Western culture and to admit a set of hypotheses postulating the source of this alienation as our secondary or auxiliary status in society. I did not need to enter the vexed lists of comparison and contrast between novels by men and women to discover in women's novels a clear sense that we are outcasts in the land, that we have neither a homeland of our own nor an ethnic place within society. Our quests for being are thwarted on every side by what we are told to be and to do, which is different from what men are told to be and to do: when we seek an identity based on human personhood rather than on gender, we stumble about in a landscape whose signposts indicate retreats from, rather than ways to, adulthood. In existential terms, our desire for responsible selfhood, for the achievement of authenticity through individual choice, comes up against the assumption that a woman aspiring to selfhood is by definition selfish, deviating from norms of subservience to the dominant gender. If authenticity depends upon totality of self—the greatest possible exercise of our capacities for significant work, intellectual growth, political action, creativity, emotional development, sexual expression, etc.—then women are supposed to be less than total selves. Sartre's quality of "mauvaise foi," the "bad faith" of avoiding human responsibility, can be chosen by men: for women it is not a matter of choice but a precondition for social acceptance.

Once I accepted our radical alienation, other feminist thinkers quite naturally challenged me for my use of theories developed by male archetypalists: given our position in Western culture, how could methods derived from it be of use in illuminating our literature? The novelistic evidence with which I was concerned made it clear to me that the masculine culture held no monopoly on archetypal patterns: configurations contrary to gender norms, such as the many rape narratives told from the woman hero's point of view, manifest themselves in women's fiction in specifically antagonistic relationship to the male perspective. Male archetypalists, alternately attracted and repelled by "the feminine," had difficulty in getting enough perspective upon it to admit it into their thinking. "It is a foregone conclusion among the initiated," wrote Jung of himself and his fellows, "that men understand nothing of women's psychology as it actually is, but it is astonishing to find that women do not know themselves." Introducing a 1933 study by a disciple, M. Esther Harding, he declares that "in this book it becomes clear that woman also possesses a peculiar spirituality very strange to man. Without knowledge of the unconscious this new point of view, so essential to the psychology of woman, could never have been brought out in such completeness."[2] Harding's "knowledge of the unconscious" derives from Jung and involves her in some blind spots about women, but she easily overcomes these biases as she delves into women's admittedly "strange" and certainly acultural experience. French feminist theoreticians are fond of a process they term "volant," usurping elements of masculine theory useful to them while discarding the biases, and I find it useful to imitate them by taking what we need from standard archetypal theory while ignoring elements useless for the analysis of women's archetypes.

As I shall indicate later in this study, Jung recognizes the power of such specifically feminine archetypes as the Demeter/Kore narrative for women's psychology. I have written elsewhere, however, about what can happen when he applies patterns derived from predominantly masculine materials and seen through a masculine perspective to a woman's dreams and fantasies.[3] The problem arises from inconsistencies in his total system having to do with his definitions of "the masculine" and "the feminine." Although he sees androgyny, involving the transcendence of gender, as a necessary element in human development, his definitions of these gender qualities tend to be rigid to the point of stereotyping. In much of his writing the unconscious *is* "female," an inner aspect of the masculine personality, the *anima*. Woman does not possess this inward feminine attribute the way a man does but, rather, the *animus*, an archetype of much less value. Erotic, emotional, and associated with the moon, the *anima*, or soul, provides the male with love, mystery, and the completion of his individuality. Logical, spiritual, and in association with the powerful creativity of the sun when present in the male psyche, the *animus* only makes a woman opinionated, masculine, and shrill. Woman's psychology, according to Jung, "is founded on the principle of Eros, the great binder and deliverer; while age-old wisdom has ascribed Logos to man as his ruling principle."[4] Since woman *is* Eros to the male, she cannot relate to an erotic other on her own or exercise eroticism for her own sake; quite the contrary, she *is* the other in a male configuration of selfhood. Women, in Jung's schema, are either exterior containers for male projections or subordinate elements of the male personality. The feminine quality becomes a prized elixir sought and usurped by the male, to whom real, individual women are objects of use. To Apollo, Daphne is not a deity or even a being in her own right: she is a container of power, a prize of war; as far as Daphne is concerned, the only way to retain her essence is to withdraw from the conflict altogether, leaving Apollo with an armful of bark.

Although Jung discovered many archetypes suggesting feminine power in ancient and non-Western cultures and recognized such figures as Mary and other feminine divinities as of value to his society, only rarely did he describe feminine archetypes as repositories of power useful to women. Like M. Esther Harding, Joseph Campbell followed Jung's footsteps at the outset of his career, making similar assumptions about woman's secondary role in male psychology, only to shift his ground in later studies to affirm the relationship between archetypes of femininity and real women. In his 1949 *Hero with a Thousand Faces* Campbell depicts women as auxiliaries to men, elements to be absorbed in masculine maturation: "woman represents the totality of what can be known. The hero is the one who comes to know." Daphne, in Campbell's early analysis, would represent a prize in Apollo's erotic quest, a goddess who provides the hero with "the supreme acme of sensuous adventure."[5] In his later *Masks of God* series, however, Campbell suggests that such rapes are explanations of Indo-European incursions into territories previously revering goddesses, elements of a widespread and traumatic replacement of agricultural settlements by warlike hordes dedicated to a "phallic moral order." He argues that the earlier Bronze Age cultures were appreciative of women and goddesses, revering them for their association with the seasons, fertility, the phases of the moon, and a universe in which life and death, light and dark, male and female were intricately intertwined. The invading Iron Age cultures, he postulates, were dedicated to the proposition of masculine superiority, allocating all that was good and ethical to themselves and all negative qualities to women. In the polar, either/or reasoning of the Greeks, all that was dark, chthonic, and mysterious belonged to women, while the dominant masculine elite reserved all that was right and good for themselves.[6] This polarism, or tendency toward dichotomous categorization, split Greek society into separate segments to the extent that Eros was considered homoerotic, men had to be forced by the state to marry at age thirty, and women were forbidden to participate in civil life or to appear unveiled on the streets and spent most of their time immured within domestic enclosures.

Insofar as we are the heirs of the Greeks and of the Judeo-Christian tradition, which propounded a similar split between men and women in all aspects of culture, the effects of repressing half of the human personality and devaluing women as the containers of that half remain with us today. Even when biased by education within this dualistic tradition, women scholars are quick to discern the power of feminine archetypes for women's own psychology. Harding starts out in *Woman's Mysteries, Ancient and Modern* (1971) declaring that autonomous women are "abnormal," that they must *be* Eros, providing an "inner moon" to men, and that femininity itself is dark and sinister in quality, "the primordial slime from which life first emerged." It is hardly surprising that feminists should want to throw the book out the window at this point. Harding goes on, however, to outline roots of authentic feminine selfhood in historical norms and customs. Looking back to cultures in which goddesses were revered as the sole powers of fertility and agriculture, she unearths a set of characteristics that deviate significantly from Western gender norms and, in the process, describes archetypes that crop up as subversive elements in a wide sample of women's novels.

Harding describes virginity, for example, as denoting a woman like a man (vir/gyn) in controlling her own body and sexuality. In the ancient world, and even in early patriarchy, she insists, young girls retained freedom over their own bodies until given in marriage: "Under our western patriarchal system the unmarried girl belongs to her father . . . but in earlier days, as still in some primitive communities, she was her own mistress until she married. The right to dispose of her own person until she marries is part of the primitive concept of liberty."[7] The clash between this "concept of liberty" and norms of monogamous, wifely chastity undermines the structure of many women's bildungsromans, or novels of development, accounting for a pervasive imagery of maiming, dwarfing, and suffocating forced upon young girls as part of "coming of age." In chapter 2 I will explore the way that adolescent heroes resist normative restrictions to their liberty by imitating Daphne's retreat into the green world.

In the second part of this book I will turn to the way that women authors treat the domestic enclosures that women accept as a condition of social survival. We shall see how wives' needs for social and economic self-determination, as well as their loss of erotic liberty, disrupt the institution of matrimony in many novels of marriage. Right down through the later years of the Roman Empire, Harding documents, women were free to express a wholly amarital Eros within the precincts of sacred temples where women's cults permitted worship of the goddess. This replenishment of the self for brief and socially disruptive periods also characterizes the behavior of wives in women's fiction, although in nearly every case the characters are severely punished and forced to conform in the denouements. In a study of archetypal patterns one might be expected to concentrate on novels in which authors make deliberate use of myths rather than to devote so much time to apparently nonarchetypal fiction of marriage and social life. My concern with these more conservative and socially accommodationist novels in part 2 of this book derives from my fascination with the way that even the most conformist of women authors admit elements of intellectual, erotic, economic, and spiritual rebellion into their narrative structures.

Perhaps Jung's most important contribution to psychology is his recognition that a fully developed individual personality must transcend gender. His recognition of the destructive effects of excessive masculinity and femininity goes beyond the psychological to the social realm, where he attributes our century of total war to the disjunctions in the repressed personality. Harding's understanding of mature eroticism springs from her similar recognition that love itself can be destroyed by being too "manly" or "womanly." She makes a distinction between immature lovemaking, an auxiliary or passive relationship for a woman who merely completes her partner's "masculinity" by being totally "feminine," and mature Eros, in which these qualities are interchangeable and transcended. The best love, she argues, takes place between persons who have passed through and beyond gender to an androgynous interchange.[8] Such eroticism is by definition antisocial, and as such it creates chaos and confusion in its frequent appearance in the novels of Eros, which I shall treat in part 3. As an expression of authentic being this "mighty deity," as Diotima describes Eros to Socrates, becomes an enabling vehicle in the humanization of both men and women. It is interesting that in the very few novels women have written where an equitable eroticism is achieved they describe it as a new and antisocial state of mind transcending gender.

The final set of archetypes that I shall treat in this study takes the hero at middle life or later through a process of rebirth in which gender becomes one among other elements in the crucible of transformation. In these rebirth novels women authors make more explicit use of feminine archetypes, although many of their elements remain fragmentary. At both ends of the spectrum of novels that I have studied we find women who consciously reject their societies and declare themselves persons in spite of it: young women not yet enclosed, on the one hand, and older women beyond bothering with the domestic enclosure, on the other. For the woman past her "prime," as for the young hero not yet approaching hers, visions of authenticity come more easily than to women in the midst of their social experience.

The task of the archetypal critic becomes complicated by the fact that the novel is a social construct and that women authors internalize gender norms from birth. A battle goes on unremittingly within the heads of most women authors between assumptions about male and female behavior norms and dreams of more gender-free possibilities. It is as if the authorial superego, or censor, preoccupied with proper conduct for women, were constantly repressing subversive desires for self-expression and development. The disjunction between an author's social conscience and her need for selfhood renders characterizations ambivalent, tone and attitude ambiguous, and plots problematic. Long ago, goddesses like Sarasvati in India, Brigid in Britain, and Nidaba in Sumer were credited with the invention of the alphabet and the creation of language and writing; these myths of the origins of culture suggest that gods usurped civilizations along with other feminine powers. We are the heirs, however, of centuries in which women, like words, have been considered symbolic objects of use in a masculine structure, linguistic tokens rather than wielders of words in our own right.[9] When a woman sets out to manipulate language, to create new myths out of old, to write an essay or to paint a painting, she transgresses fundamental social taboos in that very act. In passing I shall take note of the outcries evoked by the mildest of women writers who dared to make even the slightest rebellions against gender norms: to use our drive for authenticity in order to shape feminine archetypes into fiction, to bring elements of our inner world into consciousness and give them shape in the social form of the novel, is an act of defiance with perilous consequences.

Women's fiction manifests alienation from normal concepts of time and space precisely because the presentation of time by persons on the margins of day-to-day life inevitably deviates from ordinary chronology and because those excluded from the *agora* are likely to perceive normal settings from phobic perspectives. Since women are alienated from time and space, their plots take on cyclical, rather than linear, form and their houses and landscapes surreal properties. When we add to all this the fact that feminine archetypes of selfhood have been lost from culture and even consciousness for hundreds of years, we can understand why images and symbols appear as fragments in

women's fiction, encoded indices of a forgotten language, barely deci-
pherable hieroglyphs. My task has been to listen for these signals, to
try to piece them together into more coherent sets and systems by re-
lating them to each other. Somebody seemed to be trying to tell me
something from inside that ancient laurel tree: my difficulties were in
translation.

If Daphne were only being accosted over and over again in women's
novels, if young heroes were forever being dwarfed and our fiction
only echoed their outcries and the muffled sobs of wives entombed in
domestic life, this study would have been too dispiriting to complete.
There were many times during my research and writing, I confess,
when the constant company of mad wives, maimed adolescents, self-
blaming lovers, and dwarfed intellects became too much to bear. The
very desperateness of the outcries, however, and women authors' tendency to look at the worst of women's experiences and to satirize the
social norms that cause them derive from their insistence that there
must be better ways of becoming and better worlds of being. For
three hundred years the woman's novel has been a respository of not
merely horrors but hopes, chronicling historical facts while carrying
out speculative experiments with possibilities unheard of in our recent history. Most inspiring, and most invigorating, are the many
hints about and clues to a power capable even at this late date of
turning our wastelands once again into fruitful orchards where men
and women can walk in amity and equity.

# CHAPTER II

# THE NOVEL OF DEVELOPMENT
## (with Barbara White)

A CONSIDERABLE PORTION OF MYTHOLOGY, RELIGION, AND LITERATURE IS devoted to the quest of the youthful self for identity, an adventure often formalized in a ritual initiation into the mysteries of adulthood. Thus we have, in religion, the young Native American who fasts in the desert in order to learn his or her identity and, in literature, the plot structure in which the young hero sets forth into the world to seek his or her fortune. In fiction this quest for life's meaning shapes the bildungsroman, or novel of development, a genre in which social realism is apt to become mixed with elements of romance. This mixture of real life and fantasy, or genuine social events and imaginary adventures, is appropriate to a fictional genre that delineates a turning point in the hero's life that is of both personal, psychological import and social significance. Since the narratives most often bring the hero from childhood to maturity, moreover, the undertones of the mythic and fantastic are appropriate themes linking the free-ranging imaginative world of childhood to the more soberly social concerns of the adult.

The concept of "adolescence," as a period of some five to seven years following puberty in which a young person learns the roles he or she must play in society, is a fairly recent development, even more recent for girls than for boys. Philippe Ariès, in *Centuries of Childhood*, has pointed out that childhood itself was invented only when schooling became separate for children and adults; this separation did not occur for girls until the late nineteenth century.

Since adolescence, as a period of education, was a late development in concepts of womanhood, many early "coming-of-age" novels were structured around childhood initiation. The many eighteenth- and nineteenth-century women's novels that dealt with feminine conduct became a highly popular way of inculcating the norms of womanhood into young readers, mixing fiction and prescription in a manner that fascinated them while pleasing their parents. These novels prescribed submission to suffering and sadism as an appropriate way to prepare a young girl for life. In Fanny Fern's *Rose Clark* (1856) the six-year-old Rose is maltreated first by the cruel mistress of her orphanage and then by her aunt, who forces her to work long hours, starves her, and locks her in dark rooms. Although one would think that the result of such treatment might be madness, the author reassures us that Rose is receiving valuable lessons in humility and stoicism. Elsie Dinsmore, in Martha Finley's best-selling novel of 1868, is described as having every possible virtue—"respectful to superiors and kind to inferiors and equals, gentle, sweet-tempered, patient, and forgiving to a remarkable degree"—but she is not considered "perfect" because she has "feelings of anger and indignation" when she is unjustly punished. It is not enough for the author that Elsie suppress these feelings—she must learn not to have them at all.

The supreme goal of these novels of development is to groom the young hero for marriage, and whereas younger girls are given tests in submission in a general way, their older sisters are provided with models of behavior appropriate for success in the marriage market. Typical of this genre is Hannah More's *Coelebs in Search of a Wife*, the 1808 publication of which earned the author £12,000. One can assume from the wide sales that the hero, Lucilla Stanley, was seen as the model young woman for marriage:

> Lucilla Stanley is rather perfectly elegant than perfectly beautiful. I have seen women as striking, but I never saw one so interesting [remarks Coelebs]. . . . Her conversation, like her countenance, is compounded of liveliness, sensibility, and delicacy. She does not say things to be quoted, but the effect of her conversation is, that it leaves an impression of pleasure on the mind, and a love of goodness on the heart. She enlivens without dazzling and entertains without overpowering. Contented to please, she has no ambition to shine. There is nothing like effort in her expression, or vanity in her manner. She has rather a playful gaiety than a pointed wit. . . . Taste is indeed the predominating quality of her mind; and she may rather be said to be a nice judge of the genius of others than to be a genius herself.[1]

The series of antitheses places Lucilla on the level of moderation, keeping her from being "too" anything in excess, whether it be beautiful, witty, or bright. Her perfection results from her auxiliary nature, her obvious ability to be content with service to others. She is, to use existential terms, the model "other."

In this most conservative branch of the woman's bildungsroman, then, we find a genre that pursues the opposite of its generic intent—it provides models for "growing down" rather than for "growing up."

This disjunction between the novel of development and the woman's bildungsroman generates the textual ambivalences that characterize the genre when it falls into the hands of more rebellious woman authors. If the author wants to inject some form of protest but nonetheless must conform to her own and her society's concepts of womanhood, she has in prose fiction a number of techniques for voicing her objections while she drowns out their effect. Jane Austen, in *Northanger Abbey* (1798), was able to satirize such prescriptions as More's with textual inversions. When Catharine feels embarrassed about her drawing skills, Austen remarks:

> She was heartily ashamed of her ignorance—a misplaced shame. Where people wish to attach, they should always be ignorant. To come with a well-informed mind, is to come with an inability of administering to the vanity of others, which a sensible person should always wish to avoid. A woman, especially, if she have the misfortune of knowing anything, should conceal it as well as she can. . . . the advantages of natural folly in a beautiful girl have been already set forth by the capital pen of a sister author [a reference to Indiana in Burney's *Camilla*] and to her treatment of the subject I will only add, in justice to men, that though, to the larger and more trifling part of the sex, imbecility in females is a great enhancement of their personal charms, there is a portion of them too reasonable, and too well-informed themselves, to desire anything more in women than ignorance.[2]

Austen has provided normative moralizing ("Where people wish to attach . . . ," "A woman . . . should . . . ," etc.) while ridiculing it with bombast, pretending to be saying one thing while actually saying the opposite. Whether genial or biting, the wit serves to highlight the tensions inherent in the bildungsroman at the same time as it diverts the reader through apparently flippant "amusement."

Authors like Jane Austen, Fanny Burney, and Maria Edgeworth use the ambivalences of dual plotting to satirize excesses in courtship norms by, for example, comparing the hero's pragmatic choice of mate to a less sensible couple in a subplot. The ingénue sets forth into society, pokes fun at characters who may be excessively "male" or "female" in their behavior, sometimes disguises herself or is a victim of mistaken identity, rejects unsuitably chauvinistic suitors, and then chooses a suitable mate. In this way, the authors are able to both criticize marital norms and accommodate them, after the mode of Shakespearian "festive comedy," which combines wit and reconciliation, rebellion and return to the social fold.

The authors' varied attitudes towards young women's social devel-

opment are also reflected in the mix of genres within the broader category of the novel of initiation. In the bildungsroman proper, with its
expectation that the hero is learning to be adult, there is the hidden
agenda of gender norms, where "adult" means learning to be dependent, submissive, or "nonadult." As a result of this conflict, an imagery
of entrapment and fear of psychological invasion introduces a night-
mare element into texts that also, at the opposite extreme, manifest
yearnings for an integration of childhood hopes with adult social possibilities. Although one might expect that as it develops in the twentieth century women's fiction would resolve these antitheses, the opposite is true. Having looked into novels by such writers as Austen,
Burney, Charlotte Brontë, and Sylvia Plath in a chapter called "The
Adolescent as Heroine," Patricia Meyer Spacks concludes that

> female sexuality understandably seems to many female authors to
> mean danger rather than power; *male* sexuality is power. Female as-
> piration is a joke. Female rebellion may be perfectly justified, but
> there's no good universe next door, no way out, young potential rev-
> olutionaries can't find their revolution. So they marry in defeat or go
> mad in a complicated form of triumph, their meaning the inevita-
> bility of failure. More vividly than older women in fiction, they ex-
> press women's anger and self-hatred and the feeling that there's no
> way out. Pain is the human condition, but more particularly, these
> books announce, the female condition.[3]

The patterns of pain in the female bildungsroman are embedded in
image, leitmotif, and larger narrative patterns; their antitheses are
images of desire for authentic selfhood. These images so often involve
a special world of nature that they describe a green-world archetype,
and the figure of Eros who inhabits this world we have correspondingly identified as the green-world lover. Conversely, the villain/rapist
assault symbolizes the fulcrum of a world of enclosure and atrophy
opposite the freedom of the green world, and we call it the rape-
trauma archetype. Looking at these two contrasting archetypes, we
will first outline the more positive green-world model and then examine the way in which bildungsroman plots are nonetheless shaped by
the dominant social norms for womanhood.

### THE GREEN-WORLD ARCHETYPE

The adolescent girl, writes Simone de Beauvoir, "will devote a special love to Nature: still more than the adolescent boy, she worships
it. Unconquered, inhuman Nature subsumes most clearly the totality

of what exists. The adolescent girl has not yet acquired for her use any portion of the universal: hence it is her kingdom as a whole; when she takes possession of it, she also proudly takes possession of herself."[4] About to be conquered by "human" society, she turns to something "inhuman"; about to be dwarfed at the moment of the first development of her energies, she feels that the natural universe as a whole is "her kingdom." Taking possession of nature, she possesses *herself.* De Beauvoir's analysis of nature worship in the adolescent is worded in such a way as to suggest that the world of nature is uniquely the girl's world but one that she will no longer need when she comes into her "own." Nevertheless, the fact is that she will never come into her own; this point de Beauvoir amply explains elsewhere in her analysis. Both the girl's desire and society's discouragement are reflected in women's fiction, where, as a result, nature for the young hero remains a refuge throughout life. At the adolescent stage, however, her appreciation of nature is retrospective, a look backwards over her shoulder as she confronts her present placelessness and her future submission within a male culture. Visions of her own world within the natural world, or naturistic epiphanies, channel the young girl's protests into a fantasy where her imprisoned energies can be released.

Later, the mature woman hero tends to look back to moments of naturistic epiphany as touchstones in a quest for her lost selfhood so that when she readies herself for her midlife rebirth journey, images of the green world remembered once more come to the fore. The importance of this identification with nature is illustrated by its persistent recurrence in women's fiction. "Nature is one of the realms women writers have most livingly explored," writes de Beauvoir. "For the young girl, for the woman who has not fully abdicated, nature represents what woman herself represents for man, herself and her negation, a kingdom and a place of exile; the whole in the guise of the other. It is when she speaks of moors and gardens that the woman novelist will reveal her experience and her dreams to us more intimately."[5] The "experience" and "dreams" that are revealed in this recurrent archetypal pattern in women's fiction are of a sense of oneness with the cosmos as well as of a place to one side of civilization.

Although most authors depict the green world of the woman hero as a place from which she sets forth and a memory to which she returns for renewal, there are a significant number of novels in which nature is the protagonist's entire world. This primacy of nature characterizes both the bildungsroman and novels dealing with the development of older heroes. As I have indicated, adolescence is not the

only period of development in the lives of women heroes, and therefore in dealing with the green-world archetype we will be referring
to heroes of all ages.

In regional, or local-color, fiction (as we shall also see in chapter 7)
women often master the green world, even to the extent that some
farm it for produce, as in the case of Willa Cather's Alexandra in *O
Pioneers!* (1913), Ellen Glasgow's Dorinda in *Barren Ground* (1925),
and Sheila Kaye-Smith's Joanna in *Joanna Godden* (1921). When they
are not farming it, women in this mode are making use of it, for example, Townsend Warner's *Lolly Willowes* (1926), Mary Wilkins Freeman's Louisa in "A New England Nun" (1891), and May Sarton's
"botanizing" Ellen Tuttle in *Kinds of Love* (1970). In Sarah Orne
Jewett's first collection of stories (*Deephaven*, 1877) the two girl narrators apprentice themselves for a time to one "Mrs. Bonny," a down-
at-heels but witty and irreverent old widow who lives far out in the
woods and shares her parlor with her turkeys. "Living there in the
lonely clearing," writes Jewett,

> deep in the woods and far from any neighbor, she knew all the herbs
> and trees and the harmless wild creatures who lived among them,
> by heart; and she had an amazing store of tradition and superstition
> which made her so entertaining to us that we went to see her many
> times before we came away in the autumn. We went with her to find
> some pitcher-plants, one day, and it was wonderful how much she
> knew about the woods, what keen observation she had. There was
> something so wild and unconventional about Mrs. Bonny that it was
> like taking an afternoon walk with a good-natured Indian.[6]

The kinship between woodswomen, Indians, and nature's magical powers occurs frequently, as in Mary Austin's *Outland* (1919), where the
woodspeople are a mixture of Indian and fairy, and in English fiction,
where similar women are associated with fairies, gypsies, or elves.
This world of woodspeople is also represented in recent science fiction, by the naturistic delights and pastimes of Joanna Russ's Whileaway inhabitants, the "wind people" in Marion Zimmer Bradley's short
story of that title, and the magic of the witch-healer, "Snake," in Vonda McIntyre's *Dream Snake* (1978).

The regionalist writers of the nineteenth and early twentieth centuries, in both England and America, are thus apt to make the hero's
lifelong devotion to nature the center, rather than merely an initiatory
phase, of development. As we shall see when we come to the subject
of single women, the heroes of Sarah Orne Jewett, Alice Brown, Mary
Wilkins Freeman, and their sister writers are apt to be delightfully
happy solitaries at home with their gardens and their forests. Writers

like Glasgow, Cather, Kaye-Smith, and Townsend Warner develop mature heroes whose allegiance to the land provides them with life-long psychological sustenance.

A prototypical example of the young female hero as free spirit at one with the green world is "A White Heron," a short story from Jewett's *The Country of the Pointed Firs* (1896). While purportedly realistic, the story is full of bits and tags of fairy tale and mythology, beginning with Jewett's naming of the nine-year-old hero "Sylvia." As in many examples of "green-world fiction" the hero not only appreciates and likes nature but, through a process of metamorphosis, *becomes* an element in it: "She was not often in the woods so late as this, and it made her feel as if she were a part of the gray shadows and the moving leaves," writes Jewett, and Sylvia's grandmother remarks that " 'the wild creatur's counts her as one o' themselves.' " Sylvia goes to live with her grandmother because she has been "afraid of folks" and the "noisy town" in general and, in particular, of "a great red-faced boy who used to chase and frighten her." Jewett reverses the Snow White plot in that the sylvan girl rejects the "rescue" of the handsome stranger. At first Sylvia is fascinated. "She had never seen anybody so charming and delightful; the woman's heart, asleep in the child, was vaguely thrilled by a dream of love. Some premonition of that great power stirred and swayed these young foresters who traversed the solemn woodlands with soft-footed silent care."[7] The young man, an ornithologist, wants to shoot and stuff Sylvia's favorite white heron, and she is torn between her admiration for him and her desire to keep the heron's nesting site a secret. Through the course of the narrative it becomes clear that the nesting place—an "open place where the sunshine always seemed strangely yellow and hot"—symbolizes the selfhood Sylvia is unwilling to compromise. Her climb to the treetop in order to spot the nest suggests Psyche's climb to the sky, but Psyche sought the god of love whereas Sylvia rejects love in favor of self-knowledge. Jewett reminds us that Sylvia "could have served and followed him and loved him as a dog loves." But the young hero is not interested: the boy with his gun is too much like the "red-faced boy" of her nightmares, and she does not want to leave her green world.

Ellen Glasgow's "vehicle of liberation" (as she called it in her preface to the 1933 edition), *Barren Ground* (1925), deals with a relationship between hero, nature, and lover that enables the mature hero to use her power over nature to punish an unsuitable mate. Dorinda Oakley loves Jason Greylock, a young doctor returned to the Virginia countryside to care for his alcoholic father. At first the Elizabeth County landscape parallels Dorinda's changing moods:

He turned to look at her and his face cleared. "You are the only cheerful sight I've seen since I got here," he said.

The light had changed again and her inner mood was changing with the landscape. A feeling of intimate kinship with the country returned, and it seemed to her that the color of the broomsedge was overrunning the desolate hidden field of her life. Something wild and strong and vivid was covering the waste places.[8]

To this extent Glasgow's broomsedge is similar to Emily Brontë's Wuthering Heights and George Eliot's River Floss, a natural force that, in its variations, provides a corollary to the development of the characters. After she discovers that Jason is too mean to marry her, Dorinda's self-determination grows. The green world ceases to be a retreat and becomes something to master. After a difficult period in New York City, Dorinda achieves a crucial green-world vision at a concert. She perceives the music and the Elizabeth County landscape as guides leading her down into her buried self, where she makes her decision to return to the land: "With the flight of wings, ecstasy quivered over her, while sound and colour were transformed into rhythms of feeling. Pure sensation held and tortured her. She felt the music playing on her nerves as the wind plays on a harp; she felt it shatter her nerves like broken strings, and keep on crashing, ploughing through the labyrinth of her soul. . . ."[9]

Dorinda returns to her land, applies new methods of farming to the broomsedge, becomes economically independent, and buys all of Jason's property. At the denouement her relationship to nature prevails as the ultimate reality in her life: "The spirit of the land was flowing into her, and her own spirit, strengthened and refreshed, was flowing out again toward life. This was the permanent self, she knew. This was what remained to her after the years had taken their bloom. . . . 'put your heart in the land,' old Matthew had said to her. 'The land is the only thing that will stay by you.' "[10]

Like Jewett's Sylvia and Glasgow's Dorinda Oakley, Mary Olivier in May Sinclair's 1919 novel of that title discovers in her empathy with the natural world an inner strength with which to survive the entanglements of love. Mary's childhood is haunted by three things—her fear of Papa, "who walked in the garden in the cool of the evening, like the Lord God"; her mother's coldness (Mary overheard her remark, when brother Roddy was sick with rheumatic fever, "that it would have been better if it had been the girl"); and a passion for her brother Mark. Mary likes long walks in the English countryside, with which she passionately associates her quest for identity. Turning from the web of masculine values that surrounds her, young Mary begins to prefer nature to people: "By the gate of the field her sudden, secret happiness came to her. She could never tell when it was coming, nor what it would come from. It had something to do with the trees standing up in the golden white light. It had come before with a certain sharp white light flooding the fields, flooding the room."[11] These moments of epiphany bring her, as she matures, to an intellectual belief in pantheism that enables her to confront the patriarchal Christianity of her family. Her idea of a suitable lover is one who would have the body of various men whom she had admired but "the soul of Shelley and the mind of Spinoza and Immanuel Kant." Her intellectual convictions, built upon her earlier naturistic ecstasies, are too much, however, even for those suitors who pretend to admire them.

Mary spends the years before her fortieth birthday struggling between her desire for self-determination and the expectations of her family and suitors. When she finally meets a suitable lover, she rejects him, after a period of lovemaking and mutually passionate devotion, for the solitary life. She asks herself, "Could I give up this? If I had to choose between losing Richard and losing this? . . . If I had to choose seven years ago, before I knew, I'd have chosen Richard; I couldn't have helped myself. But if I had to choose now—knowing what reality is—between losing Richard in the way I have lost him and losing reality absolutely and for ever, my real self, knowing that I'd lost it. . . ?"[12] She finds "this reality," or self-realization, in constructing her naturistic philosophy. Like Jewett's Sylvia, she *turns away* from her lover and towards a natural "reality" that she finds less threatening to her selfhood than love.

In all of these novels, women find solace, companionship, and independence in nature. Sylvia, Dorinda, and Mary are confronted with a male antagonist who disturbs their peace; calm returns when he leaves. Nature, then, becomes an ally of the woman hero, keeping her in touch with her selfhood, a kind of talisman that enables her to make her way through the alienations of male society. Sarah Orne Jewett's women make friends and companions of wild creatures much as Mary Austin's Indian women practice the arts of foraging, pottery, and basketry; all are an assertion of feminine allegiance with nature.

Miriam Henderson, hero of Dorothy Richardson's thirteen-volume *Pilgrimage* (1915–67), is similarly moved by nature, where, throughout her journeys, friendships, jobs, and affairs, she finds her most constant solace. In the sixth volume, *The Trap* (1925), Miriam feels that "she had been dying by inches," but the seventh, *Oberland* (1927), brings her to new life through a vacation in the Swiss mountains. There, not satisfied to passively enjoy the blazing, snowbound scenery but instead learning to toboggan, ice skate, and ski in free motion through it, Miriam experiences the mountains as inviting a "thoughtless submission to their influence as to a final infinite good that would remain when they were no more seen," a submission that results in "being changed, coming back refreshed and changed and indifferent."[13] Although Miriam is an intensely social person, troubled by her feelings for men and women alike, it is nature that enables her to survive human relationships with her personality intact. Since the male world in particular offends her desire for "responsibility," she withdraws from the importunities of her male friends and lovers through naturistic epiphanies.

In most women's novels the green world is present in retrospect, something left behind or about to be left behind as one backs into the enclosure—a state of innocence that becomes most poignant as one is initiated into experience. The intensity of these moments seems to increase in direct proportion to the imminence of the hero's young womanhood, comprehended as submission to the patriarchy. Although it is so frequently depicted at the instant of its loss, heroes remember the green world with an intensity greater than mere nostalgia. When they encounter the limitations placed on their full development within society, the green-world memory erupts with the power of a struggle for personal authenticity. In the middle of her aunt's attempts to marry her off to a villain, Ann Radcliffe's Emily St. Aubert of *The Mysteries of Udolpho* (1794) consoles herself by contemplating the stars. Such sudden escapes into naturistic revery and substitutions of ideal suitors for societal ones characterize both nineteenth- and twentieth-century women's fiction. Shirley, in Charlotte Brontë's 1849 novel, escapes from her uncle's machinations to marry her against her will by fantasizing about a mythical hero, Eva, who lives alone in nature until rescued by an erotic "Son of God." In *Wuthering Heights* (1847), Heathcliff, whose name suggests a natural landscape, takes on erotic and mythological fascination for Catherine. The green-world-lover archetype may inform the mythological overtones of the Great Corn God, who carries Cather's hero Alexandra away in a dream passage in *O Pioneers!*.[14]

In such cases the young woman turns away from "appropriate" males toward fantasies of a figure, projected from within her own personality, more suitable to her needs. Such figures appear often in women's fiction, correspond to the role played by Pan, Dionysus, etc., in mythology, and constitute an archetype that I have termed the green-world lover. This figure is closely associated with the naturistic epiphany, a vision of the green world that calls up from the feminine unconscious the image of an ideal lover and almost always includes a rejection of social expectations concerning engagement and marriage. Two prototypical examples are Virginia Woolf's first two novels, *The Voyage Out* (1915) and *Night and Day* (1919), in which the heroes have difficulty reconciling their desires for self-direction with the conventions of marriage. In the first novel, Rachel meets her lover during an excursion up a South American river towards an inner heart of light (which one suspects Woolf of deliberately positing as an alternative to Conrad's *Heart of Darkness*). In a moment of realization, she sees him as her ideal, her green-world, lover but dies of a fever, having lost the will to live after contemplating her future in the world of marriage. *Night and Day* carries on the debate about whether one can marry and maintain one's creative solitude. Katharine finds the world so empty of this possibility that she retreats into the world of her imagination:

> Easily, and without correction by reason, her imagination made pictures, superb backgrounds casting a rich though phantom light upon the facts in the foreground. Splendid as the waters that drop with resounding thunder from high ledges of rock, and plunge downwards into the blue depths of night, was the presence of love she dreamt. . . . The man, too, was some magnanimous hero, riding a great horse by the shore of the sea. They rode through forests together, they galloped by the rim of the sea. But waking, she was able to contemplate a perfectly loveless marriage, as the thing one did actually in real life.[15]

Katharine splits her consciousness into the dream world, on the one hand, "a place where feelings were liberated," and a vision of conventional society on the other hand, "a stoical acceptance of facts."

Willa Cather, in *O Pioneers!*, characterizes the farmland that Alexandra Bergson loves as a "great, free spirit" and as "the Genius of the Divide," and when the hero falls sick, she has a dream in which this "Genius" visits her:

> It was a man, certainly, who carried her, but he was like no man she knew; he was much larger and stronger and swifter, and he carried her as easily as if she were a sheaf of wheat. She never saw him, but with eyes closed, she could feel that he was yellow like the sunlight, and there was the smell of ripe cornfields about him. She could feel him approach, bend over and lift her, and then she could feel herself being carried swiftly off across the fields.[16]

Later in the novel Cather suggests that this life spirit is also a death spirit: "His white cloak was thrown over his face, and his head was bent a little forward. His shoulders seemed as strong as the foundations of the world. His right arm, bared from the elbow, was dark and gleaming, like bronze, and she knew at once that it was the arm of the mightiest of all lovers."[17]

Embodying the natural cycles of fertility and drought, this masculine archetype seems to be a direct inversion of the creative and destructive feminine figure, the "Belle Dame Sans Merci," who both attracts and destroys men and who is at the center of so much male literature. Although drawn larger than life, Cather's mythological figure of Eros, with his accompanying thanatopic qualities, does not dwarf Alexandra: rather, he both complements and enhances her psyche as an expression of her desire for more than the patriarchy can offer.

The negative, or deathly, element of Cather's figure finds analogues in a destructive element that seems to accompany women heroes whenever they experience truly satisfying Eros. The ideal lover is sometimes embodied in real men during erotic epiphanies in women's fiction, but such experiences are momentary and fleeting, giving way to events that act as punishments. As we shall see in chapter 5, moments of combined naturistic and erotic epiphany between such characters as Rachel and Hewet in *The Voyage Out*, between Catherine and Heathcliff in *Wuthering Heights*, and between Martha and Thomas in Lessing's *Children of Violence* series are only momentary, the price punishment or destruction by conventional society. Rachel succumbs to a fever she contracted "up river," Catherine's love can be consummated only after death, and Martha Quest's Thomas goes mad and dies of fever in the desert. In these narratives of ill-fated love for Pan-like figures we see modern versions of the Tammuz/Adonis archetype, the desired but doomed godlike lover, a catalyst for woman's Eros too powerful for society to assimilate. We'll have an opportunity in later chapters to discuss why Eros, as embodied in the green-world-lover archetype, is too threatening to go unpunished in literature.

THE RAPE TRAUMA AS ARCHETYPE

When women heroes do seek erotic freedom, which we define simply as the right to make love when and with whom they wish, they meet all the opposition of the patriarchy. Not only is the feminine Eros discouraged, but its opposite, rape, is proffered as a substitute. The event of "rape," in that it involves the violation of the self in its psychological and physical integrity, thus becomes central to the young woman's experience even if she is to be bedded down legally, within a marriage. Social expectations for a young woman's destiny surface in women's fiction as a division of loyalties between the hero's green-world authenticity and the social world of enclosure. As I indicated in the Introduction, the plot line in which a rejected male continues to pursue an unwilling woman can be traced as far back as Greek mythology: Daphne turned into a laurel tree in order to escape Apollo, Syrinx became a reed to avoid Pan, Arethusa changed into a spring to elude Alpheus. As in novels characterized by the green-world archetypes, we see men pictured as agents of harsh disruption, and again, nature represents freedom, solace, and protection. The rape trauma, too, disrupts the green world—the hero sometimes surviving the trauma and restoring the green world—but in many instances the damage is permanent.

The pursuit narrative in mythology often involved a green-world locale, an island, "well," or grotto, invaded by men who rape the beneficent women residents—followed by an account of the destruction and theft of the area's natural value. There is, for example, the prototypical rape story of the Pays de Logres Maidens. This mythical tale describes a land where maidens appeared with refreshments to tired travelers.

> It was only necessary to go to one of the [grottoes] and state one's wishes and immediately a beautiful damsel would appear, carrying a golden bowl containing all kinds of food. . . . A second maiden would follow, with a white hand towel and a second dish containing whatever the newcomer had wished for. The maidens served all wayfarers thus, until one day a king named Amangons ravished one of them and stole her golden bowl. His people followed this bad example and the maidens never again came out of the grottoes to revive wanderers. From that time on the land went to waste. The trees lost their leaves, grass and flowers withered, and the water receded more and more.[18]

Like the rape of Persephone, this narrative involves the overthrow of a matrilinear society friendly to men and the destruction of a bountiful green world by rape and theft.

Such traumas characterize the plot structure of gothic novels where women heroes experience adventures in quest of true chivalry in combination with the horror of pursuit and victimization by male villains. Hazel Mews notes that in spite of the accusations that novel reading was causing dissipation in its early adherents,

> it is arguable . . . that adventures and horrors viewed from a safe distance in the pages of the novel may have contained an element of

> compensation for lives lived in circumstances too sheltered and con-
> fined. The events described in the Gothic Novels are such as would
> shake the bravest of men, yet they are endured by delicate young
> women. The Gothic heroes themselves seem to have been wishful
> portraits of women as their authors would like them to be, possessed
> of the qualities of person and mind most admired by society. . . .
> these young ladies were princesses in all but name, living lives of
> high adventure far away from cramping limitations and everyday
> shifts and compromises.[19]

Gothic fiction, in the late eighteenth and early nineteenth centuries, demonstrated an ambivalence towards women's roles in its presentation of heroes who in every other way embodied gender norms but who became involved in very "unladylike" adventures. The woman hero's long road of trials, in such exhaustive works as Ann Radcliffe's *The Mysteries of Udolpho* (1794), Charlotte Smith's *Emmeline* (1788), and Fanny Burney's *The Wanderer* (1814), forces her to encounter sexism in a wide variety of forms. She may marry the one she loves in the end (an act itself rebellious in the prudent world of marriage for money), but during the course of the narrative she satirizes gender norms.[20]

Let us consider in *Emmeline, The Mysteries of Udolpho,* and *The Wanderer*, for example, the way that otherwise conservative authors have included in their work feminist critiques of the socioeconomic aspects of marriage. Smith structured *Emmeline*, her first novel, according to a stock Cinderella romance of the abandoned orphan who goes through a series of seductions, escapes, and adventures before marriage to the right man, expressing much of the alienation that she experienced in her own life. "No disadvantage could equal those I sustained," Smith said of her marriage. "The more my mind expanded, the more I became sensible of personal slavery; the more I improved and cultivated my understanding, the farther I was removed from those with whom I was condemned to pass my life; and the more clearly I saw by these newly acquired lights the horror of the abyss into which I had unconsciously plunged."[21]

The author subjects her hero, the young Emmeline, to attempted seductions, first by the new steward and then by her uncle's son, Lord Delamere. Retreating from Delamere's advances to a seaside cottage, she meets Mrs. Stafford, a young bride with three children whose husband (modeled after Smith's own) is drunken, dissipated, and tyrannical. The pleas of undying courtly devotion uttered by the prurient Delamere are mocked by the two women as insincere. Emmeline and Mrs. Stafford meet a third sufferer, Adelina, who has been seduced and impregnated by Delamere's confederate Fitz-Edward. The three women help each other escape from the pitfalls of Delamere's pursuit and Fitz-Edward's importunity, aided by Adelina's brother, the kindly and affectionate Lord Godolphin. Under a great deal of pressure to marry, Emmeline declares, with full agreement from her friends, that marriage for purposes of protection, security, and finance is obscene, and she dismisses one marriage proposal with this message:

> Tell him therefore, sir (her spirit rose as she spoke) that the daughter of his brother, unhappy as she is, yet boasts that nobleness of mind which her father possessed, and disclaims the mercenary views of becoming, from pecuniary motives, the wife of a man she can neither love nor esteem.[22]

Like a number of other heroes who desire emotional autonomy, Emmeline decides to marry for love or not marry at all. She eventually chooses Lord Godolphin for a husband—a choice that underlines the contrast between the ideal lover and the more threatening men in the novel. Unlike her other alternatives, marriage to Lord Godolphin promises the greatest amount of partnership possible for the period.

While Emmeline's peregrinations are limited primarily to England, Radcliffe's Emily St. Aubert travels far, from adventure to adventure, testing her integrity against all possible odds. The novel's villains are stereotypical male tyrants, whose behavior Radcliffe satirizes. Emily's guardian, Montoni, attempts to pressure her into marrying Count Morano for financial reasons. She resists being considered an item of marital barter but finds that all her relatives urge her to obey Montoni's commands. The discrepancy between Emily's desire for autonomy and the machinations of the two villains is dramatized in a scene where Montoni tries to force her to sign away her estates to Morano. When she protests, Montoni replies, ". . . before you undertake to regulate the morals of other persons, you should learn and practice the virtues which are indispensable to a woman—sincerity, uniformity of conduct, and obedience."[23] By placing this moralizing language in the mouth of Montoni, who terrorizes the surrounding villages with his bandits throughout the novel, Radcliffe provides a satiric commentary on the way in which tyrannical men use gender norms for their own benefit.

Fanny Burney, in the five-volume *The Wanderer*, exposes her hero (known after the manner of Shakespearian festive-romance comedy as "Incognita") to a parallel series of experiences. Though she sympathetically portrays a single woman ostracized and harassed in a man's world in a manner that feminists would applaud, she nonetheless spoofs the inadequacies of radical feminism as a solution. In the course of the five volumes Burney doesn't spare any details of the indignities, embarrassments, and physical and mental torture that await the woman who attempts to support herself in a male society: much of the plot deals with Incognita's attempts to evade seduction. Incognita struggles to realize her "hope of self-dependence" by working as a seamstress and music teacher. She soon sees that economic independence, "ever cheering to the upright mind," will elude her as long as she doesn't have the initial capital outlay, but it is impossible for her to secure the money because of the improper assumptions that accrue to a woman who accepts donations from men. Her marriage at the denouement does little to mitigate the relentless portrait of one woman's attempt to survive in a totally alien environment:

> Here, and thus felicitously, ended, with the acknowledgement of her name, and her family, the DIFFICULTIES OF THE WANDERER: a being who had been cast upon herself; a female Robinson Crusoe, as unaided and unprotected, though in the midst of the world, as that imaginary hero in his uninhabited island; and reduced either to sink, through inanition, to nonentity, or to be rescued from famine and death by such resources as she could find, independently, in herself.[24]

The horrific element of gothic fiction conveys in the woman's novel the idea of women as unjustly treated by society and pictures men as agents to be feared and "the chase" as a hardship to be endured.

Elements of the rape-trauma archetype, a staple of the woman's gothic, continue to appear in more recent women's fiction. One work, Mary Webb's *Gone to Earth* (1917), deals with the coming of age and eventual destruction of the daughter of a gypsy witch and a harpist. Raised by her father in a remote, rural cottage, Hazel Woodhus inherited from her mother a number of characteristics reminiscent of a matrilinear, green-world culture. Along with her mother's book of spells, Hazel has an expert knowledge of flower, mushroom, bird, and herb, a sense of love for and unity with the natural world, and an intuition that marriage would preclude all of them. "There [in the cottage] her mother, a Welsh gipsy, had borne her in bitter rebellion, hating marriage and a settled life and Abel Woodhus as a wild cat hates a cage. She was a river, born for the artist's joy and sorrow, and her spirit found no relief for its emotions, for it was dumb." Hazel imbibed this rebellion with her mother's milk: "It was not a question of marrying or not marrying in Hazel's eyes. It was a matter of primitive instinct. She would be her own."[25]

Into this green world of liberty comes the villainous Jack Reddin on his black horse, carrying Hazel off and seducing her. She rejects the relationship Reddin offers her, and with a mixture of joy and sorrow sings "the grief of rainy forests and the moan of storm water; the muffled complaint of driven leaves; the keening—wild and universal—of life for the perishing matter that it inhabits." Her allegiance to nature thus renewed, she dies defending her pet fox from Reddin and his huntsmen.

The dramatic narrative adventures of such fiction as *Gone to Earth* and its earlier gothic counterparts persist in an internalized form in modern novels. External, physical hardships become self-imposed psychological strictures. Young women heroes in Joyce Carol Oates's novels, for example, are as likely to be driven "to earth" as Hazel Woodhus, haunted by images of enclosure, suffocation, madness, and suicide.

## THE GROWING-UP-GROTESQUE ARCHETYPE

The novel of development portrays a world in which the young woman hero is destined for disappointment. The vitality and hopefulness characterizing the adolescent hero's attitude toward her future here meet and conflict with the expectations and dictates of the surrounding society. Every element of her desired world—freedom to come and go, allegiance to nature, meaningful work, exercise of the intellect, and use of her own erotic capabilities—inevitably clashes with patriarchal norms. Attempts to develop independence are met with limitation and immurement, training in menial and frustrating tasks, restrictions of the intellect (lest she perceive her status too clearly), and limitation of erotic activity. This collision between the hero's evolving self and society's imposed identity appears consistently throughout the history of women's fiction. The heroes of radical feminist authors, such as Mary Wollstonecraft and Mrs. Opie, were overt in demanding personal freedom, but these same heroes invariably met with dismal fates.[26] Consequently, a broad sampling of nineteenth-century novels clearly advises that intellectual development should be checked in a young woman since her achievements will not receive concrete social rewards.

Caroline Helstone, in Charlotte Brontë's *Shirley*, plunges into a neurological depression when her uncle insists that she "stick to the needle, learn shirt-making and gown-making and piecrust-making, and you will be a clever woman some day." Caroline suffers from a thwarted love for Robert Moore but is aware that if she had significant work to do, she would be healthy and well. "I believe that single women should have more to do," she remarks to herself. "This stagnant state of things makes them decline in health: they are never well; and their minds and views shrink to a wondrous narrowness. The great wish—the sole aim of every one of them is to be married."[27]

Harriet Beecher Stowe observed the inequity by which boys "grow" and girls "shrink" in her regional collection *Oldtown Folks* (1869). She described four young friends—Harry, Horace, Esther, and Tina. At first they all go together to school, where the boys admire the girls' brilliance. In the episode entitled "We Enter College," however, Harry remarks to Horace that "it's rather a steep thing for girls that have kept step with us in study up to this point, and had their minds braced just as ours have been, with all the drill of regular hours and regular lessons, to be suddenly let down, with nothing in particular to do."[28]

While, in these examples, Brontë and Stowe dealt in particular with intellectual deprivation, their contemporary Louisa May Alcott examined the desire to switch gender, to become a boy and avoid the deprivations of girlhood. In *Little Women* (1869) Alcott describes young Jo as "mannish" and "manly." When Jo's conservative sister Meg says she must turn up her hair now that she is a "young lady," Jo shouts,

> "I'm not! and if turning up my hair makes me one, I'll wear it in two tails till I'm twenty. . . . I hate to think I've got to grow up, and be Miss March, and wear long gowns, and look as prim as a China aster! It's bad enough to be a girl anyway, when I like boys' games and work and manners! I can't get over my disappointment in not being a boy; and it's worse than ever now, for I'm dying to go and fight with Papa, and I can only stay at home and knit, like a poky old woman."[29]

Jo clearly perceives the irony that growing up, according to contemporary gender norms, means growing down—an atrophy of the personality, a premature senility.

Similarly, Lyndall, the hero of Olive Schreiner's *The Story of an African Farm* (1883), deplores the way young girls grow down:

> We kneel still with one little cheek wistfully pressed against the pane. Afterwards we go and thread blue beads, and make a string for our neck; and we go and stand before the glass. We see the complexion we were not to spoil, and the white frock, and we look into our own great eyes. Then the curse begins to act on us. It finishes its work when we are grown women, who no more look out wistfully at a more healthy life; we are contented. We fit our sphere as a Chinese woman's foot fits her shoe, exactly, as though God had made both— and yet He knows nothing of either. In some of us the shaping to our end has been quite completed. The parts we are not to use have

been quite atrophied, and have even dropped off; but in others, and we are not less to be pitied, they have been weakened and left. We wear the bandages, but our limbs have not grown to them; we know that we are compressed, and chafe against them.[30]

These enclosure images, associated with the eighteenth- and nineteenth-century gothic novel, surface in contemporary characterizations of young heroes "growing up grotesque." "Women writers," Ellen Moers writes, "continued to make monsters in the twentieth century. . . . 'freaks,'" she concludes, "is in fact a better word than 'monsters' for the creations of the modern female Gothic."[31] As in the early woman's bildungsroman, the young hero sets forth with wit and intelligence, only to be punished by an internalized form of self-torture with which she programs herself into atrophy and disuse.

Just as nineteenth-century authors depict the slow, inexorable process by which gender norms drive a Catherine Earnshaw, Lyndall, or Edna Pontellier to self-destruction, so in the modern period women are described as paralyzed by a sense of self-induced anomie or claustrophobia. The female adolescent hero contemplates marriage with discomfort and terror. Glee Vanney, of Dorothy Roberts's *Durable Life* (1945), believes that marriage has made her cousin "a swallowed creature who lived in [her husband] the way Jonah lived in the belly of the whale." Sylvia Plath's Esther Greenwood, of *The Bell Jar* (1963), first dislikes the idea of marriage because a wife's housekeeping duties seem to take up all her time, but she is even more upset when her boyfriend tells her that when she is married and has children, she won't even *want* time to write poems. Esther concludes, "When you were married and had children it was like being brainwashed, and afterward you went about numb as a slave in some private, totalitarian state." Molly, in Jean Stafford's *The Mountain Lion* (1947), wants to deny the existence of her body even to herself. She hates the word *body* and prefers to think of herself as a "long wooden box with a mind inside." She is so alienated that she doesn't consider her body to be a part of her "self." In *Martha Quest* (1952) Doris Lessing provides a painful example of a young woman who, in spite of her better judgment, backs into the wringer of matrimony. Marge Piercy's Beth, of *Small Changes* (1973), feels "smothered" inside a stiff, white wedding dress and veil, as if she were being stuffed into a marshmallow.

In the writings of southern American women novelists, we find intelligent, rebellious girls depicted as grotesque in their alienation from the inflexible stereotype of the lady. Flannery O'Connor's adolescents, for example, are often depicted as "freaks": the modern punishment,

Ellen Moers notes, for those who step outside or "fall from" gender expectations.[32] Two of Carson McCullers's heroes, Mick in *The Heart Is a Lonely Hunter* (1936) and Frankie in *The Member of the Wedding* (1946), hesitate between boyish and girlish behavior in reaction to the restrictions of American womanhood. Mick's fear of her sisters' "femininity" prompts her to look to her brothers for role models, but they reject and entrap her. Frankie Adams, in *Member of the Wedding*, resists " a jail you could not see." She hovers between thinking of herself as a boy (short hair, short pants) and a vamp (her fancy dress-up garb in which she barely escapes being raped) and solves her problem by trying to be a "member" of her brother's wedding, part of an adventurous threesome who will travel through the world together. The peripety occurs, of course, when she finds that the bride and groom have other plans and that she is consigned to the waiting room of adolescence until she conforms to feminine norms.

Young women growing up in poverty, like Judith Pippinger in Edith Summers Kelley's *Weeds* (1923), Marie Rogers in Agnes Smedley's *Daughter of Earth* (1929), and Anna in Tillie Olsen's *Yonnondio* (1974), feel that their biological maturity is a special curse, restricting them to marriage, childbirth, and the struggle for survival. These women feel oppressed, rather than elevated, by the arrival of adulthood. As Marie Rogers reaches maturity, she realizes that, for her father, this means she is now a marketable object. "Women had nothing but virginity to trade for a bed and food for the rest of their days. Fathers protected the virginity of their daughters as men guard their bank accounts; with a gun slung at the hips and a gleam of warning in the eye."[33] Marta Roberts's hero Concha, in *Tumbleweeds* (1940), watches in horror as her oldest daughter reaches an early puberty, fearing that she will be "ruined" for marriage.

When, in addition to her economic struggles, the working-class hero is also Black, her attempts to achieve a full personal development are hampered at every turn. The young Black hero faces a double alienation, urged to adhere to the "nice-girl" standards of white femininity while daily recognizing that, from the point of view of the white race, she is inherently "not nice." Told, on the one hand, "Don't let boys touch you," she is wrong no matter how she acts. In her world, if she doesn't fight, she will constantly be touched. Both Francie in Louise Meriwether's *Daddy Was a Number Runner* (1970) and Selina in Paule Marshall's *Brown Girl, Brownstones* (1959) are admonished by their parents to be "ladies," only to find they cannot leave their tenements without hearing the nasty epithets and remarks made about their bodies. In this atmosphere the arrival of puberty is indeed a "curse." When Marshall's Selina observes herself growing breasts and knows that she will menstruate, "an inexplicable revulsion gripped her and her face screwed with disgust. 'It's never gonna happen to me,' she said proudly." In Zora Neale Hurston's *Their Eyes Were Watching God* (1937) the hero's grandmother can protect her from sexual exploitation only by urging her into an early and unhappy marriage. To grow up Black and female is to be twice limited. As Toni Morrison's hero Claudia remarks in *The Bluest Eye* (1972), Black girls must "edge into life from the backdoor. . . ." Everybody in the world is in a position to give them orders.

As an exception to the double-jeopardy portrait, a slave-life vignette in Margaret Walker's *Jubilee!* (1966) offers a more positive picture of Black womanhood, reminiscent of green-world ideals. When the hero, Vyry, asks her mentor, Aunt Sally, what "womanhood" means, she receives the reply that "it's what makes you grow up to have younguns and be a sho-nuff mammy all your own. . . . A man ain't but trouble, just breath and britches and trouble."[34] As I shall explain in chapter 4, Vyry's pride in her womanhood is possible because of her distance from the power center of American society. She learns herbal lore, healing, and cooking from her various "Aunts" and "Grannies"; this is evidence of a matrilinear inheritance passed down from an African culture that has a more coherently formulated and positive attitude toward "womanhood" than does the American patriarchy.

Although the multiple alienation of sex, class, and race intensifies physical and psychological suffering for the young Black woman, there exists nonetheless a remarkable similarity in plot, tone, and imagery among the bildungsromans of all classes. Barbara White's dissertation, "Growing Up Female: Adolescent Girlhood in American Literature," documents the adolescent protagonist's conflict with her sexual identity; resentful of her womanhood, disgusted by her body, envious of her brothers, fearful of rape and molestation, she is oppressed by a sense of enclosure and imprisonment.[35] The female hero who undertakes to adventure into a man's world finds herself confused and isolated at best and at worst succumbs to madness or an early death.

Young heroes who look to psychiatric care for help find little solace. The psychologist in Harriet Arnow's *The Weedkiller's Daughter* (1970) is a "Grand Inquisitor" who claims that "the main desire to the normal girl is hunting and holding a mate." If her intelligence and achievement scores are too high, she must be "seeking . . . compensation for lack of popularity." In spite of the generic intent of the bildungsroman to trace a hero's progression from childhood into adulthood, the novel of development persists in mirroring a society in which such a progression is inappropriate for women. The young woman in modern society cannot "grow up": she must remain "one of the girls."

Thus, by necessity, the orderly succession of stages characterizing the male bildungsroman is disrupted since the role requirements for women are antithetical to maturation. Joyce Carol Oates, for example, says of one of her *Wonderland* (1971) heroes, "Always she had feared her body. . . . Layer upon layer the years formed her: Helene was now a married woman, the same age as her husband, and yet she was also nineteen years old, she was twelve years old again, she was a child. All the layers were intense, quivering, conscious of existing. Conscious of being a female, a little ashamed of being female."[36] Neville, the 43-year-old hero of Rose Macaulay's *Dangerous Ages* (1921), romps like a child in the first chapter, but we learn that she sacrifices her medical career for her husband and now has "a wasted brain; squandered, atrophied, gone soft with disuse." Comparing herself to her husband, Rodney, she reflects that they had "the same outlook on life. Only Rodney's had been solidified and enveloped by the contacts and exigencies of his career, and Neville's disembodied, devitalized and driven inwards by her more dilettante life."[37] Whereas Rodney has grown up into adulthood, a solid body at home in the world, Neville, having no vital role in society, has been "disembodied." Her attempts to return to her career result in the scorn of her husband and brother (now a surgeon), the misunderstanding of her children, and, at the end, a "nervous breakdown." Sheltered and protected by her husband, her development held in check despite her physical and mental capabilities, Neville atrophies into permanent neurosis. For many women, Phyllis Chesler asserts in *Women and Madness* (1972), madness and confinement are "both an expression of female powerlessness and an unsuccessful attempt to reject and overcome this fate. Madness and asylums generally function as mirror images of the female experience, and as penalties for *being* 'female,' as well as for daring *not* to be."[38]

A woman enters upon a "psychiatric career," in Chesler's theory, as a strategy for expressing an appraisal of her real position in society. Such women are "acting out," or giving dramatic form to, their insights into the dwarfing powers of the enclosure, their insanity becoming a metaphor for their social status. Women's fiction, correspondingly, is a literary strategy expressing the ironic inversion of humanistic norms by rigid gender codes. The inversion of the novel of development is an ironic reverse of gender norms that society expects of people in general. One might also postulate that the double bind underlying the structure of the bildungsroman, derived from the contrary forces of a girl's desire for authenticity and her society's desire for her femininity, also mimics the type of "split" in the personality clinically defined as schizophrenic. It follows quite naturally, then, that so many of the images and leitmotifs of the bildungsroman deal with the same sense of "suffocation," breathlessness, of being stuffed down and dwarfed, that characterizes inmates of mental institutions.

As we have seen, equally powerful drives towards free movement and naturism operate within the novel of development, working in opposition to the dwarfing forces. The need for the green world and the green-world lover intensifies at the same rate that society insists upon proffering the rapist/villain, enclosure, and atrophy as alternatives. Mediating between these two forces, the woman novelist develops strategies of image, tone, and structure. Thus, at the same time that the authors we have surveyed suggest psychic dwarfing as the inevitable destiny of young women in British and American society, they manage to introduce a considerable degree of protest into the genre through satiric portrayals of the effects of this dwarfing and through a vivid depiction of the feelings of its victims. The note of protest, accompanied by the countertone of accommodation or acceptance, stems from what Northrop Frye calls the "myth of freedom," or romance element, set against the "myth of concern," or of social conservatism.

In the genre of science fiction women authors are sometimes able to project visions of worlds where heroes dare *not* to be female, transcending the gender limitations characterizing more conventional novels. During the past ten or fifteen years a number of women science fiction authors have begun to create narrative patterns in which a hero completes a full-fledged romance quest. Ursula K. Le Guin, who began publishing short fiction in such magazines as *Fantastic* and *Amazing* in the 1960s, conceives of science fiction as a "way of seeing" better possibilities for gender equality, "a view in" to worlds in which the imagination can build social structures of its own choosing. "One of the essential functions of science fiction," she writes in an essay entitled "Is Gender Necessary?," "is precisely this kind of question-asking: reversals of an habitual way of thinking, metaphors for what our language has no words for as yet, experiments in imagination."[39] In *The Left Hand of Darkness* (1969), for example, she creates a society of ambisexual individuals who enter "kemmer" periodically, becoming male or female for sexual purposes only. Their gender may alter in successive cycles, and for the rest of the time they are androgynous.

Le Guin's *Planet of Exile* (1966), Anne McCaffrey's *Dragonflight*

(1968), and Joanna Russ's *The Female Man* (1975) all portray heroes whose adventures lead them towards an adult life as full, contributing members of society. The narrative pattern of these novels conforms to the usual definition of the (implicitly male) bildungsroman, as based on the concept of *Bildung*, or the ideal of personal fulfillment within a culture. It is not enough that the hero leave his family and undergo adventures teaching him the proper choice of friends, mate, and vocation or even that he learn to make moral choices within the reference of his society. These societal goals must be accompanied by a conscious attempt to develop the self, to realize and exercise his inner powers.

Although it is beyond the scope of this study to do a systematic comparison of male and female bildungsromans, it is plain that the male hero, as well as the female, can be alienated from his social identity. In the woman's novel of development (exclusive of the science fiction genre), however, the hero does not *choose* a life to one side of society after conscious deliberation on the subject; rather, she is radically alienated by gender-role norms *from the very outset*. Thus, although the authors attempt to accommodate their heroes' *Bildung*, or development, to the general pattern of the genre, the disjunctions that we have noted inevitably make the woman's initiation less a self-determined progression *towards* maturity than a regression *from* full participation in adult life. It seems more appropriate to use the term *Entwicklungsroman*, the novel of mere growth, mere physical passage from one age to the other without psychological development, to describe most of the novels that we have perused. Thus, even in Dorothy Richardson's *Pilgrimage*, the most affirmative of the nonfantasy novels we have studied, the survival of the hero takes place neither in the realm of larger society nor in a smaller critical enclave but within personal space, the sense of selfhood that Miriam achieves in her withdrawal *from* human relationships. It is perhaps for this reason that Sydney Kaplan has characterized Miriam's accomplishment as "a featureless freedom," using Richardson's own words to characterize the inevitable "facelessness" of a selfhood constructed upon asocial moments of epiphany. In the other major bildungsroman by a woman in our century, Doris Lessing's *Children of Violence* series, the hero manages to achieve a personal integration, or *Bildung*, within a significant enclave, but this collective exists on a remote island after the destruction of civilization. In most of the novels of development it seems clear that the authors conceive of growing up female as a choice between auxiliary or secondary personhood, sacrificial victimization, madness, and death.

The generic double bind informing these plots results, then, from society's excessive focus on gender as a determinant of social roles and character. The tone of protest conforms, in Frye's terminology, to the romantic tendency to associate everything "demonic or regressive" with society and everything revolutionary or "progressive" with the "individual, the hero or heroine, who has the vision of liberation."[40] Such a dichotomy between liberation and society is wholly appropriate for heroes moving out of a free space into an enclosure, their "vision of liberation" intensified by its imminent demise. Young women heroes begin outside the enclosure into which they must be drawn. In that they are looking *into* a trap *from* a space of doomed authenticity, these are among the most extrasocietal heroes I considered in this book, and it is for this reason that at its roots the bildungsroman is essentially a novel of selfhood rather than of social conformity.

# PART II

# ENCLOSURE
# IN THE PATRIARCHY

> *For you and me, to think may be to be angry, but remember, we can surmount the anger we feel. To find oneself like a young tree inside a tomb is to discover the power to crack the tomb and grow up to any height.*
>
> ELIZABETH BOWEN, *The House in Paris*

# CHAPTER III

# NOVELS OF MARRIAGE

IN THE WOMAN'S BILDUNGSROMAN TENSION BETWEEN THE HERO'S DESIRES and society's dictates results in archetypal narrative patterns of pursuit and submission, accompanied by images of suffocation, dwarfing, and mental illness. In novels of marriage similar archetypes occur, the authors depicting matrimony as one of the primary tools for dulling a hero's initiative and restraining her maturation. Like the rape trauma in the bildungsroman, marriage becomes the turning point in the hero's life, and once again she protests; however loudly she argues, though, these novels remain primarily accommodationist, the authors either undercutting their criticisms with conformist denouements or punishing rebellious heroes with tragic fates. Although many novels depict wives as debilitated or insane, a few suggest that men and women can transcend gender norms to create authenticity within marriage. These equal-marriage novels, which I will discuss at the end of this chapter, provide a bright spot in an otherwise bleak landscape of marital politics.

The conflict between conformity to and rebellion against gender norms that characterizes women's novels of marriage reflects a fluctuation in courtship standards during the past several centuries of the patriarchy. Laurence Stone, in *The Family, Sex and Marriage in England, 1600–1800* (1977), documents two significant shifts in these standards. In sixteenth-century England decisions about marriage were made by family and kinship groups; in this system marriage, at both the top and the bottom of the social scale, was "primarily a contract between two families for the exchange of concrete benefits, not so much for the married couple as for their parents and kin." As early as 1660 a move towards accepting "personal affection, companionship, and friendship" as marital motives, along with allowing the prospective couple a final veto of parental choices, became popular. This development, however, halted abruptly at the end of the eighteenth century with the "revival of moral reform, paternal authority, and sexual repression" to the extent that even the middle classes, which had been the most stalwart supporters of marriage for affection, were swayed by motives of economic and social prudence. Stone hails the popularity of Hannah More's *Coelebs in Search of a Wife* (see above, p. 14), which outlines the model of wifely compliance and submission, as evidence of the "end of an era in husband-wife relations."

Even at the height of the affectional-marriage era there were elements eroding women's authenticity that help to account for persistently dismal portraits of matrimony even to the present day. Stone notes that the shift from motives of power, status, and money to the "imponderables of affection" did not give women full freedom in courtship since they were prohibited from initiating a relationship. Once married, a man and his wife were "one," but only in the sense that the man was the "one"—his desires, needs, and interests subordinated hers.

A second factor limiting women's full development in affectional-marriage relationships was the profound taboo against feminine sexuality. Chastity has been high on the list of wifely virtues for centuries, accompanied by modesty, obedience, prudence, constancy, etc.—all qualities enhancing subordination. "Romantic love" (love at first sight, a passion carrying one way from oneself) and physical attraction (eroticism), writes Stone, were considered "unsafe bases for an enduring marriage, since both were violent mental disturbances which would inevitably be of only short duration."[1] Sexlessness, which Germaine Greer calls "eunuchry," assures propertied men of their biological heirs. Thus, any woman who initiates courtship, or any wife who unconventionally enjoys her sexuality, becomes a threat to the inheritance system; she is "ruined" economically, "fallen" in the scale of social values, and "abnormal" in the sense of acting in an antinormative manner. We shall see, however, that women novelists insisted upon a hero's right to romantic love and that society was quick to condemn such heroes as subversives.[2]

The campaign for romantic love was an act of protest, an attempt to wedge some modicum of equity and Eros into the matrimonial enclosure. While women have achieved a measure of marital and reproductive freedom in the twentieth century, the clash between social norms and individual desires persistently underlies archetypal narrative patterns and images in women's fiction. These archetypes remain intact because the alienation in which they originate still exists. The modern novel of marriage continues to picture a patriarchy that controls economic and political activities, a wife as subordinate to husband, and feminine sexuality as a target of fear and loathing.

Walter Houghton, speaking of Victorian novels, agrees with Stone that novels promulgating affectional relationships were not mere day-dreams but, instead, were pleas for a greater acceptance of passionate feelings between men and women and "a bitter arraignment" of the system that ignored these feelings.[3] Authors developed fictional strategies that encouraged affectional marriage while fully aware of the difficulties that *any* marriage entailed for women. Jane Austen, for example, was concerned with the debilitating effects of bearing many babies. "Anna has not a chance of escape," she wrote of a woman she knew.

> Her husband called here the other day, and said she was *pretty* well but not *equal* to so long a walk; she *must come in her Donkey Carriage*. Poor animal, she will be worn out before she is thirty. I am very sorry for her. Mrs. Clement too is in that way again. I am quite tired of so many Children—Mrs. Benn has a 13th. . . . Good Mrs. Deedes!—I hope she will get the better of this Marianne, and then I would recommend to her and Mr. D. the simple regimen of separate rooms.[4]

Reviewers soundly condemned Charlotte Brontë for allowing Jane Eyre to take the initiative with Mr. Rochester. After *Jane Eyre* (1847) was published Brontë wrote to a friend that "no young lady should fall in love until the offer has been made, accepted, the marriage ceremony performed, and the first half-year of wedded life has passed away. A woman may then begin to love, but with great precaution, very coolly, very moderately, very rationally. If she ever loves so much that a harsh word or a cold look cuts her to the heart, she is a fool."[5] Whereas Austen was concerned with the physical strain of marriage, Brontë's fears, here, relate to the emotional vulnerability of a woman who has placed her well-being in the hands of a husband. In an authorial comment couched in a tangle of negative constructions in an alternative ending to *Middlemarch* (1871–72) George Eliot wrote:

> It was never said in the neighborhood of Middlemarch that such mistakes [Dorothea's marriage to Casaubon] could not have happened if the society into which she was born had not smiled on propositions of marriage from a sickly man to a girl less than half his own age.[6]

This desire for equity in marriage accounts for the rebellion underlying much of women's fiction.

Twentieth-century authors have been equally perturbed by the dichotomy between love and marriage. Contemporary novelist Katherine Anne Porter calls herself a "Western romantic," finds the idea of love within marriage a "charming work of the human imagination," but wonders how "Romantic Love got into marriage at last, where it was most certainly never intended to be."[7] Like a number of other modern authors—Elizabeth Bowen, Doris Lessing, Fay Weldon, Jean Rhys, for example—Porter's fiction consists of an intrepid but perennially frustrated quest for a relationship in which a hero can achieve equity, authenticity, and Eros.

The nineteenth-century author's desire for affectional marriages and the twentieth-century author's desire for romantic and erotic ones inevitably lead them to create textual constructions and narrative strategies that emphasize these themes. Although, as I have stated in the Preface, in-depth textual studies of works by major authors are beyond the scope of this book, it will be useful to note the techniques employed by writers like Austen and Eliot. Austen's fiction is uniquely concerned with the question of marriage for money: "All of Jane Austen's opening paragraphs, and the best of her first sentences, have money in them," remarks Ellen Moers.[8] Austen approaches marriage by balancing critique with acceptance, using wit, humor, and satire to spoof the worst marital abuses and then to proffer an affectionate *and* financially prudent model husband. Another Austen plot strategy matches a minor character in an undesirable marriage while the dismayed hero looks on and strives to do otherwise. "Mr. Collins, to be sure, was neither sensible or agreeable," reflects the girl who has decided upon a prudent marriage in *Pride and Prejudice* (1813).

> His society was irksome, and his attachment to her must be imaginary. But still he would be her husband. Without thinking highly either of men or of matrimony, marriage had always been her object; it was the only honourable provision for well-educated young women of small fortune, and however uncertain of giving happiness, must be her pleasant preservative from want.[9]

A similar plot strategy, which involves a comparison of undesirable unions with desirable ones, characterizes Eliot's *Middlemarch* as well as a great number of nineteenth-century and turn-of-the-century novels. In the "double-marriage plot" an unsuitable alliance is proffered or consummated but, fortunately, terminated by either jilting or death so that a more equal norm may be achieved. This second marriage or engagement, however, is rarely depicted; picturing it as the festive goal of the denouement, the author rarely details its actual dimensions. Using comic conventions, many authors spoof the foibles of married life so soundly as to make marriage a target of satire. This is true of such humorists as Nancy Mitford and Angela Thirkell, who carry on in a minor vein many of the turns of wit and satire developed by Austen and Eliot.

Not all marital plotting is comic, however; many women authors, as we shall see, develop so bitter a portrait of matrimony that their heroes are destroyed by it, worn down by society's pressure for non-affectional, economically viable marriages, or turned outcast because they demand more of the institution than the patriarchy can permit. Tragic plots characterize the novels of not only Edith Wharton, Charlotte Perkins Gilman, and Elizabeth Stuart Phelps but also a number of more recent women writers, like Jean Rhys and Joan Didion. Finally, as in the case of the bildungsroman, many women develop extended metaphors of insanity, likening effects of matrimony to madness and incarceration.

## MARRIAGE AS ARCHETYPAL ENCLOSURE

Since *Bildung*, or true maturation, is as rare for the married hero as for the adolescent one, many of the archetypal images and patterns characteristic of the novel of development persist in the novel of marriage, the perspective differing only in the sense that the heroes are now *within* the wedded circle. Each attribute of authenticity meets with its opposite: freedom to come and go is abrogated; early, ideal lovers are banished, to be replaced by a husband who resembles the gothic villain; erotic freedom is severely limited; intelligence becomes a curse, and, correspondingly, too much consciousness of one's situation leads to punishment or madness. Defined as "normality," mental abnormality shapes an archetype antithetical to the virgin goddess— the mad wife. Authors describe the golden circle of marriage, symbolizing an eternity of mutual love, as a tarnished enclosure. I touch here upon some typical examples of these novels. Once again, I will principally deal with minor novelists, although similar themes and images can be found in the works of more recognized authors.

Freedom to come and go, which involves the right to make decisions about one's own time, work, and other activities, is a basic element of authenticity. The irony that permeates so much of women's fiction results from a recognition of the discrepancy between premarital dreams of authenticity and marital realities. During courtship, in the novel of marriage, the quest for mutuality often leads men to promise more freedom to their fiancées than traditional patriarchal marriage permits. This disappointment of expectations characterizes Elizabeth Stuart Phelps's *The Story of Avis* (1877), in which the hero takes long, happy walks over the fields, fosters her ambition as an artist, and falls in love with a man who promises that he will hamper neither her freedom nor the development of her talents. Her doubts produce a frightening proposal scene: " 'I suffer because I love you,' " she remarks. " 'It is like—death.' "[10] The young husband quickly limits Avis's freedom, and her health atrophies as she realizes her decorative function within the enclosure of marriage.

Gertrude Atherton depicts a similar disappointment in *American Wives and English Husbands* (1898), building her plot upon the notion that American girls are given much more freedom than British ones, who are carefully groomed for submission. Lee meets Cecil in America and falls in love with him for both his intellect and his attractiveness, only to find that he expects her to take a subordinate, auxiliary role. Belittled by the domestic duties expected of the British wife, Lee experiences "moods" of boredom. Cecil derides her American "spoiled child" need to "be an individual," upset that she has been brought up to consider herself rather than serve a husband. Lee finally exercises her talents after her father-in-law squanders her money, and she helps to rescue the estate. Unlike Phelps, Atherton thus restores her hero to some degree of authenticity within marriage.

Women authors sometimes point out that the new generation is as bound by patriarchal norms as the older. Ruth Suckow, in *Country People* (1924), depicts a family so thoroughly ruled by a merciless German patriarch that his wife dies because she is not permitted to send for a doctor without his leave. "When they were married," remarks Suckow of such women, "they found themselves cramped up in someone else's existence and having to order their own lives by what someone else was able to do. That was Mama's life—wasn't it? Doing double work, and at the same time actually dependent upon Papa, upon what he, not she, was able to make—having to fit all her efforts into that."[11] If a young woman escapes to "sexual emancipation" in the big city, however, she finds that the patriarchy still limits her ability to make choices. Margaret, in *The Folks* (1934), leaves her German immigrant family only to fall in love with a man who behaves just like her father. On the one hand, she recognizes that "regular marriage meant being like the folks, presenting a united front to the world, neither one doing as he or she wanted to do" and that wives like her mother were "womenly women, who were nothing on their own, made out of the rib of man." On the other hand, she submits herself to a married lover who keeps her firmly in her place.

In Atherton, Phelps, and Suckow, the taming of the free "virgin," to use the term in the sense of a self-motivated, self-determined being, includes images of cramping, diminished stature, and psychological "moods" resulting from the dwarfing of the personality. Katherine Anne Porter, in *Ship of Fools* (1962), creates a complex, extended metaphor of many enclosures within a single enclosure of a German passenger steamer crossing the Atlantic in the 1930s. Bearing passengers of many nationalities straight into the maw of fascist Germany, the ship has cabins that contain men and women whom Porter sees as "necessary enemies," who hate each other as if sexual warfare were a "kind of virtue."[12]

The ship carries German couples involved in sadistic, but often pathetic, marriages; Spanish couples fighting over the women's earnings as prostitutes; and several Americans, including Jenny and "David Darling," lovers locked into a situation typifying disappointed young American women on the quest for "emancipation." During the voyage, Jenny realizes that all of the choices in their relationship are in David's hands: he even has the right to read her letters, although he has denied her all access to his private life. Even though David jealously watches Jenny's friendship with Freytag, these two men enjoy greater mutuality than do the lovers. At the denouement Jenny sees them shake hands in parting and realizes that she is witnessing "the wordless affirmation of pure male complicity, complete understanding from far depths of instinctive being . . . from which she was excluded by natural law, in their inalienable state of manhood." Not only are women rendered secondary in their relationships to men, but they must also watch their lovers engage in the very mutuality and authenticity that they are denied.

Porter's David Darling shares an ironic trait with the husbands in Phelps's *The Story of Avis* and Atherton's *American Wives and English Husbands*—he is not overtly destructive but, rather, "perfectly nice," a lover who apparently will bring out the best in both himself and his partner. Under the guise of "green-world lover," these young men only gradually become repressive. This slow transformation of seemingly appropriate mates into guardians of the enclosure inundates twentieth-century women's fiction. Harald in Mary McCarthy's *The Group* (1963) only gradually reveals his inability to love Kay; Douglas Knowell in Lessing's *Martha Quest* and *A Proper Marriage* (1954) appears as quite a liberal fellow to the hero, who later must painfully move toward authenticity through divorce. Both McCarthy and Lessing use the discrepancy between their heroes' expectations and marital realities as a structural irony, turning the apparently nice young husbands into satiric targets.

In Josephine Herbst's story of "The Man of Steel" and in Christina Stead's *The Man Who Loved Children* (1940) the husbands' "niceness" itself, exaggerated by hyperbole, is destructive. Herbst's Truax gives his wife presents as a substitute for love, and Stead's Sam Pollitt is a paragon of sweetness and light, planning programs for his children's education and physical development. In both cases the wives feel neglected, locked within marriages that, while appearing ideal to the outsider, in reality allow them no room for growth. Most important, their autonomy is watched, their movements limited, their every trip to town monitored. This invasion deprives the heroes of personal space until they either divorce or die of "suffocation." " 'You beast, you pair of beasts,' " shouts Stead's Henny as she drinks the poisoned tea her daughter has prepared for her. " 'My womb is torn to pieces with you—the oil is everywhere and your dirty sheets falling on me to suffocate me with the sweat, I can't stand it any more— she's not to blame' " (of the daughter), " 'she's got guts, she was going to do it.' "[13] There is absolutely nothing "wrong" with Henny's mind, even at this point: her wild behavior is merely a logical reaction to her husband.

## COMPLICITY

The sense that these heroes have entrapped themselves and freely chosen their guards/husbands emphasizes the irony in this fiction. Like Katherine Anne Porter, Joyce Carol Oates and Mary McCarthy seem convinced that women are fated to make these terrible decisions, will-lessly driven into postures of masochism and submission. Husbands who are depicted as gothic villains in so many novels of marriage do not intrude from some terrible otherworld over which the heroes have no control; rather, the heroes submit to the invasions of their authenticity as if such invasions were completely unavoidable, even "normal." Thus McCarthy describes Miles, villain of *A Charmed Life* (1954), as having the "method in his madness" of making "his wives choose between him and common sense, between him and ordinary decency," engulfing them in his megalomaniacal perspective.

> He made his wives his accomplices; that was why they could not escape him. They had to stand by and watch him abuse the servants, hold back their wages, eat their food, accuse them of robbing him. He insisted that his wives lie for him, to his creditors, to the insurance company, to the tax people. He had no sense of limit or of other people's rights. Nothing was safe from his meandering appetites: the maid's time off, her dinner, her birthday box of candy, the cooking sherry, the vanilla. He even, Martha remembered, used to eat Barrett's lollipops. . . . His outrageousness had a purpose: by a cam-

paign of calculated "frightfulness" he broke his wives' spirits. She herself could never live down, in her own mind, not what he had done to her, but what she consented in.[14]

However horrific McCarthy's portrait, Martha consents to her dilemma, sexually submitting to Miles even after her divorce and remarriage, and as an indirect result she dies. In Oates's fiction, similarly, many heroes surrender themselves to husbands who turn them into passive zombies. Programmed to be wives, mothers, and helpmates when they would rather remain single, childless, and celibate, woman after woman in Oates's work imprisons herself within escape-proof enclosures. Helen, the second of three doomed, feminine generations in *Wonderland* (1971), forces herself into marriage because she knows society expects it of her, although she is dimly aware of a tension between her predilections and her self-policing:

> All her life she had felt wild rushes of expectation and fear. *To be a woman. A Wife.* You needed a man to complete you; that was obvious. In order to be a woman, a wife. She had been afraid to think about love, about loving a man, because it had seemed to her impossible, ugly, brutish. She had resisted thinking about it the way she resisted thinking about death. It was too ugly. She had grown up with a dislike of being touched, even by her parents. Yet she knew she must be touched eventually. She must be touched, loved, completed by a man and made over into a woman. *A woman: a wife.*[15]

Helen cannot be a woman, in her own estimation, until she experiences a physical invasion that she equates wtih death. Once again, Helen does not *have* to marry Jesse (who is one of the "perfectly nice" school of husbands); she does not have to marry *anybody*. Her daughter, Shelley, correspondingly, takes a sadistic lover who declares that he has reduced her to a "Shell," to a part of his brain: " 'That girl is my property,' " he declares. " 'She willed herself to me.' "

Because women were property, as reflected in early inheritance laws, chastity remained a norm for wives until the beginning of the present century. The sexual emancipation heralded in the 1920s, however, has been as likely to free a woman for further enslavement as to encourage sexual freedom. Heroes like Suckow's and Porter's leave country families for the city, only to have affairs or marriages that duplicate familial paternalism; other novels describe women making attempts at adultery, merely to return, disappointed, to the original marriage; or, as a variation on the theme, heroes engage in affair after affair (or marriage after marriage) without finding erotic satisfaction.[16]

Sexual repression, a sense of physical frustration and unmitigated desire, becomes one among other discomforts typifying enclosure.

When a character battles a force outside herself (like Lessa, in McCaffrey's *Dragonflight*, in her foray against the extraterrestrial "thread"), she is able to call upon an inner strength and sense of self-worth. When heroes in the novel of marriage internalize dictates from the patriarchy, rebellion is more difficult, and when, in addition, the hero has a heightened consciousness, the ironic boon of intelligence, her discomfort becomes even more excruciating. For the adult hero, as for the adolescent one, critical intelligence is a curse. In *The Dream and the Business* (1906), John Oliver Hobbes (Pearl Craigie) develops a subplot in which the wife, Tessa, succumbs to her own self-knowledge, leaving the way clear, after her death, for her husband to marry another woman. Tessa, dissatisfied with the role of social hostess, would prefer "to move on a larger stage and take part in some heroic drama." She forces herself to be domestic and thinks of herself as a "Sleeping Beauty": " 'Is not the fairy tale of the Sleeping Beauty the story of every girl who is intelligent and well-guarded?' " she asks. " 'She is sent to sleep lest she should think too much and too soon.' " Tessa cannot keep herself from thinking about her marriage, likening herself to a "songbird in a cage," unable to find outlets for an "uncontrollable new force within her . . . crying out for more liberty, more experience, and more response." Subject to fits of futile weeping, she withers away from a mysterious illness remarkably like Betty Friedan's feminine mystique, the disease with no name: "She seemed to droop and perish as a starved plant."[17]

Not all novels of marriage employ death as a punishment for intelligence: many detail the development of a hero's consciousness and then leave her in contemplation of the dimensions of her enclosure. Neville, in Rose Macaulay's *Dangerous Ages*, complains of "her active but wasted brain. A good brain, too; she had easily and with brilliance passed her medical examinations years ago. . . . But now a wasted brain; squandered, atrophied, gone soft with disuse." She is unable to escape her auxiliary role in her husband Rodney's life: "She 'helped Rodney with the constituency' of course, but it was Rodney's constituency, not hers; she entertained his friends and hers when they were in town. . . . Yet her nature was stronger than Rodney's, larger and more mature; it was only his experience she lacked."[18] Rodney, a full-fledged citizen of society, has been educated for decision making and for political leadership. Neville's experience limited her to the enclosure of wifehood, her immurement as psychologically delibitating as if she had been kept in purdah. Julia, in Elizabeth Taylor's *At Mrs. Lippincote's* (1945), is also plagued by intelligence, by her "strange gift of coming to a situation freshly, peculiarly untarnished by preconceived ideas, whether of her own preconceptions or the world's. Could she have taken for granted a few of the generalizations invented by men and acquiesced in by women . . . she would have eased her own life and other people's."[19] Julia, like Neville, suffers from her authentic, inner voice. Questioning patriarchal expectations, authors imply, is a painful, sometimes fatal experience.

## INSANITY

Complicity and repressed critical intelligence thus are associated with the other experiences of wifehood—limitations on freedom, submission to husbands, diminished eroticism—that split these heroes' personalities between authentic selfhood and social dictates for femininity. In fiction describing the mad wife, women authors create their most complex embellishments on the enclosure archetype. Depicting wifehood as a cause or condition of madness, they develop extended metaphors linking normal households and insane asylums, not only using real insane asylums but also picturing individual rooms, suites, floors, and entire houses where women are driven mad by dehumanizing gender norms. The prototypical mad wife of this type is Antoinette Rochester, in Charlotte Brontë's *Jane Eyre*, wild, alcoholic, and imprisoned in the attic of Thornfield Hall. Although Brontë sympathizes with Rochester (whose relatives forced him into an emotionally unsuitable but financially useful marriage), Jean Rhys, in *Wide Sargasso Sea* (1966), recreates the story, blaming Rochester for mistrusting Antoinette's eroticism. In Rhys's account, Rochester awakens her sexuality, only to be disgusted by it, horrified that a wife should enjoy sex. " 'She'll moan and cry and give herself as no sane woman would,— *or could,*' " he declares to a friend. Rochester's society condones his assignment of the "crazed" Antoinette to his attic, and as a result she becomes violent. The world outside, she decides, is "cardboard," the world of her enclosed space her only reality. Although she is perfectly sane to begin with, her growing madness seems a self-fulfilling prophesy.

Rhys's irony pivots on the discrepancy between social expectations and Antoinette's personal realities. "If you say my eroticism is insane," such heroes might say (or "my critical intelligence" or "my desire for freedom to come and go"), "then, indeed, I will show you, I *will act mad.*" A similar irony underlies the plot of Charlotte Perkins Gilman's "The Yellow Wallpaper" (1892), emphasized by Gilman's use of the careful, meticulous diarist as first-person narrator. Gilman presents a "perfectly nice" husband, John, who calls the narrator "little girl" and "blessed little goose," incarcerating her fondly in a second-floor nursery (she would have preferred a sunny downstairs room) to help her recover from "nerves." The chief causes of her weakened state of mind, he feels (and, because he is a physician, she finds it hard to dissuade him), are her excessive longings for social life and for using her imagination in "fancies" and in writing. These activities are forbidden, and with her normal outlets atrophied the narrator focuses her attention on the nursery's wallpaper. At first merely aesthetically displeased by its illogical patterns ("a toadstool in joints, an interminable string of toadstools, budding and sprouting in endless convolutions") and its smell (of "foul, bad yellow things"), she gradually begins to hallucinate. Perceiving a split in the wallpaper, she decides that there is an "outside pattern" and a "subpattern" and determines that her own meaning exists in their interaction. "I *will* follow that pointless pattern," she declares, "to some sort of a conclusion." To this end, she tears away at the outside pattern, trying to liberate a woman imprisoned within it. "I didn't realize for a long time what the thing was that showed behind, that dim subpattern, but now I am quite sure it is a woman."[20] In the final scene of the novella the nice husband falls into a dead faint, finding his insane wife crawling around the nursery, tearing away at the wallpaper.

Clearly, Gilman intends the wallpaper as an analogue to the institution of marriage. The outside pattern corresponds to society's expectations that good little wives do not gad about and write; the subpattern contains the heroic but imprisoned symbol of authentic personality. It is also clear that the narrator will be sent away to a lunatic asylum as a result of her response to her confinement. Narratives in which a hero can only rebel with the ironic but futile "acting out" of the unfeminine behavior that society finds "insane" are staples of women's fiction. Thus Tina, the hero of Sue Kaufman's *Diary of a Mad Housewife* (1967), bemusedly accepts her insomnia, drugs, drinking, crazy hours, freakish outbursts, and veiled rebellions as necessary conditions of marriage to her hard-working husband. In spite of her critical intelligence, she comes to believe that "mad" and "housewife" are synonyms. Maria, hero of Joan Didion's *Play It as It Lays* (1970), feels that "if Carter [her husband] and Helene [his lover] want to think it happened because I was insane, I say let them. They have to lay it off on someone. . . . One thing in my defense, not that it matters: I know something Carter never knew, or Helene, or maybe you. I know what 'nothing' means, and keep on playing."[21] Maria accepts the accusation that her insanity has led to Helene's husband's death, preferring to act out the role of madwoman than to live in the world outside, which seems even more irrational than the world within.

The outside world in mad-wife fiction provides little encouragement to the deviant hero who wants to escape her enclosure since its norms are the very ones that make human behavior "abnormal" for women. Nor are husbands the only gothic villains presiding over such enclosures: they are aided and abetted by the heroes' relatives, including their mothers. Women novelists frequently make use of two, and sometimes even three, generations of mothers and daughters to show how heroes are punished by their closest role models. Thus, in Doris Lessing's *Children of Violence* series, as in Macaulay's *Dangerous Ages*, the mother's neurotic behavior is detailed as one among other causes of the hero's difficulties. Diane Hamilton, hero of Blanche Boyd's *Nerves* (1973), can look back to three women as models for her own feeling of neurosis: her mother, who had a nervous breakdown because she felt that her identity had been "erased" by marriage; her mother's friend, who leaves her husband, has an affair, and commits suicide; and her aunt, a pathologically lonely widow. "I will never be crazy," repeats the adolescent hero to herself. "I will never get killed. I have to grow up." How she can grow up, when feminine adulthood clearly entails debility, remains an open question.

There is no question about the condition of wifehood, however, in the novel of marriage. Authors paint intensely negative portraits of husbands, mothers, and marital realities, devastating portraits that point to a traumatic rift in matrimonial ideas. It is striking, furthermore, that the men and women—Kaufman's housewifely Tina, McCarthy's "hysterically" rebellious Kay, their husbands, Jonathan and Harald—are not presented as inherently deviant but as hyperbolic exaggerations of normative feminine and maculine behavior. Their marriages, presented with enough gothic imagery to suggest torture chambers or iron maidens full of spikes aimed at the human spirit, are not fantastic or intrinsically pathological relationships but perfectly "normal" marriages. Women authors tenaciously portray matrimony as a negative institution, utilizing archetypal patterns of trauma and enclosure analogous to those found in the novel of development. Such representations lead one to wonder whether there is anything worth salvaging of the institution of matrimony; this prescriptive question is seldom addressed in women's fiction. Although few in number, there do exist novels in which men and women seek, and sometimes achieve, authenticity and equity within marriage.

## POSSIBILITIES OF TRANSCENDENCE: THE EQUAL-MARRIAGE NOVEL

In 1927 Gertrude Atherton brought out *The Immortal Marriage*, a meticulously researched historical portrait of the sexual politics of Classical Greece, and of Aspasia, a Doric woman who defied Athenian misogyny in her lifelong love relationship with Pericles. Atherton discovered that love between men and women shocked a culture that allowed passion only in relationships between men; this discovery raises the problem of whether, in a totally male-dominated culture, there can be equal love between a man and a woman. " 'True love,' " remarks one man whose male lover is seduced away by a woman friend of Aspasia's, " 'can exist between intellectual and high-minded men only. It is but the meaner sort of love that a man may feel for a woman, who is without virtue; or with only those lesser virtues which are necessary in the house. I realize that I am talking to a woman, but I am also talking to Aspasia. You have the mind of a man and it was due to the strange oversight of the gods that it passed into the form of a woman.' "[22] Although he deeply loves Aspasia, Pericles fears that if he marries her she will automatically become childlike, as is suitable for inferiors: "Must he live to witness Aspasia's love change to that of a dutiful daughter?" By the end of the novel (although not without much debate and personal struggle to overcome Greek sexual prejudice) Pericles's fears prove unfounded. Atherton portrays Aspasia as feminine and as capable of love and of intellectual and political activities without detracting from the quality of their passion.

Marriages in this genre do not begin as "equal" but involve a man and a woman in the process of struggling through societal obstacles to equal partnership. In *The Home-Maker* (1924), Dorothy Canfield Fisher examines the ill-fitting marital roles of one unhappy couple, allowing them to reverse roles so that the wife becomes the breadwinner and the husband a contented housewife. The first half of the book consists of a detailed description of the familial chaos caused by Evangeline Knapp's compulsive housekeeping. Constantly angry, nervous, overwrought, and covered with eczema, she is destroying her youngest son by the wrong kind of attention and has undermined the health of her two elder children with excessive fussing. Husband Lester hates his career so much that he tries to kill himself by jumping off his roof while supposedly putting out a chimney fire. He survives but is confined to a wheelchair. Lester joyfully cooks, cleans, and cherishes his children, realizing "how unhappy she [Evangeline] must have been before, like a Titan forced to tend a miniature garden; forced to turn the great flood of that inherited, specialized ability of hers [business acumen] into the tiny shallow channels of the infinitely minute detail of child-care; forced, day after day."[23] Evangeline, meanwhile, goes to work in Lester's department store, loves the commercial world, and realizes, from hearing other women's accounts of male brutality, how lucky she is to have the androgynous Lester, whom she had previously considered a Milquetoast.

When Lester begins to regain the use of his legs, he realizes that if he fully recovers they could not continue their new life-style.

> He knew that this was impossible. The instant he tried to consider it, he knew it was as impossible as to roll away a mountain from his path with his bare hands. He knew that from the beginning of time everything had been arranged to make that impossible. Every unit in the whole of society would join in making it impossible, from the Ladies' Guild to the children in the public schools. It would be easier for him to commit murder or rob a bank than to give his intelligence where it was most needed, in his own home with his children.[24]

This equal marriage survives only because Evangeline, Lester, and the doctor agree to pretend that he is permanently paralyzed: he would rather never walk again than return to the monstrosities of "normal"-male-role behavior. In this way his "paralysis," like insanity, becomes a metaphor for prescribed sex roles; only by becoming functionally asocial can Lester achieve authenticity.

Fisher's concern with the effects of sex-role changes on the male character reflects an economy that had historically reserved "money-making" and personal worth for the male. In *Spellbinders* (1922), Margaret Culkin Banning deals with the visit of a single "strong-minded woman," Margaret Duffield, to her old college friend, Helen Flanagan. Upset by Margaret's skepticism about their marriage, Helen's husband, Gage, loathes Margaret for her feminism, which he calls a " 'horrible conscious-self-consciousness. Their nervousness. Their aggressiveness.' " Helen, encouraged by her feminist friend, carries out her lifelong political ambitions and confronts the limitations of two seemingly unreconcilable alternatives: sacrificing sexuality for a career, on the one hand, or sacrificing a career for sexuality, on the other. Helen must also deal with Gage's criticism of her fast-developing political career, and without giving up an inch of that career she resolves to be more tender. He, in turn, realizes that her femininity will not be lost in her new-found happiness:

> As he looked he saw upon her the marks of the work she had done and would do, the new definiteness, the look of being headed somewhere. But his rancor seemed to have burned itself out and with it had gone the old possessive passion. He stirred restlessly. Some phoenix was rising. . . . Whether they could work it out through his storms and hers ceased to gnaw at his thought of her. He saw her strong, also self-sufficient. . . . The delight of the adventure, the indestructible adventure between man and woman remained. His mind moored there.[25]

As in *Immortal Marriage* and *Spellbinders*, a struggle must take place before reciprocity can be achieved. Gage moves through fear and anger at Helen's human needs into a state where he is one part of "some phoenix . . . rising." Banning uses this archetype of the androgynous bird regenerating itself from its own ashes to represent the transcendence of "masculinity" and "femininity" that must take place before men and women can achieve truly reciprocal authenticity. Rarely has the vexing question of whether a woman could have both a man's love and a career received so positive a treatment in women's fiction.

Pamela Hansford Johnson, like Gertrude Atherton, chose a historical setting for her *Catherine Carter* (1952). Most of the action takes place during a premarital affair, and the resulting marriage traumatizes the relationship. Johnson shows actor Henry Peverel and protegée Catherine Carter trying to reconcile their great passion for each other with their careers in the Victorian theater. Henry, determined never to be upstaged by a woman, gives Catherine minor parts throughout their love affair. Johnson describes the childhood insecurity underlying his terror of equality and shows Catherine persisting in her determination to succeed despite the anguished knowledge that she may lose Henry's love. At the denouement they play a scene from Shakespeare's *Antony and Cleopatra*, finally breaking out of their prescribed sex roles in a triumph of passionate reciprocity:

> "There's beggary in the love that can be reckon'd!" cues Henry. She retorted: "I'll set a bourn how far to be belov'd!" He hesitated for a second, staring at her. His laughter died into a look of such passionate intensity that it drew the mirth from her own face. His voice deepened. He said, almost roughly: "Then must thou needs find out new heaven, new earth."

Henry remarks to himself, at this point, that it is his acting that is "bearing her up." "But," remarks Johnson,

> it was not merely that, she was not a cramped swimmer, borne up by him upon these sparkling seas: she was rising to his side, powerful as he and as joyful. Her love for him fused into love for Antony. She spoke each line as if it had sprung freshly to her lips, as indeed it had, for she had never known it before. She was no longer afraid of smallness: she had the spirit of height, of muscle, of sovereign energy.[26]

Johnson characterizes Catherine's maturation with images antithetical to those of enclosure: instead of cramped and atrophied muscles we have healthy limbs, free breathing, and a sense of filling one's own space without being suffocated in it. To grow up fully, without being constricted by "femininity," is so unusual a denouement that Johnson must also project the archetype of a "new heaven and a new earth" as a more suitable setting than the society we already know. Like Banning's phoenix, Johnson creates a futuristic figure, suggestive of the powerful force necessary to transcend gender in heterosexual relationships.

Fully cognizant of the difficulties of equal love within the patriarchy, Banning and Johnson nonetheless project the possibility that such a love *might* exist if men and women could conquer those inner, or encoded, voices that dictate "male" and "female" behavior. Each character reaches a consciousness where reciprocal Eros becomes possible, but only after looking inward, coming to terms, in Woolf's phrase, with the "manly" in the woman and the "womanly" in the man. It is interesting that both Banning and Johnson look carefully at the problems faced by the men, as well as by the women, in a gender-rigid society. "The adequate meeting of the two worlds," posits Daly,

> cannot be imagined as a simple one-to-one relationship between humanity's two halves, for half a person never really can meet the objectified other half. The adequate "cosmosis" will require a breakdown of walls within the male psyche as well as within the female. It will require in men as well as in women a desire to become androgynous, that is, to become themselves.[27]

The enclosure of marriage limits male, as well as female, development, and, conversely, the alternative of androgynous reciprocity benefits both sexes. Human selfhood, in Daly's analysis, is not a matter of balancing two eternally cycling and rigidly defined opposites. Rather, androgyny results from the negation of gender stereotypes, the absorption of positive qualities of "masculinity" and "femininity" into the total personality, and thus the development of a selfhood beyond gender dichotomies. The equal-marriage novel embodies this dialectical process in its narrative structure, taking its heroes from destructive gender norms towards more authentic selfhood. Though so very few in number, such novels perform the same prescriptive and prophetic function as feminist science fiction, building the promise of new worlds from the destruction of the old.

# CHAPTER IV

# THE NOVEL OF SOCIAL PROTEST

WE HAVE SEEN HOW WOMEN AUTHORS, IN NOVEL AFTER NOVEL, DEPICT heroes struggling for authenticity against the limitations of familial and marital enclosures. In many cases the hero has so thoroughly internalized extrapersonal, societal norms that she is fighting against behavior patterns encoded in her own consciousness. In the novel of social protest, in contrast, authors treat the family and marriage as enclaves within a wider enclosure, as individual prisons bounded by the walls of a larger community. Since modern society itself is the object of awareness and target of satire in these novels, authors censure impersonal economic and social forces as responsible for the oppression of women. As we shall see, however, women embrace Christianity, socialism, and communism as alternate systems, only to find that these systems, too, are undermined by the sexual politics of patriarchy.

## THE CHRISTIAN HERO

The nineteenth century witnessed a surge of evangelical Christianity that was often promulgated in the form of didactic "tracts" or nonfictional pamphlets promoting both social reform and religious conversion. Many actively Christian women writers found fiction more effective than these tracts in reaching souls and sought narrative formulas that would appeal to the widest possible audiences.[1] The traditional Christian morality play, in which Everyman battles the Devil while Virtue confronts Vice, proved a popular format for women evangelists. It was a natural transition from the hero of gothic fiction, the young girl struggling against the machinations of the villain, to the reformist hero tilting against the evils of industry. The character familiar to us as the witty, satiric virgin plays the role of Virtue, challenging the Devil as industrial combine while urging Everyman to end capitalist exploitation of the workers. At the denouements of this fiction a festive reconciliation between Virtue, Everyman, and the Devil takes place in the form of a marriage between the ingénue and her repentant industrialist suitor, and the couple then sets forth to build a benevolent, Christian, company shop.

Elizabeth Gaskell's prescriptions in her sociologically astute *Mary Barton* (1848) follow this morality formula: aware that the shutdowns and layoffs in the Manchester shops have been caused by fluctuations in the cotton market, she calls not for economic planning but for religious attention. The mill owner, Mr. Carson, is to be reformed in such a way that he comes to "acknowledge the Spirit of Christ as the regulating law between both [owner and working] parties," resulting in a Christianized company shop in which the workers will be educated and "bound to their employers by ties of respect and affection, not by mere money bargains alone."[2] Similarly, Charlotte Brontë uses this formula of a Christian optimism in *Shirley*. Brontë describes two heroes, one the more liberated, free-wheeling Shirley and the other her friend Caroline, a timid, conservative, but nonetheless sensitive and courageous girl. They fall in love with two brothers: Robert, an industrialist Everyman, and Louis, Shirley's former tutor. Using the Luddite riots of the Napoleonic era as a background of economic history, Brontë has her heroes observe the negative effects of fluctuating trade conditions upon the mill workers and their families. The two friends try to modify Robert's single-minded mercantilism, urging him to behave more humanely with his workers.

For Charlotte Elizabeth Tonna, as for Gaskell and Brontë, fiction was a weapon for the Christian reform of industrial conditions, in *Helen Fleetwood* (1841), her major novel, and in such stories as "The Wrongs of Women" (1843). Permitted and indeed encouraged to concentrate upon religion as one among other wifely duties, activist Victorian women used Christianity in their push for a more humane society. "We may shower Bibles like hail over the earth's wide surface," remarks Tonna,

> we may exhibit in our own conduct and conversation a very model of all that Christian women ought to be; but this one thing God requires of us, and will not acquit us if we refuse to do it, whatever worthy deeds we may choose to do, that we enter our strong, urgent unanimous protest against the frightful degradation of our sisters, and demand from those who have the power to accord it the boon of their emancipation.[3]

Far from meekly religious, women authors seized upon the prophetic and humanistic aspects of religion as contrary to industrial practices. Such fiction enjoyed widespread popularity, as in the case of Mrs. Humphrey Ward's *Sir George Tressady* (1896), in which the male hero establishes the New Brotherhood of Christ in the London slums. A similar formula informs Mary Wilkins Freeman's *The Portion of Labor* (1901), in which the hero, Ellen, falls in love with the factory owner, manages to minimize a worker's wage cut, and then marries the owner at the denouement. This formula persisted in the twentieth century with Phyllis Bentley, a Yorkshire writer, who clung throughout her long writing career to the conviction that Christian heroes could reform the world. "I can see that not till men have learned the mutual love which casts out fear," she concluded in her 1934 *A Modern Tragedy*, "can the economic problem be solved."[4]

Religion sometimes has such an appeal to the hero in her quest for social reform that she gives up marriage in order to pursue a career of agitation. This is the case with Elizabeth Stuart Phelps's *The Silent Partner* (1871), in which the festive marriage-denouement of the morality formula is aborted by the hero's excess of Christian virtue. Perly Kelso, the daughter of the mill owner and fiancée of the partner's son, breaks her engagement as a result of a new awareness of her economic status as a woman. Through her curiosity about the life of a factory woman, Sip Garth, Perly learns about conditions in the mill. She asks her fiancé and his father for a partnership in the concern, and in a chapter entitled "A Game of Chess" they tell her that although her property is invested in the mills, she must remain economically mute, with "nothing to do but to spend the money and let [them] manage it. That's all it amounts to." When she complains that the workers are unfairly being forced to work extra time when the demand for cotton is high, they reprove her, insisting that " 'the state of the market is an inexorable fact . . . before which employer and employe, whose interests, of course, are one, have little liberty of choice. The wants of the market must be met.' "[5]

Discontent with such answers and with the inhumanity of laissez-faire economics, Perly makes use of an acceptable role as charity worker by visiting workers' homes, setting up reading rooms, and playing the lady bountiful in an authentic, if not widely effective, manner. She breaks off her engagement (in a chapter entitled "Checkmate") and also refuses the offer of marriage from Garrick, a third, reform-minded partner who has risen from the ranks. The climax of the plot occurs when father and son are unable to avert a riot and Perly steps into the breach by going out before the workers. She accepts the laws of supply and demand, however, and persuades protesting workers that a production slowdown is inevitable, given the market. Perly returns to Christian preaching and convinces her protegée,

Sip, to follow her example in urging the workers to Christian piety and renunciation.

In *Uncle Tom's Cabin* (1852) Harriet Beecher Stowe took advantage of the values of Christian piety to urge eradication of slavery. Her arguments in the novel are strictly along Christian, and even patriarchal lines—she deplores the plantation system's disruptive effect upon family relationships. In her historical novel about the slavery, Civil War, and Reconstruction eras, Margaret Walker (*Jubilee!*, 1966), depicts her Black hero, Vyry, as a devout Christian, opposed to violence, whether it stems from the Ku Klux Klan or the revolutionary activities of her husband. Having endured years of racial abuse, Vyry emerges at the denouement as a powerful model, "a living sign and mark of all the best that any human being could hope to become." She refuses to internalize racial hatred, militating against white racists, and succeeds in creating a world apart: nonetheless, Vyry fails to target patriarchal values as a root cause of her difficulties.

Writing about the origins of feminism and Protestantism, Sheila Rowbotham argues that the two forces were in alliance, giving women the opportunity to both enhance their personal salvation and criticize an oppressive culture.[6] As the examples suggest, although heroes used Christianity to aid in social reform, these reforms did not extend to a radical alteration of patriarchal structures. The morality formula provided a forum for dissent *within* traditional boundaries and in this accommodationist sense made limited contributions to feminism. However, the very fact that it could be used as a tool for dissent at all represents a new development in woman's self-consciousness.

### THE SOCIALIST HERO

In the late nineteenth and early twentieth centuries Christianity and socialism were often complementary forces militating against industrial capitalism; this alliance was exemplified by the fact that Eliza Lynn Linton's *The True History of Joshua Davidson, Christian and Communist* became a best-seller in 1873. Even though socialists were often agnostic or atheistic, the morality formula found its way into narratives dealing with the formation of unions, the fomenting of strikes, and the organization of workers into viable pressure groups. The Devil was still the unreformable magnate, industrial abuses were still evil, but the hero had become a virtuous socialist and Everyman a fellow agitator. No longer willing to reform the magnate with marriage, the hero now chose to remain single or divorce him to marry the socialist Everyman.

In Mary Johnston's *Hagar* (1913) and Zona Gale's *A Daughter of the Morning* (1913), thus, socialist heroes escape dominating fathers, avoid marriage to chauvinistic suitors, become involved in both suffrage and labor reforms, reject further capitalist suitors, and, after much soul searching about marrying at all, wed sympathetic, socialist equals. In this formula, Everyman and Virtue go forth to battle the forces of Evil, manifested in industrial machinations against union organization. Everyman and Virtue battle side by side in such novels as Amabel Williams-Ellis's *The Big Firm* (1934) and Clara Weatherwax's *Marching! Marching!* (1935), solidarity between workers more important to the cause than intersex divisiveness, but sometimes Virtue remains a solitary martyr to the cause. In *Men and Steel* (1920) Mary Heaton Vorse describes the women of the steel towns battling industry under the leadership of Fanny Sellins, an organizer who is murdered by company gunmen. "The picture of her bruised face," Vorse explains, "is hung in every organizer's office." In *Strike!* (1930), Vorse models the character of Mary Lewis on the life story of Ella May Wiggins, a folk balladeer martyred for the cause of union solidarity.

In novels of social protest the festive denouements of Christian-hero novels have their counterpart in a climactic rally during which proponents of socialist virtue openly confront the forces of capitalist evil and workers unite across generational and sexual barriers to force better wages and working conditions from their employers. The limitations of these campaigns, however, are vividly portrayed in problematic resolutions. Thus, in *Marching! Marching!* we see the whole town full of workers singing "Hold the Fort for We Are Coming/Workingmen Be Strong!" while marching straight into a company militia armed with machine guns. At the denouement of *The Big Firm*, similarly, Williams-Ellis's Everyman and Virtue marry after attempting to sabotage her family's shipments of arms to the Spanish fascists, but they must leave England. At the conclusion they visit an old aunt for a blessing, which she gives in the form of two lines from Milton's *Paradise Lost*:

> They, hand in hand, with wandering steps and slow,
> Through Eden took their solitary way.

It is ironic that the blighted Eden they must abandon is their own country, the reason for their exile not original sin but the alliance between British industrialism and European fascism. The realities of twentieth-century industrialism discourage socialist collectives; in fiction, men and women who desire such utopias are shot, imprisoned, or exiled.

## SEXUAL POLITICS IN UTOPIA

Although women authors explore Christianity, socialism, and communism as alternatives to capitalism, they ultimately recognize that the promised equalities of each are undermined by the overriding concerns of the patriarchal system. Perly Kelso's Christianity alone cannot make her an equal business partner with her fiancé and his father, nor can shared socialist convictions enable a man and a woman to surmount gender inequity. In the same way that the novel of marriage subverts the institution of matrimony, the social-protest novel digs away at the sexual politics within socialism, labor agitation, and communism, undermining their viability as reform institutions. Beatrice Bisno, in *Tomorrow's Bread* (1938), openly criticizes the marital politics of union organizer Sam to the point that Sam becomes an antihero, suggestive of the "perfectly nice" husbands in the novel of marriage. Although she details Sam's longing for an effective garment-workers' organization for Russian Jewish immigrants, she also catalogues his oppression of his wife, Bessie. He espouses, for example, Emma Goldman's doctrine of "free love" in order to rationalize his multiple, careless affairs. When his wife protests that " 'then what is marriage, a business proposition only?' " he continues to ignore her, leaving her to express her frustrations through conspicuous consumption.

In *Pressure* (1927) Margaret Culkin Banning examines the relationship between sex and capitalism, connecting businessmen's campaigns to keep women consuming in the home with an overall plan for control of national politics and economics. Blaming themselves for "not keeping our eyes open" during the passage of the suffrage amendment, the capitalist Paget and his cronies scheme to bring psychological, financial, and social pressure on their employes to keep their wives in line. Although the hero, Annette, and her lover, David, become aware of Paget's machinations and intend to break away from his economic shackles, they go forth at the novel's conclusion, like Williams-Ellis's heroes, into problematic exile.

In her trilogy—*Pity Is Not Enough* (1933), *The Executioner Waits* (1934), and *Rope of Gold* (1939)—Josephine Herbst takes note of the sexual politics threatening the marriage of two intrepid socialist reformers, Victoria and Jonathan Chance. Like a number of broken marriages in the trilogy, the heroes' mutual love suffers from intersex divisiveness, which mimics the politics of ownership. Jonathan's insecurity springs from his family, who consider him less than an American (economically viable) male because of his devotion to communism. His especial need for trust makes him unable to love Victoria after he begins to suspect that she has slept with someone else. Whereas, on the one hand, Herbst spends a good deal of time showing the reciprocity of this essentially equal marriage, the language with which she describes Jonathan's jealousy suggests that the disintegration occurs as a result of his ownership instincts. Although Victoria struggles to convince Jonathan that she loves him, "it did not keep him from accusing her bitterly of never having loved him and of *always having lived for herself.*" In spite of the fact that he admits to his own affairs, Jonathan cannot tolerate Victoria's free expression of sexuality, which would represent a "life of *her own*" (italics mine).

Victoria finally realizes that "she had not annexed Jonathan like a piece of land; he was a whole human being with lungs and heart, and it was too true she had wronged him. She too belonged to herself, she thought proudly, and the words seemed part of some unearthly bargain that had witlessly betrayed them."[7] The alienation between the two lovers springs from mistaken attempts to deny each other's totality of self, to destroy each other's authenticity. Sexual ownership, Herbst suggests, even in the heart of a left-wing Everyman, is inextricably meshed with the concept of property.

Marie Rogers, the protagonist of Agnes Smedley's *Daughter of Earth* (1929), also finds the men she marries more interested in patriarchal norms than communist ideals. First married to a fellow traveler, then to a proponent of Indian revolution against the British, Marie learns that both husbands disapprove of her retaining her own name, holding jobs, and striving for equality within marriage.[8] The communist and revolutionary collectives for which Marie and her husbands agitate do not promise utopia for women and, in fact, as in Bisno, Banning, and Herbst, promise only a corrupt and false Eden.

When women writers turn to the description of conditions among the proletariat, they deal with the way that the relationships between men and women are damaged by economic forces beyond individual control. One of the principal difficulties that their heroes face is victimization at the hands of angry husbands frustrated by economic and social impotence. Mirroring in a more violent way the rifts dividing men and women in the novels dealing with the middle class, these marriages are destroyed by capitalist expectations for white male success. Marta Roberts, in *Tumbleweeds* (1940), illustrates how hero Concha's self-respect deteriorates as she watches her beloved husband destroyed by alcoholism and unemployment. The Chicana hero's efforts to feed her family collide with both patriarchal and capitalist norms.

In the Black novel, gender despair also informs characterization and conflict, intensified by the added limitations of racist stereotypes. Most Black women authors do not depict the protagonist's problems as wholly racial, however. Like their white counterparts, they characterize heroes whose fates are shaped by the interdependence of economics and sexual politics. In Ann Petry's *The Street* (1946), for example, both white and Black men beset and destroy the hero with a combination of sexual, racial, and economic victimization. Lutie's every attempt to remedy her poverty plunges her into deeper difficulties. Like Concha, Lutie's work first alienates her husband and then keeps her away from her son, who learns to steal; desperate for money, she tries to sell herself to a Black night-club operator, only to find that he has already sold her to the white barman.

Sarah Wright, in *This Child's Gonna Live* (1969), depicts a strong Black woman, Mariah Upshur, struggling with the abject poverty of a Maryland coastal town. Mariah says of her dispirited husband, "he was just weak, weak, weak, that's all there was to it—and always hiding behind the Lord. If the crops failed, it was the Lord's will. If the children stayed sick with the colds, it was the Lord's will." She sees clearly that the colds come from poor living conditions, and after two of her three children die she wants to leave for the north, but her father says that things are bad all over for the "colored man." To this Mariah rejoins, " 'But what about the colored *woman*? . . . All I keep hearing is you all talking about the hard time a colored *man*'s got.' " " 'See my scars! See my scars!' " shouts the father. " 'Colored woman's always been more privileged than the man. You ain't got no hard time in this community.' "[9] At this point he urges Mariah's mother to beat her with a stove-lid lifter; later in the novel, Mariah repeats this violence within her own family. By the denouement, clearly, she has internalized racist and sexist norms until she hates both herself and those around her.

Whether the husbands are labor organizers, Communist party members, fellow travelers, Indian revolutionaries, or unemployed Chicanos and Blacks, their rage in these novels is fueled by a sense of gender failure. Shulamith Firestone has argued that since males in every recorded political system have perceived women as "others," then control of the means of *reproduction* must be a more radical source of human alienation than control of the means of production. Offering an alternative to the Marxist view that materialism alone undermines the equal distribution of goods and services, she argues that sexism and materialism are interdependent parts of patriarchal culture.[10] This marriage of economic viability to gender identity—men "feminized" by failure, women "masculinized" by success—points to the preeminence of sex roles in social organization, and women's fiction corroborates Firestone's theory of gender-norm primacy. Authors' explorations of alternatives to capitalism illuminate the inevitable inequalities of any socioeconomic system bounded by the all-encompassing, ever-present patriarchal enclosure.

## WOMAN AS OUTSIDER

Indeed, the modern woman's novel is extraordinarily clear and bitter about the inexorable power of patriarchal capitalism over women in our times. The most radical look at this situation, but one by no means atypical, is that taken by Virginia Woolf in her essay *Three Guineas* (1938). The typical woman, she declares, is an outsider:

> " 'Our country,' " she will say, "throughout the greater part of its history has treated me as a slave; it has denied me education or any share in its possessions. 'Our' country still ceases to be mine if I marry a foreigner. 'Our' country denies me the means of protecting myself, forces me to pay others a very large sum annually to protect me, and is so little able, even so, to protect me that Air Raid precautions are written on the wall. Therefore if you insist upon fighting to protect me, or 'our' country, let it be understood, soberly and rationally between us, that you are fighting to gratify a sex instinct which I cannot share; to procure benefits which I have not shared and probably will not share; but not to gratify my instincts, or to protect myself or my country. For," the outsider will say, "in fact, as a woman, I have no country. As a woman I want no country. As a woman my country is the whole world."[11]

A number of novelists depict heroes quite as Woolf describes them, aliens within their own land, trapped by dependency upon male whims. Should they in any way disentangle themselves from wifely behavior, they are cast out of even the flawed enclosures of the family and household. In *Sula* (1973) Toni Morrison constructs a contrast between two Black women in an Ohio town between 1919 and 1941: Nel, who gets married and lives a proper life, and Sula, who remains independent of men, having many affairs and no marriage. Sula attempts to live out her own desires without interference, but, as in so many novels where women engage in amarital sexuality, she is severely punished for her independence. At the denouement she dies slowly, all alone in a filthy room, from cancer. Nel visits her and insists, " 'You *can't* do it all. You can't be walking around all independent-like, doing whatever you like, taking what you want, leaving what you don't.' "

Sula replies from her deathbed, "'Yes, but my lonely is *mine*. Now your lonely is somebody else's. Made by somebody else and handed to you. Ain't that something? A second handed lonely.'"[12] At a very high price of pain and isolation, Sula has attained a true "lonely," a sexual and personal authenticity. She pays the price, nonetheless, of total outsiderness.

Vyry, the hero of Margaret Walker's *Jubilee!*, is an outsider in a different and more hopeful way. A law unto herself, ultimately able to rescue her family with a combination of Christianity and honesty, Vyry has a heritage of herbal lore and nursing skills that comes to her from a line of women who have never been included in American society. It is as if that most radically alienated space in America, the slave quarters on a white plantation, had achieved a potency of its own by its very removal from the dominant culture. Vyry completely rejects white culture and embraces the matrilinear powers that enable her to create her own world. Her milieu is so marginal that the patriarchy ultimately fails to subvert it.

White women authors, through the intensity of their critique of modern society, also create heroes who become outsiders. Jean Rhys's first novel, *Quartet* (1928), shows what happens to a young woman in Paris who is left to her own devices after her husband, a petty Polish thief, goes to jail. A couple takes her in, and using her as a football in their marital battle, they consign her to a ghastly, mauve suite where she is expected to make love to the husband. "'I don't think women ought to make nuisances of themselves,'" the wife warns her. "'I don't make a nuisance of myself; I grin and bear it, and I think that other women ought to grin and bear it, too.'" Marya finds enclosure within this marriage unendurable, but when they abandon her she still feels imprisoned, like a fox in the zoo, running up and down in its cage:

> each time it turned it did so with a certain hopefulness, as if it thought that escape was possible. Then, of course, there were the bars. It would strike its nose, turn and run again. Up and down, up and down, ceaselessly. A horrible sight, really.[13]

Without money, as Virginia Woolf noted in *A Room of One's Own*, women have no choice but to accept their dependence upon the "large and imposing figure of a gentleman, which Milton recommended for [their] perpetual adoration."

Rhys's novels detail the hopeless struggles of determined, brave women to escape from inexorable enclosures.[14] Fay Weldon's fiction also deals with "down-and-out" heroes. In *Down Among the Women*

(1972) and *Female Friends* (1974) she creates group portraits of women whose friendships are based upon sharing the horrors of their relationships with men:

> Marjorie, Grace and me.
> Fine citizens we make, fine sisters!
> Our loyalties are to men, not to each other.
> We marry murderers and think well of them. Marry thieves, and visit them in prison. We comfort generals, sleep with torturers, and not content with such passivity, torment the wives of married men, quite knowingly.
> Well, morality is for the rich, and always was. We women, we beggars, we scrubbers and dusters, we do the best we can for us and ours. We are divided amongst ourselves. We have to be, for survival's sake.[15]

These women begin, at the denouements, to achieve some sense that they might be able to band together as a group of self-admitted "outsiders." In *Female Friends* Chloe decides to raise the various children of the group on her own; the generations of women in *Down Among the Women* seek roots among each other. "Scarlet walks like a zombie. Regard Scarlet's personality as if it were a plant. Come the winter it goes underground. Come the spring it will force its way up, cracking concrete if need be, to reach the light." "I think," ponders a woman on a park bench watching the generations of women flow by, "perhaps we are in the throes of an evolutionary struggle which we must all endure, while we turn willy-nilly, into something strange and marvellous. We gasp and struggle for breath, with painful lungs, like the creatures who first crawled out of the sea and lived on land."

The sufferings of Rhys's caged heroes and the sense of enclosure and breathlessness of Weldon's describe women's sex roles as so stifling that, as in the novel of marital rebellion, the human consciousness chooses to eradicate them or perish. Or, as Weldon concludes *Down Among the Women*:

> Byzantia, like her grandmother Wanda, is a destroyer, not a builder. But where Wanda struggled against the tide and gave up, exhausted, Byzantia has it behind her, full and strong.
>
> Down among the women.
>
> We are the last of the women.[16]

If Weldon's heroes are "the last of the women," she suggests that personhood must be a better tool for survival. Gender norms, for poor women as for rich ones, are so destructive that they should be abandoned and alternatives explored. The suffocating sense of enclosure, the gasping and struggling for breath, is thus not absolute but transitional, part of adaptation to a new environment where "maleness" and "femaleness" no longer undermine the development of the human personality. Just as in the novel of development and in the equal-marriage novel, the only possible abrogation of sexual politics is to project other worlds of being: Weldon envisions an extrasocietal solution eccentric in the root sense of the word. Transcendence necessitates passing through and beyond sexual politics to a new environment, a new kind of space. This visionary fiction depicts the process by which the patriarchy's most marginal heroes attain a centricity within a wholly apatriarchal space.

Heroes in novels dealing with women's quest for Eros also encounter this apatriarchal space. In this fiction, moreover, characters behave in such a way as to eject themselves out of the enclosure, to become scapegoats, outcasts, or deviants in the punishment denouement and wry social commentators in the more problematically terminated novels. As in the case of those enclosure novels which depict a fully realized personhood for women, those few novels of successful heterosexual, lesbian, and solitary passion occupy a paradoxical place both inside and outside the patriarchal enclosure.

# PART III

# EROS AS AN EXPRESSION OF THE SELF

*Society considers the sex experiences of a man as attributes of his general development, while similar experiences in the life of a woman are looked upon as a terrible calamity, a loss of honor and of all that is good and noble in a human being.*

*Those who, like [Ibsen's] Mrs. Alving, have paid with blood and tears for their spiritual awakening, repudiate marriage as an imposition, a shallow, empty mockery. They know, whether love last but one brief span of time or for an eternity, it is the only creative, inspiring, elevating basis for a new race, a new world.*

*In our present pygmy state love is indeed a stranger to most people. Misunderstood and shunned, it rarely takes root; or if it does, it soon withers and dies. Its delicate fiber can not endure the stress and strain of the daily grind. Its soul is too complex to adjust itself to the slimy woof of our social fabric.*

EMMA GOLDMAN, *The Traffic in Women and Other Essays on Feminism*

# CHAPTER V

# LOVE BETWEEN
# MEN AND WOMEN

IN NOVELS OF DEVELOPMENT, MARRIAGE, AND SOCIAL PROTEST WE HAVE seen how patriarchal expectations thwart the heroes' quests for totality of self to the extent that they become alienated not only from the enclosures of society and marriage but also from their own bodies and minds. The tiny particle of "self" that they retain becomes a cause for further punishment, and only in very few cases do heroes find some way to exist eccentrically or antisocially, transcending gender norms. In considering the history of marriage, I have taken account of the social insistence that potential wives be totally chaste lest they be "ruined" for the marriage market; that wives limit themselves not only to monogamy but, through much of our history, eunuchry; that adulterous wives are especially cursed; and that women engaging in sexuality outside of marriage are "fallen," "abnormal," or "whores." I feel that these extreme prohibitions spring from a fear of feminine sexuality rooted in the early history of the human race. In the first chapter I outlined the possible dimensions of apatriarchal societies in which women are free to engage in whatever sexuality pleases them. Such a virgin priestess as Medusa, who displeased the goddess Athena by appropriating her lover; such deities as Daphne and Syrinx, who were transformed into the green world rather than submit to rape; and such a tragic figure as Medea, who murdered her children in response to Jason's betrayal, are all archetypes of womanhood whose sexuality, like the "Moon Goddesses" described by M. Esther Harding, is intimately related to their power of being "one-in-themselves."[1]

This goddesslike quality of self-determined, or authentic, Eros has a way of cropping up in women's fiction even though it is clearly alien to ordinary marital norms. One of the most striking aspects of the fiction in which women authors deal with heterosexual passion is that the fates of the heroes depend upon patriarchal norms forbidding passion for women. The tragic denouements result from a flaw that would not be fatal in a male hero, namely, the desire for sexual fulfillment.

In classical or Shakespearian tragedy mere Eros does not bring about the catastrophe, which finally results from a combination of the hero's error and complicated ethical circumstances. In women's love fiction, in contrast, the denouements are likely to result from the ethically uncomplicated circumstance of a human being behaving normally. This turnabout of events in which eroticism becomes criminal results from the radically different position that men and women occupy in society.

The persistent drive for Eros in women's lives and literature undoubtedly derives from its primacy in the development of the human personality. Distinguishing it from mere "mechanical" sex, whose goal is only "gratification and relaxation," Rollo May describes Eros as

> a desiring, longing, a forever reaching out, seeking to expand . . . the drive toward union with significant other persons in our world in relation to whom we discover our own self-fulfillment. Eros is the yearning in man [sic] which leads him to dedicate himself to seeking arête, the noble and good life.[2]

I have suggested during the course of this study that Eros is one of the primal forces leading the personality through growth towards maturity, as necessary to human development as intellectual growth and the opportunity for significant work. Whereas the intellect and the capacity for work find their outlets in the world of social activity, however, Eros springs from the inner realm of unconscious experience. Indeed, fully experienced Eros demands the capacity for moving down into and returning from the deepest realms of the libido. A woman whose educational and work experiences are limited by sexual politics can move into a private, albeit bounded, realm of being, but the denial of erotic outlets eliminates even this remnant of personal space.

We have seen how in the novel of development young heroes experience ecstasies in relation to both the green world and those naturistic figures, whom I have termed green-world lovers, who call up libidinal powers that signal maturation. Throughout my analysis of the novels of enclosure, however, I have noted prohibitions against Eros for women: the limitations on sexuality placed upon adolescents, the monogamous strictures for married women, and the degradation accorded both married and unmarried women who make love out of wedlock. To seek Eros, clearly, is to cast oneself beyond the bounds of the enclosure. In dealing with heterosexual and lesbian love I will thus describe a continuum or gradation from novels in which Eros is fatal for heroes to those, once again few in number, in which it flowers in a new, inevitably apatriarchal space.

The greatest problem facing the woman writer of love fiction is not so much society's resistance to her revolutionary subject matter as her own internalization of social norms. Authorial ambivalence in combination with the necessity for drowning out the nature of her hero's true feelings creates a labyrinthine twisting of attitudes in this genre, most often manifest in the author's encoding of self-doubt and blame into the hero's consciousness. Apt to be convinced that whatever happens to her as a result of her eroticism is "her own fault" and that she has her punishments "coming to her," the hero of this fiction is, like her author, a victim of both external, societal structures and self-flagellation.

Although the element of romance, of the quest for one's heart's desire, is important in these novels, the denouements are likely to be tragic or inconclusive. In romance, traditionally, the hero returns at the end to a small enclave of society, although he sometimes winds up as a hermit. In women's love fiction the denouement of social isolation persists, but the *Liebestod*, or love death, traditionally dealt out in medieval fiction for extramarital love often replaces survival. Such punishments continue, even for minor infractions, to the present day, and the cause of the love death is not a mutual passion, as between Tristan and Isolde, but the mere existence of the hero's eroticism. In addition, the denouements of many love novels that are not strictly tragic nonetheless are clouded by authorial ambivalence towards the subject matter, manifested in split characterization, mixed points of view, and tonal ambiguity—literary effects used to jam messages that the authors fear are antisocial. Even in the very few examples of freely exchanged, reciprocal Eros the heroes remain alienated from their societies.

PUNISHMENT

The novel, as we have seen, has been a perennially social form, a literary convention that, for all of its flights into romance and fantasy, is grounded in social reality. Throughout the early history of the novel death has been a staple of love fiction, meted out not only for the more flagrant extramarital crimes but also for any gesture suggesting that the hero is less than totally passive. As early as 1791 and 1797 novelists like Susanna Rowson and Hannah Foster were able to tap a widespread popular fascination with "the fatal effects of seduction" in *Charlotte Temple* and *The Coquette*, titillating their audience on the one hand and providing the catharsis of pity for the heroes' deaths on the other. The young ingénue, misled by boredom with socially acceptable suitors and with ordinary feminine life, runs away with an exciting and apparently gallant lover, only to find herself "ruined," consequently perishing in childbed or through suicide. As Helen Papashvily remarks of the scores of novels that imitated Rowson's and Foster's, ". . . death, at home or abroad, seemed the only possible solution under the circumstances. The ignorant and gullible, the stupid and silly, the clever and rebellious, it made no difference—whoever broke the rules forfeited her life, not so much to an avenging God as to an implacable society that provided no respectable way to live on."[3]

This formula occurs not only in the lesser-known novels of the eighteenth and nineteenth centuries but also in a number of works by major women authors. The necessity of punishing a hero for aspiring to be human leads, sometimes, to puzzling denouements. George Eliot concludes *The Mill on the Floss* (1860), for example, with her hero, Maggie Tulliver, drowning with her brother in a flood. Only when one recognizes the central problem in Maggie's maturation as the deadlock between her emotional and intellectual authenticity and her culture's insistence upon dutifulness and passivity for women and then calls to mind Tom's assumption that it is his duty to force Maggie to conform to these feminine norms can one understand the irony, and the tragedy, of this outcome. The event is ironic in that Maggie has remained loyal to Tom in spite of his cruelty and thus sets out dutifully to rescue him. The tragedy, as well as the symbolic import of their deathly embrace, derives from the fact that *only* in death can such a conformist brother and such an authentically human sister be at one: alive, in society, they can only play the roles of arbiter and victim of gender norms. Similar fates meet the heroes of Olive Schreiner's *The Story of an African Farm* and Kate Chopin's *The Awakening* (1899), the heroes' flaw their desire for the freedom to love as they will. Both Lyndall and Edna enjoy green-world ecstasies and visions of naturistic lovers, and both perish as a result of trying to pursue their apatriarchal visions.

If we look at the characters of the heroes of these novels, we find them punished, thus, for qualities that society rewards in men: Maggie Tulliver is remarkable for her mind and spirit, and Lyndall and Edna are more than ordinarily sensual. Frye has characterized romance as a genre in which ideal worlds are polarized against abhorrent ones and in which the hero battles for a vision of good against a countervision or antithetical world of evil. In women's love fiction, remarkably, the world of abhorrence is not so much the world of the seducer as society itself. Visions of hell are not needed here, nor even is very much of the gothic: the iron hand of the patriarchy constitutes the evil force against which the heroes struggle in vain.

Even though the hero is duly punished, such fiction elicits a backlash from reviewers and social pundits. Although Schreiner and Chopin surely intended to make their novels socially proper by means of the tragic denouements, the reviewers were not placated in the least and attacked the authors as having perpetrated social crimes. The public, on the other hand, read away delightedly. "For every suburban matron who took [*African Farm*] up in the tongs and put it in the fire, as at least one reported doing," writes Colby, "and for every village library that yielded to the pressure of a local vicar or schoolmaster and took it off the shelves, there were hundreds of eager readers."[4] When an author modifies the tragic denouement even slightly by permitting a "fallen" hero to live on, the hue and cry is similarly severe. This was the case after the publication of Elizabeth Gaskell's *Ruth* (1853), in which the seduced hero and her bastard son survive and the hero dies a socially useful death nursing villagers (including her seducer) in a typhoid epidemic. "I *have* been *so* ill," wrote Gaskell during the period of public reactions to the novel.

> I do believe it has been a "Ruth" fever. . . . I . . . cd not get over the hard things people said of Ruth. . . . I think I must be an improper woman without knowing it, I do so manage to shock people. Now *should* you have burnt the 1st vol. of Ruth as so *very* bad? even if you had been a very anxious father of a family? Yet *two* men have; and a third has forbidden his wife to read it.[5]

Even more surprising, but nevertheless symptomatic of the severity of the social threat posed by even the slightest deviation from norms of feminine eunuchry, were the violent outbursts occurring upon publication of books in which the heroes err only by quite modestly expressing their love for a chosen mate. All that the heroes of Charlotte Brontë's *Jane Eyre* and *Villette* did to provoke the wrath of the patriarchy was to overtly declare their affections. Jane and Lucy transgressed a supreme injunction aganst declaring one's love; this prohibition is based on the fear that a woman's rating on the marriage market would fall should she be known as immodest. Recent feminist critics have sometimes taken such heroes as abject figures hurling themselves at the feet of "superiors," but contemporary reviewers saw the homely little governess who announces her love and the schoolteacher pining for her professor as innovative and revolutionary figures in women's fiction. In those instances in which the author did not sufficiently torment her hero, the reviewers set out to punish the author herself.

It is paradoxical that the drive toward acceptance of woman's eroticism should lead to effects that were the direct opposite of its intentions. The turn-of-the-century discovery that women indeed had sexuality of their own led not to greater freedom of sexual choice for women but to greater insistence that they make themselves sexually active or else risk neurosis, complexes, and an even more severe social ostracism than the accorded celibates in previous centuries. By the 1920s women who did not participate in sexuality were warned that they might become riddled with complexes; men cited popularized Freudianism to aid sexual conquests, and women found that the sexual emancipation they thought that they had won was likely to mean sexual availability.[6]

The maddening contradictions of twentieth-century sexual norms, according to theoretician Shulamith Firestone, result from a dialectic between ideal love and its debasement by the patriarchy. Ideally, it is "being psychically wide-open to another. It is a situation of total emotional vulnerability. Therefore it must be not only the incorporation of the other, but an *exchange* of selves. Anything short of a mutual exchange will hurt one or the other party." In a society in which men see women as inferior, she argues, they tend to project their own feelings of inferiority upon women. When women try to overcome their own sense of inferiority, moreover, they are likely to do it not by identifying with other (inferior) women but with a (superior) male. Since they live in a society that recognizes only men as primary existents and women as auxiliaries, they feel more secure in subordinating themselves to and identifying with some man. The result, which we see reflected in the state of mind of many characters in modern fiction, is that woman's life becomes "a hell, vacillating between an all-consuming need for male love and approval to raise her from her class subjection, to persistent feelings of inauthenticity when she does achieve his love. Thus her whole identity hangs in the balance of her love life. She is allowed to love herself only if a man finds her worthy of love."[7]

As a result of the persistence of social condemnation of feminine eroticism in the modern era many contemporary English and American novels have the same tragic plotting as their nineteenth-century predecessors. The severity of modern punishments parallels the traditional death from childbirth, hanging, or drowning. For example, in Willa Cather's *Lucy Gayheart* (1935) the hero fortuitously drowns, having only desired a passionate relation to her dead lover, and thus Martha, in Mary McCarthy's *A Charmed Life*, pays the price of pregnancy for one hour in bed with her former husband and dies in a head-on collision on her way to an abortion. Jean Rhys, as I've noted, traces Mrs. Rochester's madness and eventual death, in *Wide Sargasso Sea*, to the fact that her husband becomes disgusted with her after he has awakened her sexually, her only crime her passionate response to his titillation. But horrific denouements do not have to be fatal: Edna O'Brien punishes the hero of *August Is a Wicked Month* (1965) for one paragraph of fully satisfying Eros with desertion by her lover, the death of her son by mangling, and two deeply frustrating one-night stands, one with an impotent man and the other with a man who leaves her with gonorrhea. Upon returning to her home she rejects the original lover, partially because of her "shame" at contracting the disease and partially because she has decided that autonomy and Eros are incompatible.

With older women, like Antoinette Rochester and Edna O'Brien's hero, being rewarded with madness and gonorrhea for enjoying sex, it is hardly surprising that young women growing up are shown becoming aware, simultaneously, of their erotic desires and the price society exacts for erotic fulfillment. In Olivia Manning's *The Camperlea Girls* (1969) the price of youthful initiation is death by rape for the hero's good-looking friend Vicky. The hero, who had been attracted to the same man, realizes that she is alive only because she is less attractive than her friend. Ellie Parsons, in Manning's *The Doves of Venus* (1955), similarly, has her quest for erotic initiative thwarted at every turn by the sadism of her married lover, who says that girls are "soft as doves" but treats them well only if they totally submit to his will. Ellie, who had happily celebrated the loss of her virginity, escapes into what she hopes is an equal marriage after discovering that sensuality leads to either madness (as in her lover's wife) or masochistic submission. Or, as one male in the novel remarks, " 'Surely, my dear girl, you've discovered by now that you're living in a man's world. You must try to gain things by your charms. We men are delighted to reward you, but we won't disarm ourselves in your favor. Why should we? Eh?' "[8]

Punishments for extramarital love, moreover, are as damaging to the psyche as the matrimonial enclosure of the novel of marital rebellion. What we have in these novels is love as seen from the point of view of "the other woman." A favorite popular category of this genre is the "office-wife" novel, in which the "office wife" faces two counts of sex-role violation: work and extramarital sexuality. These denouements usually involve the hero in a choice between quitting the job to marry the boss or quitting men entirely to marry the job, abrogating either her employment or her sexuality. One example is Faith Baldwin's *The Office Wife* (1930), in which, as the title suggests, the hero acts as the business equivalent of the boss's homebody wife. She marries the boss, but only after giving up her job, with the dubious honor of being allowed to pick her successor. Tess Slesinger's Miss Betty Carlisle, of "The Mouse Trap," makes a different choice: having considered herself her boss's pal all during a crucial day while he thwarted a strike among the lesser staff, she flees when he demands that she have intercourse with him. Heroes who decide to become mistresses suffer for it heavily: Ray Schmit, in Fannie Hurst's *Back Street* (1931), gives up a good career to become the mistress of a married man but, when he will not divorce his wife, winds up starving in a ratty French hotel.[9] In another novel, *Imitation of Life* (1933), Hurst pictures her hero as a successful businesswoman who ends up alone as a result. She once loved a man, but he left her out of preference for a more "natural" woman. The moral of these widely read stories is resoundingly clear: a working woman is a wicked woman. The double standard of role expectations is equally clear: men can combine love and work as two facets of "normal" lives, but women must subordinate their love and work to male priorities.

The response on the part of reviewers to modern women's love fiction is marked with the same intensity and distortion of earlier centuries. Norah James's *Sleeveless Errand* (1929) was censored in England and labeled by counsel for the prosecution as "a collection of degrading muck." James was accused of dealing with "persons entirely devoid of decency and morality"; this sentiment was echoed by Arnold Bennett, who declared that the novel was "an absolutely merciless exposure of neurotics and decadents."[10] The bemused reader, perhaps expecting a woman's version of *Fanny Hill,* finds only a very depressed girl who is her own vicious counsel for the prosecution. Paula has been left by her lover in a long-standing affair and is planning her suicide when she meets a man who has just found his wife in bed with another man. She succeeds in dissuading the husband from suicide but drives herself over a cliff. In 1934 Ruth Suckow found herself under attack for her portrayal of Margaret Ferguson, in *The Folks*, who, we will recall from chapter 3, escaped marriage only to be bullied in her love affair. Suckow had noted that such criticism results from choosing a "dark lady" as a hero rather than one of those "fearful tomb[s] of 'female virtue' who is usually the heroine of fiction."[11] In 1935 Pamela Hansford Johnson was amazed to find herself the center of a "*succès de scandal*," labelled for *This Bed Thy Centre*, her first novel, as "out-spoken," "fearless," and "frank," the twenty-two-year-old author led to understand "that I had disgraced myself and the entire area of Clapham Common."[12] In 1944, simply for letting her hero take a lover while her husband is away at war in *Till the Boys Come Home*, Hannah Lees was dubbed a "nymphomaniac," and the *Times Literary Supplement* grieved over the publication of *The Golden Notebook* for Lessing's loss of a "clean discrimination" and giving of herself over to a "drooling, exhibitionist hysteric Anna Wulf." Most puzzling are those contemporary reviewers who hail novelists like Erica Jong, Edna O'Brien, and Cynthia Buchanan as "pornographic," telling it "like it is" from the female sexual viewpoint, "at long last."[13]

The structural characteristics perennial in women's love fiction result from the author's persistence in the face of this kind of public disapproval and misunderstanding. In the nineteenth-century novel the author tended to rely on such time-honored devices as the double-marriage or double-suitor plot, in which an impossible but socially accepted male fortunately perishes or is rejected, to be replaced by a more equal partner. Thus we have Anne Brontë's *The Tenant of Wildfell Hall* (1848) (in which the alcoholic husband dies and the hero marries someone nicer) and George Eliot's *Middlemarch* (in which Casaubon, whose suit seems highly appropriate to the inhabitants of Middlemarch, dies and is replaced by Will Ladislaw). This doubling of husbands and suitors parallels the tendency of romance fiction to split the hero's love into two figures, a "dark" one and a "light" one, "a polarization," as Frye defines it, "between the lady of duty and the lady of pleasure." In women's fiction, similarly, many heroes must marry normative males while taking pleasure only in antisocial, amarital lovers.

This tension between a hero's passion for an unacceptable lover and her dutiful marriage characterizes Emily Brontë's *Wuthering Heights*, where, as we have suggested in chapter 2, Heathcliff takes on the qualities of the green-world-lover archetype. The plot structure is determined by Cathy's overt conformity to gender norms in marrying the insipid Edgar Linton—a prototypical "gentleman of duty," to apply Frye's formula—while remaining attached to Heathcliff, her true lover. Cathy grows up torn between a desire to emulate the passive, spotless femininity of Edgar Linton's sister, Isabella, and her identification with the spirit of Heathcliff. Her transformation from a free existent to a young lady is only skin deep, of course, and *Wuthering Heights* is thus, among other things, an anatomy of the damage done to woman's psyche by repressive gender norms. As Carol Ohmann has

illustrated, the book is about "freedom, or at least the will to freedom," in that it raises the question of whether any young woman can
grow up into "a life of love and adventure . . . the freedom to feel and
to act. And to die grandly, or grandiosely, as the sun goes down."[14]

Even among the "erotic" school of turn-of-the-century novelists a
hero's rebellion is unlikely to be full fledged. Gertrude Atherton's heroes indulge in declarations of their right to love fully, only to submit
themselves to "superior" males, and George Egerton's heroes tend to
rebel against sexual frustration in oblique or symbolic, rather than direct, form. As Showalter notes, Egerton (Mary Chavelita Dunne) often puts her heroes' rebellions into the "mouths of minor characters
on the fringes of the narrative" or turns their antagonism against figures not directly responsible for their fates.[15]

## PUZZLEMENT

The socially unacceptable status of Eros as a natural force in the
human personality automatically places woman in a puzzling double
bind. On the one hand she experiences Eros as an aspect of her natural maturation; on the other hand such an experience for a woman
is considered "unnatural." The gender norms for feminine behavior
that should provide signposts to adulthood are obscured, destroyed, or
reversed. Modern women's love fiction reflects this situation in a disjunction of narrative structure characterized by quests gone awry, labyrinthine wanderings, and a general tone of confusion and perplexity.

A number of novelists in the early modern period found it convenient to contain their ambivalent attitudes towards their heroes' eroticism by using a semidetached narrative persona for their point of
view. Willa Cather, for example, is likely to choose a narrator somewhat innocent of the world in order to express her ambivalence toward the sensuality and materialism of her woman characters. A narrator like Niel in *A Lost Lady* (1923), for example, can be both
drawn to and repelled by the beauty and allure of a Mrs. Forrester;
Don Hedger, in "Youth and the Bright Medusa" (1920), can observe
(albeit from the closer perspective of a lover) the character of the
singer Eden Bower. These personae provide the same kind of perspective on women having extramarital affairs that Jim Burden does on
Ántonia. What Cather seems to be doing with her stories of opera
singers and theater women is indulging her interest in these very feminine, very ambitious women whose work means a great deal to them
and who are also passionately involved in deeply sensual relationships.
She thus transgresses both work and sex prohibitions for "true woman-

hood" and deflects her enthusiasm for these Aphrodites, Bright Medusas, and self-supporting, sensual career women by using either an "odd woman" or a moralistic (if infatuated) young man to comment upon their careers.

The practice of disguising authorial accommodationism in slightly detached narrators persists throughout the modern period. In Margaret Drabble's *The Needle's Eye* (1972), for example, the complex character of Rose Vassiliou is seen through the eyes of Simon, a bemused third-person narrator; in a novel by Joanna Glass, *Reflections on a Summer Mountain* (1974), the first-person narrator is the son of a woman who, during the summer of her fortieth year, had plunged into the one deeply passionate love affair of her life. In Drabble and Glass, as in Cather, the device of the bemused narrator disassociates the author from the hero and leaves the reader free to choose whether to approve her vagaries and passions.[16]

When a woman author dispenses with the on-the-scene and infatuated narrator and plunges into the moils of the action more directly, she still manipulates her point of view to allow for ambivalence about Eros. In her construction of *The Waterfall* (1969), for example, Margaret Drabble creates an ambiguous hero who alternates between a first-person, sensible point of view about her affair and the third-person attitude of the submissive mistress. Doris Lessing achieves a similar detachment throughout her works by assuming an ironic and frequently omniscient point of view, as of a goddess hovering over the mortals toiling in the wheel of Eros. She introduces "Not a Very Nice Story" (*The Temptation of Jack Orkney and Other Stories*, 1972) with a rumination over this problem:

> This story is difficult to tell. Where to put the emphasis? Whose perspective to use? For to tell it from the point of view of the lovers (but that was certainly not their word for themselves—from the viewpoint, then, of the guilty couple) is as if life were to be described through the eyes of some person who scarcely appeared in it; as if a cousin from Canada had visited, let's say, a farmer in Cornwall half a dozen unimportant times, and then wrote as if these meetings had been the history of the farm and the family.[17]

Here Lessing, as in most of the other short stories in this collection, maintains the tone of author as omniscient (if puzzled) commentator. Her predominant attitude about love is voiced by Anna in *Play with a Tiger* (1962): "Put your arms around one other human being, and let the rest of the world go hang—the world is terrifying, so shut it out. That's what people are doing everywhere, and perhaps they are right."[18]

In her stories, similarly, Joyce Carol Oates creates men and women who tend to be victimized by their marriages and infidelities, just aware enough of something "odd" or awry in their lives to exist in a limbo of emotional malaise, as in a story entitled "Puzzle":

> I shake my head no, no. No. I go to him and put my arms around him, his head and his shoulders, and he presses himself against me, exhausted, hot, breathing hard. He hides his face against me and I can't see him. What is this puzzle of people!—what have they to do with one another? They can't help one another. They are better alone.[19]

Given the predominance of either punishment or puzzlement in women's fictional characterization of passionate heroes, it is easy to understand why some feminist theoreticians consider romantic love an opiate that dulls a woman's self-determination. Although ambivalent in their attitudes, women novelists nonetheless persist in upholding the experience of Eros as a quest in which women have both a need and a right to participate. Thus even in Lessing, whose fiction provides portrait after portrait of the destructive effects of Eros, we see the drive towards a meaningful, passionate love as a constant force motivating characters. Like Katherine Anne Porter, Lessing goes right on deploring love's effects while lauding its possibilities, convinced that "it is only in love and in war that we escape from the sleep of necessity, the cage of ordinary life, to a state where every day is a high adventure, every moment falls sharp and clear like a snowflake drifting slowly past a dark glistening rock, or like a leaf spinning down to the forest floor."[20]

It is in the same spirit that Mary McCarthy, in *The Company She Keeps* (1942), takes her character Margaret Sargent through a series of short stories in which the complexity of modern love is explored, analyzed, and left unresolved. In a series of eccentric acts like those characterizing the heroes of Lessing and O'Brien, Margaret has taken a young man and thus brought on a divorce from her first husband, made love on the train to Reno with a man in a Brooks Brothers' shirt, and finally, after a second marriage, accounts for her lifelong career of sexual "accidents" to her psychiatrist in "Ghostly Father, I Confess." She has been playing an elaborate game in which she replaced her father with one man after another in order to relive the trauma of a motherless Catholic childhood. McCarthy's portrait of her hero exemplifies erotic inauthenticity: Margaret has played at "being a woman" by acting *like* one, by flirting, getting raped (she feels most "womanly" when mounted by a man she doesn't want), and arranging marriages that will perpetuate her pretense.

In the last story in the collection Margaret stops playing these games and, in a dream, comes to a frightening vision of herself:

> She could not disown the dream. It belonged to her. If she had not yet embraced a captive Nazi, it was only an accident of time and geography, a lucky break. Now for the first time she saw her own extremity, saw that it was some failure in self-love that obliged her to snatch blindly at the love of others, hoping to love herself through them, borrowing their feelings, as the moon borrowed light. She herself was a dead planet. . . . At the end of the dream, her eyes were closed, but the inner eye had remained alert. She could still distinguish the Nazi prisoner from the English milord, even in the darkness of need.
>
> "Oh my God," she said . . . "do not let them take this away from me. If the flesh must be blind, let the spirit see. Preserve me in disunity."[21]

By learning to value consciousness of her own "duplicity" Margaret begins to transcend blind immersion in destructive love affairs; as yet unable to control her choices, she agonizes over their inauthenticity.

Like McCarthy's hero, Anaïs Nin's Sabina, in *A Spy in the House of Love* (1954), hovers between a quest for self through love and self-punishment for the false self that she constantly assumes as she pursues the quest. On the one hand, Sabina changes herself to each of her many lovers' requirements: becoming a childlike innocent for her husband, Alan, a "bad woman" for her Black lover, Mambo, a mother figure for the impotent Donald, and a fellow in madness to the crazed airplane pilot, John. On the other hand, in each of these encounters Sabina feels herself to be on a venture in which the boundaries of self are expanded and transcended.

Sabina's sexual adventures are thus intended to be flights of self, quests for an expanded personal universe, but they are grounded every time by the expectations of her male lovers. This raising of erotic expectations followed by an anticlimax of patriarchal misunderstanding recurs throughout the plot in a rising-and-falling narrative sequence resulting from the clash between Sabina's desire for authentic Eros and the enclosure. As long as she seeks to exercise her libidinal drives with social conformists, she will fail to achieve totality of self, and at the denouement she longs to find herself in one individually satisfying love. Nonetheless, like Lessing's Anna and McCarthy's Mar garet, Sabina realizes that, however painful the knowledge of her disunity, it is more authentic than compliance to gender norms.

## PASSION

As in the case of the novel of equal marriage, the novel of true love is rare in women's fiction. What is more common is a continuum, whether in an individual novel or in an author's total works, from punishment through puzzlement to a consciousness of repression. Such a process characterizes the total works of Rosamond Lehmann, who devoted her oeuvre to various stages of this pilgrimage. Whereas Sabina's loss of self resulted from her fragmenting acts of love, Lehmann's heroes experience Eros not only through others but as an enhancing personal experience. Between 1927 and 1953, Lehmann's characters are devoted to living out a full gestalt of erotic and intellectual faculties, and in both the attempt and the results they are the heirs of Jane Eyre, Lucy Snow, and Maggie Tulliver. As women in love, "dark women" telling their own stories, they approach the erotic from a new angle in literature.

*Dusty Answer* (1927) is basically a novel of punishment. Judith seeks the love of three brothers and a college classmate, all eventually failing her: her favorite of the brothers is killed, and she is seduced and dropped by another and engaged to a third. A woman classmate, for whom she develops a deep passion, betrays her for an older lesbian lover. She finally realizes that she has been a kind of "sport" or hunted animal for all of them, a rabbit like those her fiancé shoots. She nonetheless transcends both love and loneliness by achieving an authentic solitude: "She was rid at last of the weakness, the futile obsession of dependence on other people. She had nobody now except herself; and that was best."[22]

Olivia, the hero of both *Invitation to the Waltz* (1932) and *The Weather in the Streets* (1936), becomes self-reliant because she is not like the other girls, lacking something of "femininity." In comparing herself to her sister Kate she feels unwomanly: "All these dainty devices, so natural to Kate, seemed when she performed them to become unreal, like a lesson learned by heart, but not properly understood."[23] The "dainty devices" are the primping and preparations with which the two young sisters make ready for the ball that is their initiation into "society." Like the American adolescents in Barbara White's study, Olivia feels herself to be freakish, ungainly, and unsuited to womanhood. Like adolescent heroes, moreover, Lehmann's women are policed by mothers, sisters, friends, and other women. In *The Weather in the Streets* (1936), for example, Olivia is policed by her conservative married sister and by her lover's mother, Lady Spencer. She has fallen in love with Rollo Curtis while separated from her husband, Ivor. Rollo is married to a mysteriously sick (or hypochondriacal) Nicole, and the novel details the rise and fall of the love affair. The turning point occurs when Olivia returns from a trip to Austria with Rollo, finds herself pregnant, and has to go through an abortion alone. Realizing that Rollo cares more for his pleasure than for her, she prepares to end their relationship. These complexities and tawdry details make her long for a life disentangled from sex altogether: "If I could escape to a new country, I'd soon strip off these sticky layers, grow my own shape again."[24] The implication of *The Weather in the Streets*, as of *Dusty Answer*, is that love within the patriarchy involves too much false selfhood to enhance the hero's personal development.

In her subsequent novels, however, Lehmann makes it clear that despite its shortcomings she considers the experience of erotic love central to human life. In *The Ballad and the Source* (1944) she uses the initially detached persona of a child, Rebecca, to portray an emancipated woman, Sybil Jardine, whose "freedom" has wrought destruction all around her. Sybil's unhappy early marriage led to the commission of her daughter to an insane asylum; now she wants to rescue her granddaughter. She is portrayed as a scheming female but also as revered and loved by both the narrator and an artist, Gill. Lehmann, in her ambivalence, recognizes women's double bind: women who transcend the selflessness of gender roles will be considered "selfish," but to deny their own selfhood is destructive both for themselves and succeeding generations. "'As a girl she was always one to go on about women's rights,'" remarks an old family servant. "'She got 'er bellyful all right.'" Sybil is punished for seeking "The [Erotic] Source" of the title:

> "The source, Rebecca! The fount of life—the quick spring that rises in illimitable depths of darkness and flows through every living thing from generation to generation. It is what we feel mounting in us when we say: 'I know! I Love! I *am!*' . . . One day, Rebecca, women will be able to speak to men—speak out the truth, as equals not as antagonists, or as creatures without independent moral rights—pieces of men's property, owned, used and despised. It may begin to be so in your lifetime. What am I saying?—it has begun."[25]

The quest for this elixir, as illustrated in Sybil's life, is hemmed with traps and destruction. The Eros these heroes seek transcends sensual gratification, providing a spring of creative energy that, activated in their sexuality, radiates to all of the facets of the fully realized personality.

This variety of Eros infuses Lehmann's penultimate novel and the consciousness of its hero, Dinah. In *The Echoing Grove* (1953) Dinah and Ricky, her brother-in-law, are deeply in love, and she and her woman friend Corrigan plan to take Dinah's baby to a new country, where they will all be free: "As soon as she was out of the hospital she was going off to France with the baby and Corrigan. Somewhere in Provence they were to compose a unit dedicated to freedom, creative freedom and responsibility; Corrigan painting, Dinah writing, the child to be nourished on sun, milk, wine, and happiness. Ricky to send funds."[26] This dream collapses, however, when the baby dies and Ricky's health fails due to his inability to leave his wife. In this novel, Lehmann recognizes that the failure of love lies in the restrictive social dictates that define it. " 'I can't help feeling,' " concludes Dinah, that

> "it's particularly difficult to be a woman just at present. One feels so transitional and fluctuating. . . . I believe we *are* all in a flux—the difference between our grandmothers and us is far deeper than we realize—much more fundamental than the obvious social economic one. Our so-called emancipation may be a symptom, not a cause. Sometimes I think it's more than the development of a new attitude toward sex: that a new gender may be evolving—psychically new— a sort of hybrid. Or else it's just beginning to be uncovered how much woman there is in man and vice versa. . . . It's ourselves we are trying to destroy when we're destructive: at least I think that explains the people who never can sustain a human relationship."[27]

For the seeker of Eros and the seeker of equal marriage the obstacle is the same: the breakthrough that Dinah cannot achieve is the birth of the androgynous self, the self beyond "male" and "female" roles. The necessity of transcending gender roles before true Eros can be achieved, implicit in Lehmann, echoes M. Esther Harding's theory that mature love springs from personalities that have come to terms with their own androgyny and that, conversely, those personalities too one-sidedly feminine or masculine are incapable of it. In Lehmann's fiction the attempt to transcend sex roles is stillborn, the result symbolized, as one critic remarks, in the frequent appearance in her novels of dead babies, which seem to "be an image of death in life; . . . [and to] symbolize the dilemma of modern women, aspiring to liberty but enslaved by physical processes."[28] Until only very recently, the biological price of erotic initiative has been unwanted pregnancy or abortion, and the psychological price paid by the woman who indulges in her own sexuality, an abortion of selfhood.

The woman author and her hero have internalized the social dictates against erotic authenticity to the extent that they experience Eros as a "shadow" or a denial of individual aspirations. Self-censorship, both conscious and unconscious, drowns the revolutionary power of Eros in these novels of love between men and women. This, it seems to me, accounts for the puritanical attitude that both Lessing and Oates maintain toward their heroes' few moments of fully realized passion. That the bright, sunny, and self-enhancing experience of passion should seem to the modern writer to be a cold, darkening force preventing the development of self is a result of centuries of internalization of norms allocating feminine sexuality to the realm of the feared and the dreadful. Sometimes women heroes survive only by projecting punishment upon their lovers: in two instances in *Children of Violence* where Martha seems to achieve a full orgasm, her lovers eventually perish or go mad, Thomas dying in the desert and Jack becoming a sadistic corrupter of young girls for the prostitute market. In *Dusty Answer* the hero sees her lover as a "shadow" that is "laid on a screen and then wiped off again" and as part of a process in which her past may be "completed now and be ready to be discarded." In the consummate sexual experience of *The Golden Notebook* (1962) Anna dreams of herself and Saul as negatively androgynous figures, shadowy freaks of nature: "We came together and kissed, in love. It was terrible, and even in the dream I knew it. . . . it was the caress of two half-human creatures, celebrating destruction."[29]

The rebirth of Elena in Oates's *Do with Me What You Will* (1973) also involves understanding sexuality as an evil force: "And now if she wanted Morrissey she would cross over into adulthood to get him, into the excitement of evil. Extending her freedom, as men do, making a claim . . . claiming a man . . . almost against his will, forcing him. It saddened her, it was degrading. Spiritually, she loathed it. As a Woman she loathed it" (ellipses hers).[30] Elena's quest ultimately leads her to recognize that fully individualized selfhood includes the exercise of erotic initiative: she sees herself, nonetheless, as loathsome and evil. Erica Jong, similarly, in *Fear of Flying* (1973), presents a series of erotic experiences that the hero forces herself to undergo as part of her quest for rebirth and transformation—"what I really wanted was to give birth to *myself*." Although the book, as I have mentioned, was hailed as a breakthrough vision of feminine eroticism, the three lovers are exemplars of erotic horror: Brian never stops babbling but stops making love, the reticent Bennet never stops having intercourse long enough to find out if his partner is enjoying it, and Adrian Goodlove, bringing the quest full circle, is "into" open marriage but sexually impotent.

Whereas Jong's Isabella ends her journey at the beginning of a quest for rebirth through erotic experience and her own poetic creativity, Jane Gray, in Margaret Drabble's *The Waterfall*, begins where Isabella leaves off. Drabble intends in this novel to develop a full portrait of Eros, of a "sublime, romantic passion" experienced by a woman hero. Perhaps because of her straightforwardly antisocial intention Drabble splits her point of view into two voices, that of the assertive, self-conscious "I" and that of the more submissive, self-abashed "Jane." With her "I" voice, which corresponds to Martha Quest in her more lucid moods and to McCarthy's narrator at the end of "Ghostly Father, I Confess," the hero sees with horror the meaninglessness of her parents' marriage and her own. In her marriage to Malcolm she has retained both erotic and spiritual virginity through intercourse and childbirth alike. Totally dependent and passive immediately after the birth of her second child, Jane sleeps with another man. With him, and with the "Jane" voice protesting her astonishment all the time, the hero achieves psychological integration, deliverance from her past through the experience of mutual orgasm:

> Reader, I loved him: as Charlotte Brontë said . . . the world that I lived in with him—the dusty Victorian house, the fast car, the race tracks, the garages, the wide bed—it was some foreign country to me, some Brussels of the mind, where I trembled and sighed for my desires, I, a married woman, mother of two children, with as much desperation as that lonely virgin in her parsonage. Reader, I loved him. And more than that, I had him. He was real, I swear it, and I had made myself a true loneliness, and in it, I had him.[31]

As in the case of Elena, Jane "comes to herself" by being "brought to herself" through Eros, a stage that she achieved by rejecting her cold parents, cold husband, and all that they have stood for.

Drabble clearly does not suggest mutual orgasm as the only way towards personal development. " '*The Waterfall*,' " she explains in an interview with Nancy Hardin,

> "is a wicked book, you see. I've been attacked really very seriously and I can only respect the attack by people who say that you should not put into people's heads the idea that one can be saved from fairly pathological conditions by loving a man. People say that's not how I can approach my life. There's no guidance in that for me. And that's true. As Doris Lessing would say, there are not all that many men in the world these days who are worth looking for. She

said in *The Golden Notebook* that the Englishman isn't worth tuppence and that no Englishman knows how to love. Well, that's very true. And if a woman happens to meet one of the few men available, good luck to her. But I mean it's luck."[32]

It is within this context of the paucity of decent lovers—described by Rhys, Weldon, and Lessing—that Drabble launches her novel of passion, well aware that this modern delineation of Charlotte Brontë's "Brussels of the mind" reflects not so much the rest of her own oeuvre as an older tradition. The fact that Jane Gray thinks of herself as a Jane Eyre (and, significantly, as a Maggie Tulliver) and that the Jane/James/Lucy triangle is quite similar to Lehmann's Ricky/Magdelene/Dinah or Olivia/Nicole/Rollo plots seems a result of Drabble's deliberate building along a fictional gradient or continuum, adding brick by brick to the historic portrayal of women's quest for authentic sexuality.

Drabble has not left *The Waterfall* to stand alone in her oeuvre as an isolated account of successful Eros but has gone on, in *The Realms of Gold* (1975), to picture a hero successful in passion, intellectual achievement, and spirit. Drabble seems to have conceived this novel as a dialogue with both *The Waterfall* and *The Golden Notebook*. Whereas Lessing's Anna was able to integrate her life only partially, leaving a character whose intellectual and erotic needs were unsatisfied, Drabble's Frances is a successful archaeologist who creates realms of gold in her mind and then becomes professionally and financially successful by going forth and discovering them in reality. Her refugee lover, Karel, parallels the absconding Michael in Lessing's novel, but the events of the book take place not according to a narration of their breakup, as in *The Golden Notebook*, but of their reconciliation. In full consciousness of the punishment she should accord such successes Drabble portrays Eros with geniality and humor. In her affair with Karel, Frances promotes love as an apt substitute for the "holy love of God," which she has not "the spiritual capacity for." Eros is serious but treated comically. For example, Frances treasures Karel's discarded false teeth as a love token:

She carried them around for ages, then put them in a drawer by her bed with his letters. Later, when she had left him, she got them out again, and when she returned to Africa and started again upon social life she had taken to putting the teeth down the front of her brassiere. She liked the feel of them, Karel's teeth resting gently and delicately and wirily against her soft evening breast, they kept her company. She had one low cut dress that she was rather fond of, a soft black one, soft black wool, and one night at a party she caught a man in the act of staring down her cleavage and meeting, entranced and horrified, the sight of Karel's glaring teeth, the guardians of her virtue.[33]

"Silly, really," remarks Drabble, "the things she had found herself doing since she fell in love with Karel."

Drabble's geniality does not completely permeate her portrait of society, one should note: in two key subplots she counterpoints the dreadful marriages of the cousins Janet and Stephen to the happier affair. Janet's situation seems unchanged at the end of the novel, the only hope for her implicit in the degree to which her relationship to Mark resembles Frances's earlier marriage; Stephen, unable to accept the ills of modern society, commits suicide and kills his baby. Finally, a good part of the plot centers around the pathetic death by starvation of Frances's Aunt Connie, an "odd woman," a hermit, whose cottage she finally inherits. These negative elements provide complications that are resolved festively nonetheless: although the world outside their love and their immediate family seems characterized by "toil and subsistence, cruelty and dullness," an enclave of erotic reciprocity and humanism survives.

In a thoroughgoing analysis of the relationship between love and feminism, Ti-Grace Atkinson's *Amazon Odyssey* (1974) poses the question of whether "love" is not *itself* the key to woman's inability to break free from patriarchal bondage. Atkinson sees love as based on "magnetism" and magnetism as based on "friction," or conflict, between the two sexes, whom society has placed in unequal roles, the one inferior and the other superior. Since women continue to choose to live with and subordinate themselves to the "Oppressor" and since in most cases compliance is voluntary, "it must be," Atkinson reasons, "that the internal coercion within the female to maintain the female role is not essentially biological in nature but psychological." The root of coercion, she feels, is the concept of "love."

> I propose that the phenomenon of love is the psychological pivot in the persecution of women. . . . it is not difficult to conclude that women by definition must exist in a special psycho-pathological state of fantasy both in reference to themselves and to their manner of relating to their counterclass. This pathological condition, considered to be the most desirable state for any woman to find herself in, is what we know as the phenomenon of love.[34]

"I recount these things as proof of my madness," remarks Jane Gray in her "I" lucidity. "In extenuation. As indictment. Perhaps merely as a record; in case I should forget. And it was worse, it was worse than I can ever say."[35] Atkinson's theory of romantic love as psychopathology is certainly borne out by the catatonic manner in which so many heroes of the modern novel back into marriages or rebel against marriages into identically destructive love affairs. It is also borne out in the schizophrenic "splits" that turn up in a Mattie/Martha syndrome in Lessing or an "I"/Jane pattern in Drabble, as well as in the manic pursuit of unsuitable and personally destructive Eros on the part of characters in Oates, Porter, Jong, Lehmann, and Lessing.

Are the women of the modern Eros novel to be allocated, then, to a class of mad lovers analogous to the heroes of mad-wife fiction? "These cross-sexual alliances," remarks Atkinson,

> because they are definitively inequitable, and because they thus necessarily alienate women from their natural class interest [e.g., other women] are anti-feminist. The tension created by the male/female role confrontation and the pseudo-alliances across these role interests has the structural appearance of a web of boxes with a single woman trapped in each one.[36]

Is the libidinal drive that woman directs towards man in heterosexual relationships of value *at all* in her development, or, as Atkinson implies, has it become destructive to the modern psyche? Students of Western romantic love like Joseph Campbell, Abraham Maslov, Rollo May, and Denis de Rougemont have traced its existence through Western history as a positive value, even to the extent that Frederic Jameson, in *Marxism and Form*, characterizes Eros, or the libido, as a source of not only individual enhancement but revolution. Eros, they imply, drives both individuals and societies towards a better vision and a richer life. The individuals whom these philosophers describe are assumed, of course, to be male, the object of their passions to be female. But if we turn the equation around and suggest that the transcendent energy characterizing Eros is of great positive value to the feminine psyche as well as to the masculine one, would we not, if we adhered to Atkinson's condemnation of heterosexual passion, be throwing out a very important baby with our bathwater?

We can resolve this problem, it seems to me, by recognizing that the destructive attributes of romantic love stem from the friction in what Atkinson describes as the "male/female *role* confrontation" but not from its heterosexual quality per se. I have demonstrated that whenever there are excessive "male" qualities in a man's approach to love (e.g., Adrian in *Fear of Flying* or Miles in *A Charmed Life*), they are apt to be counterpointed by pathologically submissive "female" behaviors in the woman character (e.g., Isabella's hurling herself into the affair with Adrian and Martha's destructive bedding down with Miles). In novels of erotic fulfillment, however, we find that characters like James and Jane in *The Waterfall* and Henry and Catherine in *Catherine Carter* are described as achieving authenticity after stripping off false roles, breaking through the grid of societally imposed "male" and "female" behaviors. "Indistinguishable needs," remarks Drabble of James and Jane's achievement of erotic mutuality. "Her own voice, in that strange sobbing cry of rebirth. A woman delivered. She was his offspring, as he, lying there between her legs, had been hers." It is no coincidence that the authors of the few equal-marriage novels and novels of erotic fulfillment talk of phoenixes, of androgyny, or of, in Lehmann's phrase, a "new gender," a state of consciousness in which individual men and women shed the destructive attributes of gender and reach towards those moments of truly human exchange.

As in the science fiction novel of development and in the equal-marriage novel, heroes transcend gender norms in the novel of true love only in asocial and bizarre conditions. In *Wuthering Heights*, in which Heathcliff takes the role of the archetypal green-world lover, he and Catherine consummate their passion only in a burial together, after traditional marital expectations have destroyed them. Lehmann's heroes know that they can consummate their passions only in isolated enclaves or by assuming wholly "new genders," and Drabble's lovers succeed by what she terms a freak of "luck" or "grace." These lovers have broken out of the enclosure and tread a new space eccentric to the culture that rejects them. We shall see in the following chapters that when novels depict women loving women or seeking Eros and rebirth in solitude, women authors must create new spaces and new worlds of habitation.

# CHAPTER VI

# LOVE AND FRIENDSHIP
# BETWEEN WOMEN

*(with Andrea Loewenstein)*

ALTHOUGH WOMEN HEROES IN NOVELS OF HETEROSEXUAL, LESBIAN, AND solitary passion act, by definition, in an antisocial way, much of their revolutionary spirit is tempered by conflict with patriarchal values. Battles about dominance and submission, self-punishments, and despair before gender norms characterize many novels of love and friendship between women—often resulting in excessively punitive denouements. The lesbian novel, as a result, does not always create new worlds for its protagonists since they face the same battle with gender norms as those of other novels we have examined. The genre reflects a radical polarity of experience: the intensity of the hero's anxieties and punishments, on the one hand, and, on the other, a great sense of regeneration, of freshness, when lovers successfully break through into their unique "new spaces."

## THE NOVEL OF FRIENDSHIP BETWEEN WOMEN

> "Chloe liked Olivia," I read. And then it struck me how immense a change was there. Chloe liked Olivia perhaps for the first time in literature. Cleopatra did not like Octavia. . . . Suppose . . . that men were only represented in literature as the lovers of women, and were never the friends of men, soldiers, thinkers, dreamers; how few parts in the plays of Shakespeare could be allotted to them, how literature would suffer! . . .
>
> For if Chloe likes Olivia and Mary Carmichael knows how to express it she will light a torch in that vast chamber where nobody has yet been. It is all half lights and profound shadows like those serpentine caves where one goes with a candle peering up and down, not knowing where one is stepping.[1]

Chloe had been liking Olivia for several centuries before Virginia Woolf noticed it: we need only to recall the deep, passionate, and mutually supportive friendship between Emmeline, Mrs. Stafford, and Adelina in Mrs. Charlotte Smith's *Emmeline, The Orphan of the Cas-*

*tle* or the alliances between sisters, wives, and friends in Jane Austen's, Charlotte Brontë's, and George Eliot's novels to recognize a strong, if muted, bonding among women who draw together to outwit their lords and masters. For all its ambivalence women's fiction has not always muted the depth of women's feelings for each other: "A good deal of the passion felt by Mrs. Ward's female characters," remarks Vinetta Colby,

> is sublimated in relationships that modern readers would immediately designate as Lesbian. To Mrs. Ward, however, these served as decorous outlets for her characters' passions while, at the same time, they were not only proper but even poetic and elevating. Such relationships flourished both in fiction and in real life in the nineteenth century. George Eliot, Mrs. Browning, Dinah Mulock Craik and Jane Carlyle had circles of adoring female friends and disciples. Mrs. Ward herself, apparently fulfilled in her marriage and in motherhood, had ardent female admirers.

In fact, Colby notes, Ward's last book (*Harvest*, 1920) was about two women who are in love with each other and running a farm together. "One must acknowledge," she concludes, "that the total effect of such implied, latent, or merely accidental sexuality helped to sell her books."[2]

In this great moralist of the Arnold clan we see an author able to write about deeply passionate feelings between women because actual physical sexuality between them was so unheard of that its presence went unsuspected. Women's interest in reading about women's friendships probably derived as much from the self-enhancement that the mutual support suggested as from latent sexual undertones: as any avid reader of the material will attest, a scene in which two women outwit a chauvinist idiot is just as titillating as a scene of the profoundest eroticism. After 1920, moreover, it became far less acceptable for woman authors to exhibit strong feelings between their heroes than during the previous era because an acknowledgement of lesbian sexuality had become more prevalent. It thus became more questionable to exhibit attractions between women than when the general public thought that women had no sexual urges and should be punished for taking a sexual initiative at all, even towards men.

A large number of novels written by women between 1920 and the present deal with close friendships between women and demonstrate the importance of these friendships to the heroes' personal growth and development. As a result of the twentieth-century backlash against feminism and a gynophobic fear of lesbianism, authors have implied that the flame of these friendships results from either only very extreme circumstances or a group of women living in isolation from "real" society—in a girl's school, for example, or a women's boarding house or college. As an example of this mode of novels of women's friendship in extreme circumstances we might take Shirley Jackson's *We Have Always Lived in the Castle* (1973), in which Merricat and Connie, two sisters, love each other and want to live together. Merricat, who is a witch, had poisoned her entire family in order to live alone with the quiet and gentle Connie, who had been tried and acquitted for the crime. Their happy world is threatened, however, when their cousin Charles arrives to take over Merricat's "male" duties and persuade Connie to be "normal" (i.e., "female"). Merricat sets the house on fire with his pipe, rescuing her sister from this "fairy Prince." The "idyll" of Merricat and Connie can take place only after they have barricaded themselves in the wreckage of their house, the townspeople having attacked them as insane. In May Sarton's *As We Are Now* (1973), similarly, the hero can permit herself to love a woman only in her old age, and when it is alleged that her love is "dirty," she burns the nursing home down. In Joan Haggerty's *Daughters of the Moon* (1971) the denouement involves a similarly rigid punishment: two married women who are both pregnant and have broken up with their husbands find deep comfort in each other, but one of them has to die as a result of childbirth.

In novels depicting groups of women living together, at least before 1970, we find that mutual friendships and passions between women are often treated either as passing phenomena on the road to marriage or ironically, with a high degree of spoofing. In *The Girls of Slender Means* (1963), Muriel Spark depicts women living together temporarily in the "May of Teck" club at the end of World War II. Like McCarthy's Vassar "Group" the May of Teck girls lose touch with their own solidarity, isolated from each other by competition for the goals of love and money. The brief energy that they are able to share characterizes only a transitional period in their mutual quest for male appropriation. Their bonding experience thus becomes ironic, like the collective farm run by soldiers' wives in Margaret Shea's *The Gals They Left Behind* (1944), which must be abandoned as soon as the men return from war.

When the plot of a novel of friendship between women does not occur within the context of "insanity" or a transitional emergency, the author may adopt a particularly satiric tone towards it, mocking the foibles of women while describing the relationships between them. This occurs in both Ivy Compton-Burnett's *More Women Than Men* (1933), where women jockey with each other for the affections of a new schoolmistress, and Brigid Brophy's *The Finishing Touch* (1963). However, although Compton-Burnett and Brophy spoof lesbians, among other people, the satiric aim does not target lesbianism as such. Considering the lord chamberlain's censorship of Lillian Hellman's play *The Children's Hour*, which deals with precisely the same subject, it is remarkable that Compton-Burnett and Brophy were able to treat lesbianism as openly as they did.

In fact, these novels convey the suggestion that friendship between women generates a unique energy and strength essential to the woman who tries to survive in the male world. In Elizabeth Bowen's *The Little Girls* (1963), the hero, Dinah, calls together a reunion of two girlhood friends to dig up a treasure box they buried in the garden. The treasure is their own lost personalities, but Dinah becomes both mentally and physically ill during the plot to retrieve the box and emerges with a new sense of herself only *through* the mediation of her two close friends. Dinah could not have achieved this passage to a new identity alone or in her relationships with men.

The fact that rebirth, rejuvenation, and full personal individuation can occur through friendships with members of one's own, as well as with those of the opposite, sex underlies the evolution of May Sarton's total work, an oeuvre that plays a role in this genre similar to that played by Rosamund Lehmann's in the novel of love between men and women. Starting her novelistic career in 1938, Sarton was well aware that she did not live in a culture that allows a woman novelist to dwell upon friendship between women as a major theme without adopting a tone of satire and wry spoofing: in *Mrs. Stevens Hears the Mermaids Singing* (1965) she has the writer-persona transpose the love relationship between women that inspired her first novel into the story of a heterosexual affair. Throughout her writing career Sarton continued to divert attention from this important theme until, in 1965, she brought out a fully overt lesbian novel, much to the horror of her publishers. "The fear of homosexuality is so great that it took courage to write Mrs. Stevens," Sarton admits, "to write a novel about a woman homosexual who is not a sex maniac, a drunkard, a drug-taker, or in any way repulsive. . . . The danger is that if you are placed in a sexual context people will read your work from a distorting angle of vision. I did not write Mrs. Stevens until I had written several novels concerned with marriage and with family life."[3]

In looking at the theme of friendship between women in some of Sarton's novels we do not want to distort our vision with too narrow a focus: a novelist of ideas, Sarton's oeuvre covers a wide variety of ways in which the individuals—men, women, or bisexuals—search for the meaning of life through a dialectic of solitude and relationships. Her first novel, *The Single Hound* (1938), dealt with three aging teachers, one of whom has been married and two of whom have not, living together happily. *The Small Room* (1961), similarly, deals with the relationships between women at a women's college, but in this case Sarton assumes that one cannot achieve intellectual excellence without sacrificing the experience of passion. The ingénue hero, Lucy Winter, must choose between a career and a marriage as either/or alternatives. Indeed, the most towering intellectual figure at Appleton, Caryll Cope, remarks that "in my heart of hearts I have to agree that the intellectual woman, as Dr. Johnson said of the woman preacher, can only be compared to a dog standing on its hind legs." While suggesting that intellectual profundity cannot go hand in hand with womanhood, Sarton portrays deep, long-lived friendships between the women teachers, particularly between Caryll Cope and Olive Hunt, a college benefactor. She does not describe these friendships in detail, however, their depth merely implicit; the dichotomy between intellect and Eros persists in Lucy's realization that "only from immense inner reserve, only from the secret life, the dedicated life, could such moments [of great teaching] be created. They came from innocence, deep as a well, the innocence of those who have chosen to set themselves apart for a great purpose."[4] Women in love, in contrast, are seen as so embroiled in passion that they become irrational, far too emotional to be intellectually productive.

Nonetheless, even in a purportedly domestic novel, *Kinds of Love* (1970), Sarton gives equal weight to friendships between women and to the central marriage relationship. Christina and Cornelius Chapman have retired to a small New England town, where Christina renews her friendships with the dying botanist Jane Tuttle and with her old friend Ellen. In an interesting subplot, moreover, a vision of the women of the town as the real force in its history emerges. During the course of research for the town's bicentennial celebration, Christina discovers letters that show that during the Civil War the women had bonded together on a farm, managed happily, and written the men letters in which they hid their new self-sufficiency.

Although as both novelist and poet Sarton has dealt with a variety of relationships, it seems likely that her immense popularity with women readers springs from their response not to any salacious message encoded in her works but to her simple portrayal of the possibilities of mutual renewal. For many years, however, her works have been ignored by a society that disapproves of a woman author who dares to describe things as they are. "If sometimes unlucky in the critics," she writes,

> I have been lucky in slowly getting my books through, across them, like secret agents, into the territory of the readers. There I know that I am welcome. The welcome is not measured in sales—now always respectable but never enormous—but in little things that have come to my attention, such as the fact that in the Detroit Public Library my books have to be rebound every six months. . . . The admiration of a fellow writer brings a flush to the cheek, like getting an A in school, but for me it is even more heartening to be told that a farmer's wife has pinned a poem up over her sink. The rage comes in when reviewers and critics put up a wall between the writer and such a woman. How is one to get through the wall? Only by going quietly on one's way sending out the secret agents.[5]

Because of the development of feminist criticism and a new sense of the novel as a mirror of women's status, Sarton, after a lifetime of encoding her messages within her writings, has found not only that her messages have been received but also that such heavy secrecy may no longer be necessary.

### THE BORDERLINE

The necessity of disguise, encoded messages, and secret agents in novels of friendship recurs in the lesbian novel, where heroes must find their way through the labyrinths of sexual politics in both the external world of male society and the internal world of woman's embattled psyche. The continuum from borderline to new spaces that we will describe is not a straight line but a series of bends and turns, of feints and diversions, as can only be expected in a guerrilla mode within an already suspect genre of women's fiction.

Although Sarton's *Mrs. Stevens Hears the Mermaids Singing* and Marge Piercy's *Small Changes* (1973) are by authors very different in background, age, and personal and political perspective, they approach the subject of love between women in a similarly careful manner. In Sarton's novel we see the aging poet Hilary Stevens's encounter with Mar Hammer, a young man who has left college in panic over a homosexual affair with a teacher. The two are drawn together, and Mar asks her what " 'sort of love are you talking about' " in the poems. Mrs. Stevens at first evades (" 'All kinds, I suppose' ") but then gives in: " 'When I was your age I had been madly in love with a woman a good deal my senior, with an old man, a doctor, briefly with a nurse in the hospital, and then of course . . . with the man I married' " and goes on to insist that " 'it's people that matter, Mar, not sexes or ages.' "[6]

Hilary Stevens has been a successful poet and a passionate lover of both men and women. In an interview, she continues to vacillate between an evasive attitude towards her own past and the desire to reveal it in its naked energy. The interviewers want to know about her "muses," but she tries to depersonalize them as much as she can. One reporter, Peter, asks her, " 'The epiphanies you have told us are behind each book—are these actual visitations of the Muse? An incarnate Muse?' " to which she replies, " 'Of course, you idiot. Naturally,' " and reminisces to herself about the lovers who were the midwives to her work.[7] The first of them was her governess when she was fifteen, with whom she had felt "the sensation of being inhabited by powers she could not understand or control, a thick mass of electric energy with no outlet"; this love, though unconsummated, "stretched all her powers, it was as if the whole outer world also resounded in her."[8] As she remembers other books of poems and other novels, each of which emerged from a similar "epiphany" with a lover, Mrs. Stevens realizes the source of her creativity and at the same time recognizes a falseness in her work that resulted from conformity. " 'But I sometimes wonder whether if I had quelled the censor, I might not have done better,' " she admits. " 'Women are afraid of their daemon, want to control it, make it sensible like themselves.' " For Mrs. Stevens, the necessity for disguise was self-imposed, automatic, and inevitably limiting. That she should question the ultimate value of the disguise itself points to her growing strength and independence.

In *Small Changes* Beth seeks to find her individuality first in her relationship to a man and then to a woman. Beth is from the working class and enters half-heartedly into a stultifying marriage in which the only model for sex is rape. Her individuation begins with her withdrawal from this marriage into a self-healing isolation and celibacy, living alone at first and then moving into a women's house in Boston.

It is against a background of close female friendships that Piercy gives us Beth's lesbian relationship with Wanda. "[Wanda] . . . talked about the need for women's rituals, for making each other strong, for giving each other power, for feeling each one her own beauty with the other." Working with Wanda, who is the director of a woman's theatre, Beth at first attempts to mythologize her, setting her up as a strong, invincible earth mother, but Wanda refuses to allow this: " 'Don't try to make me something up there. . . . I'm a woman the same as you are, and it isn't easier for me to fight and survive and to get things done than it is for you. . . . I get to feeling sorry for myself.

. . . I want to be cuddled and coddled and fussed over. . . . I'm still lonely and somewhere inside it's cold.' "⁹

Theoreticians of lesbianism have tended to see it as a "childish" phenomenon resulting from an intense emotional need left over from a childhood deprivation, "maladaptive," as Chesler summarizes it, "regressive, and infantile: even if it isn't, it leads to undeniable suffering, and is *therefore* maladaptive, regressive, etc."¹⁰ In refusing to be or to play "mother" and in demanding an equal interchange of strength and weakness Wanda breaks this stereotype in positing an equal relationship: "Making love with Wanda was natural. . . . They were close physically in bed and out—no sharp differences." This results, for Beth, in a freedom from nonenhancing "box shaped intimacy," so that "she was a tree in the strength of love, she dreamed, standing high on a hill in New Hampshire, and hung with flowers and fruit at once." Here again we have the contrasting images of enclosure and of free organic growth, of a woman turned into a tree of life after having escaped from her husband into the green world.

## THE LESBIAN NOVEL

Although the critical reactions to *Small Changes* were mixed, none of the reviewers labelled it a "lesbian novel." Critics were not in doubt, however, about Radclyffe Hall's *The Well of Loneliness* (1928), which was one of the first openly emergent and sympathetic lesbian novels to appear in the English language. Such authors, in abandoning accommodationist concerns, are abandoning the male/female social framework and exposing themselves to societal opprobrium. By "emergent" we mean an author's character has discarded the aim of finding and keeping a male as a life partner. "Emergence" does not imply, as a result of this stepping through the grid, a tone and attitude of happiness and content any more than does the depiction of women driven mad by sex roles in the novel of marriage. Emergence, thus, as in Hall's case, is as likely to provide misery and despair for lesbian characters as is nonemergence.

The first "doom" to fall on authors' heads is the rage and disgust of the critics. The authorities who banned *The Well of Loneliness* in England were principally outraged that "not one word suggests that anyone with the horrible tendencies described is the least bit blameworthy";¹¹ this omission deviates from the standard treatment of lesbians as "grotesquely hermaphroditic, transvestite, or so absurdly butch and pathetic as to be the object of great hilarity, ridicule, or instant revulsion. She would also need to be sadistic, outrageously promiscuous, and totally male-imitative."¹²

Internalization of social disgust, paralleling the heterosexual heroes' internalization of gender norms for women, makes the hero of *The Well of Loneliness* a figure alienated from herself. Her mother had desperately wanted a boy, and Stephen, from early childhood, grew too large, clumsy, and strong for the British feminine model. As a young woman, Stephen falls in love with a flirtatious woman neighbor, to whom she writes, in a state of mental self-hatred, that "I'm just a poor, heart-broken freak of a creature who loves you and needs you more than its life. . . . I'm some awful mistake—God's mistake—I don't know if there are any more like me, I pray not for their sakes, because it's pure Hell."[13] Her mother discovers the letter, announces that "this thing you are is a sin against creation," and drives Stephen away from her childhood home to London, where she begins to write novels. Stephen meets and falls in love with Mary, and together in Paris they share a painful love affair, surrounded by a group of self-hating male and female homosexuals. Stephen ends the relationship by encouraging Mary to choose a man who can offer her protection, children, and normality, whereas Stephen herself can offer only "the pitiful . . . lot of a girl, who herself normal, gives her love to an invert." The book ends with a passionate plea to God to " 'acknowledge us . . . before the whole world. Give us also the right to our existence!' "[14]

Like Stephen, who manages to preserve some sense of life and self-worth in her career as a novelist, Jan Morales, in Gale Wilhelm's *We Too Are Drifting* (1935), is a sculptor whose work gives her strength in a life of overt lesbianism. The art world of New York City provides an unusually accepting and nonjudgmental environment, and Wilhelm's sophisticated discussion of lesbianism outshines Hall's literary naïveté. But both the sense of desperation and the pronounced butch/femme roles dominate *We Too Are Drifting*, as they do *The Well of Loneliness*. Strong, independent, and beautiful in a "male way," Jan's sculpture is often mistaken for the work of a man, and she attracts "feminine" women. After an initial sexual involvement with an elegant, cloying society woman Jan falls in love with an unreliable ingénue.

Jan's longest friendship is with the male sculptor Kletkin, but when he is killed in a riding accident, she is left totally alone, caught between "male" and "female" since she is too "tough" to call out for help from her particular well of loneliness. Her world, moreover, is one in which only male artists produce, and the bone that society throws out to her, artistic creativity, is won at the price of her feminine identity. In spite of the realistic punishment and misery that Jan experiences, critics discounted the book because it did not deal with "the normal world, the only arena that could give it life."[15] Other novels appearing during the twenties and thirties involving lesbian heroes were marked by a similar internal alienation of their heroes and external damning by the critics. Naomi Royde-Smith's *The Island* (1930) and Sheila Donisthorpe's *Loveliest of Friends* (1931) are especially punishing and stereotypical, and more sophisticated novels, like Virginia Woolf's *Orlando* (1928), sections of Dorothy Richardson's *The Pilgrimage*, and most of Gertrude Stein's oeuvre drown explicit references to lesbianism in difficult literary styles that make the books' purpose unavailable to all but the most subtle readers.[16]

One way of avoiding the pitfalls of self-alienation and attack from the critics was for women authors, rejecting the extremes of those who feel that lesbianism is a pathology, to write books in which lesbians are carefully portrayed as "just people" who have chosen a love partner of the same sex but who differ from heterosexual people in no basic way. "We would remind you," write Del Martin and Phyllis Lyon of this attitude, "that the Lesbian is first of all a person; secondly, a woman; and only thirdly, a Lesbian. That the third often becomes first is because of societal pressures which you have the power to lift."[17] This neutralization of the alarming subject results in a fiction based on the calm assumption that love between women exists as an accepted fact, the unhappiness and difficulties experienced by the characters resulting from life in a difficult world rather than from the inherent misery of doomed, aberrant creatures.

Sometimes the neutralization of the lesbian theme occurs because the hero already belongs to an even more alienated group within contemporary society. This is the case for the hero of Sharon Isabel's autobiographical *Yesterday's Lessons* (1974), who finds lesbianism secondary to her primary identification as a working-class woman. Although Sharon's love relationships repeatedly disappoint her, so do her friendships with "straight" women. Sharon (who identifies herself as "butch") enjoys one fairly long-lived relationship with a "feminine" woman who returns her love and to whose children she becomes a good "father" and wage earner. The book ends bitterly, however: rejected for another woman, Sharon consoles herself with drink and sad songs.

Sharon's attitude towards her lover falls within the tradition of heterosexuality, and what she desires is a long-term, ideal "marriage" relationship. This parallels the lesbian novels of Jane Rule and Isabel Miller, which, like the Beth/Wanda relationship in *Small Changes*, project a utopian, fantasy world. Isabel Miller's *Patience and Sarah* (1973), for example, describes the unhappy experiences of two nineteenth-century New England heroes. These women survive the abuse and misunderstanding of the male world, and the book ends with the couple intending to spend their lives together in happy isolation on a farm. Unlike Stephen Gordon, Jan Morales, and even Sharon Isabel, Patience and Sarah do not feel that they have to take on "male" or "female" roles but find, rather, that their relationship enhances their mutual "womanliness." In this novel, although society puts obstacles in the way of the relationship, there are no interior conflicts: stereotypes, power struggles between the women, and the possibility of competition, unfaithfulness, or boredom do not exist. The setting in another era makes it slightly more plausible to the modern reader, who may reason that if such innocence is no longer possible, it may have been "back then," making of *Patience and Sarah* moving lesbian fantasy.

Jane Rule's lesbian romances, after *This Is Not For You* (1970), contain enough detailing of interior hardship to seem more realistic. *Against the Season* (1971) pictures a remarkably calm and happy acceptance of homosexual residents by a New England coastal town. Here the heroes, Rosemary and Dina, move *from* rigidly defined butch/femme, upper/lower-class, tough/weak role playing towards erotic equity. In an earlier novel, *The Desert of the Heart* (1964), Rule had assailed in a similar way the standard concept that love between an older and younger woman had to be on a mother/daughter basis. The two women, an English professor and a young cartoonist, look very much alike and must move from the attitudes imposed by their age differences towards reciprocity. At the outset, "Evelyn looked at Ann, the child she had always wanted, the friend she had once had, the lover she had never considered. Of course she wanted Ann."[18] Once they establish their love, however, they have to face returning to their jobs and life-style as well as the pain and terror of societal opprobrium. The doubts and risks of this decision are not minimized: as the limiting "butch/femme" roles in *Against the Season* had to be worked through, so here both the "narcissism" and "unmothered child" roles are overcome. Like the other characters in this category, however, these lesbian lovers strive to exercise full play of their erotic, intellectual, and artistic potentials and at the same time maintain a place in a marriage-oriented society.

### THE NEW SPACE IN LESBIAN FICTION

In lesbian novels written from the borderlines of the new space, women's right to love one another was itself so deeply in question that both authors and characters were occupied with a frantic defense of lesbianism. Though less energy was expended on this problem in the "neutral" novels just treated, where a world in which women loved one another was a given and not the primary issue, a good deal of effort was put nonetheless into the portrayal of lesbians as "just people." As we have seen in the equal-marriage novel, however, when the rules of the sex-role game are suspended, when the characters are allowed to break through the grid of depersonalizing sexual politics without the fear of being abnormal, new territories of human possibility are achieved. This same phenomenon occurs in the lesbian novel when the strength to be different, to reach for a new world without gender restrictions, frees the heroes to move into a new space.

Whereas theoreticians like Charlotte Wolff, Del Martin, and Phyllis Lyon were limited by their acceptance of standard psychoanalytical theory about narcissism and abnormal mother-child relationships, Jill Johnston, in *Lesbian Nation* (1973), posits a new world for women beyond the boundaries of "just people," long-term marriagelike relationships, "normal" love, and career orientation. Johnston feels that accommodation to these standard life patterns entraps the lesbian just as mercilessly as it does her "straight" sister. Each of them, she writes, has "been profoundly conditioned to orient herself toward accepting a single partner around whom her life would center in a 'marriage for life' and for whom she waits in suspended animation as for the storybook prince who will arouse her love and sexuality simultaneously." She admits that she herself was "just as hopelessly addicted to the ultimate oedipal for life romantic fantasy stuff as any straight girl" and concludes, thus, that the lesbian who "retains the tragic oedipal and monogamous and role-playing solutions of the straight heterosexual institution . . . is not necessarily any more liberated into her sexual autonomy than the straight feminist."[19]

The novels that emerge into the new space, like earlier heterosexual examples, are not fully occupied with detailing that space, but they do spend a great deal of time portraying heroes trying to get there. For example, Rita Mae Brown's *Rubyfruit Jungle* (1973) chronicles the development of Molly Bolt, who knows from the very beginning who she is and what she wants from life. Growing up as an unwanted, adopted child in a working-class Florida family, she refuses to conform to traditional social expectations: when she overhears her high school lover declaring that whereas Molly is masculine acting, the lover considers herself " 'not like that at all. I just love Molly. That doesn't make me queer,' " Molly says furiously, "A delicate whiff of hate curled round my nostrils. I'd like to bust her feminine head." Later, she rejects the "sick" labelling of the college dean, saying, " 'Hell, at least I'm honest about what I am.' " When she arrives in

New York City to take up a career in film, she is equally dissatisfied with the "butch/femme" stereotyping of the gay bars, reasoning, " 'What's the point of being a lesbian if a woman is going to look and act like an imitation man? Hell, if I want a man, I'll get the real thing. . . . I mean . . . the whole point of being gay is because you love women.' "[20]

The quality of consciousness in women's self-sufficient world—a world of erotic, intellectual, and emotional nurturance—was not "new" in 1974 but had already been described in Gertrude Stein's lesbian novel, *Things As They Are*, which was written in 1903 but published only in a limited edition in 1945. Stein's novel traces the relationship between three wealthy young women, detailing their striking honesty with minute sensitivity and insisting upon a world defined on its own terms—fully in the manner of Brown sixty-one years later. Adele and Helen move into a difficult, new sexuality: the two women alternate in the roles of lover and loved and strain to throw off the roles altogether. "Their pulses were differently timed" both physically and mentally, but they work hard to understand and surmount these differences. They must also deal with Helen's preexisting relationship with Sophie and absorb its existence rather than deny it. At one point Helen tells Adele that " 'I tried to be adequate to your experiments . . . but you had no mercy. You were not content until you had dissected out every nerve in my body.' "[21] This note of pain does not signal resignation, however, and by the end of the book, pain clearly has become a necessary part of the new woman's experience, shifting and growing in a fluid experiment, beyond the societal definitions of women, heterosexuality, monogamy, and despair.

Novels of the new space often violate not only sex-role expectations but also traditional fictional structures, in a mingling of autobiography, theory, journalism, and dreams that makes them a new genre between fiction and nonfiction. This is the case with Elana Nachman's *Riverfinger Woman* (1974), in which she combines straight autobiography, dream and fantasy, reflections, letters received and sent, and journal entries in her portrayal of Inez Riverfinger, a twenty-two-year-old lesbian. Nachman's use of authorial intrusion and nonlinear chronology, as well as mingling both political and personal material, also characterizes such nonfiction as Jill Johnston's *Lesbian Nation* (1973) and Kate Millett's *Flying* (1975) and such fiction as June Arnold's *The Cook and the Carpenter* (1973) and Joanna Russ's *The Female Man* (1975). Although Inez loves Abby throughout the book, she does not deny other relationships and refuses to participate in closed-off monogamy. Her love affairs with other women are thus not "substituting" or "second best" but openly positive acts of affection. The women do not restrict their love to sexuality, moreover, and extend it to "straight friends." These women draw strength from this sharing. In many novels of this type, in fact, there are passages that duplicate the experience of being mother, daughter, sister, friend, and lover all at once: "We are each other's children now, we will bring each other out of the uterus fresh, with only an infinite tenderness." Writing her mother a letter, Nachman asserts that the change in her life is not only personal but political: "They are afraid because we are no longer separating out our private lives from our public lives." She writes of reactions to her life-style, "To be a lesbian is to be implicitly revolutionary and I am just beginning to find out what that means and so the slick men question and where they can they jail or hospitalize. I'm not making this up, mother, I've seen it."[22]

Successfully combining interpersonal relationships and revolutionary politics, June Arnold's *The Cook and the Carpenter* explores the consciousness of women living in a *literal* new space, a radical feminist community in a small Texas town. The pronouns "he" and "she" are discarded for "na," and the reader has to figure out for herself that all of the principal characters (except, perhaps, some of the children) are women, thus moving herself into the new-space experience. Early in the book the carpenter conceptualizes the connection that she feels between personal and political experience:

> Look, I really don't believe that anyone can work for a revolution separate and distinct from nan own personal happiness or love-needs. Such a person wouldn't have any way of knowing the difference between what is true and what is false. It isn't that we're trying to do two things at once—set up a counterlife and work for a revolution; the two are halves of the same whole and the absolutely essential thing is to keep juggling them.[23]

The book itself juggles the interpersonal relationships between commune members and, in turn, between the commune and the Texas town. The commune members are highly introspective, constantly redefining their connection to each other and to revolutionary reality.

The women in Arnold's world try to relate to one another and to make decisions free of traditional male hierarchies and power struggles. They regard children as responsible members of the community instead of burdens or appendages. Loving has moved beyond its usual boundaries of monogamy and exclusiveness. Not one of these aims, naturally, is easily or smoothly achieved: there are disagreements over the legitimacy of violence in self-defense; the cook's child, Nicky, becomes a problem; and, finally, the love between the cook and the carpenter, instead of bringing freedom and joy, often brings constraint and suffering. The lovers' balance of power prompts a painful personal and political awareness: "'It's about big and little, isn't it?' The cook was little and the carpenter was big. Their own group was little and the men threatening to come Saturday were big. 'Or we just assume they are big because we're used to thinking of ourselves as little,' the cook said."[24]

The commune itself, in bringing the individuals into a group consciousness, has strengthened possibilities for new ways of life:

> They were joined to each other like petals of a five-pointed flower, dependent upon the joining for any life at all. . . . The space they had created (up until now) for themselves had formed a vacuum wherein they could scatter and diverge, where shape was unnecessary. . . . For now, they locked their hearts into each other and felt love like the focus of the poles.[25]

This moment of militant unity characterizes the still center of the communal structure, the fountainhead of the novel's energies. None of the participants, as evidenced by the breaking up of the collective at the end, expects to share such ecstasy for more than a brief time. As the cook explains:

> "sometimes forging into new territory or allowing yourself new boundaries preserves your sanity but then you have to live in them and that's entirely different. Maybe too hard. I was afraid that where I had been . . . was a pinnacle of the mind on which I could balance for a minute but not live. I had to come back down."[26]

Just as in the lives of its characters, the structure of the new-space novel itself revolves around epiphanic moments, or peak experiences, of erotic or metaphysical vision or both of a better world beyond genders, beyond sexual politics; the material of characterization, plot, imagery, and detail focuses upon the heroes' struggle out of patriarchal marginality toward a new hub. In the lesbian novel, as in the other genres we have treated, such epiphanies can be only temporary; they will soon be invaded and surrounded by a world totally contrary to the new space. Fictional postulations of better enclaves thus have a transitory quality, given the inexorability of their patriarchal context. Once again, however, the genre of science fiction provides a mode for projecting better worlds while keeping sight of social reality, for postulating romantic lands of hearts' desire while detailing the wastelands one must traverse to attain them.

I have noted earlier how Ursula Le Guin constructed *The Left Hand of Darkness* as a "*Gendankenexperiment*," or thought experiment, in which the action takes place in a world of ambisexual androgynes. Her hero, however, is a male heterosexual and his adventures by no means lesbian. Even earlier, in *Herland* (1915), Charlotte Perkins Gilman had constructed a hilarious spoof of gender norms by conducting three patriarchal males through a land entirely inhabited by women, but in this case the highest sentiment was maternal rather than erotic. In *The Female Man* we find Joanna Russ depicting a world similarly controlled by women, who are now unabashedly erotic in their relationships to each other. Russ uses the genre of science fiction to project new states of mind necessary for new ways of living in a strictly feminine space.

The new space of the novel is the land of Whileaway, where a plague has killed all of the adult males. Although children are born by artificial means, love is a very important element of this world and is characterized by all of the distractedness, panic, and ecstasy usually associated with Eros. There are "marriages," but they, as in the worlds of Nachman and Arnold, are not to be violated by monogamy, and everyone shares the work and child rearing.

Whereas a utopia presents the best possible aspects of a world imagined by the human mind, a dystopia functions as a warning, displaying the worst aspects of one's present society. The action of *The Female Man* alternates between Manland, a dystopia, and the utopian Whileaway, thus maintaining a tension between the actual and the desired. Just as Arnold's lesbian commune is surrounded by a small Texas town, the world of Whileaway clashes with the patriarchy; this conflict Russ portrays with irony and wit. There is the world of "male" and "female": " 'I love my body dearly and yet I would copulate with a rhinoceros if I could become not-a-woman,' " remarks "Joanna" (the first-person authorial voice who unabashedly intrudes whenever appropriate).

> There is the vanity training, the obedience training, the self-efface-ment training, the deference training, the dependency training, the passivity training, the rivalry training, the stupidity training, the placation training. How am I to put this together with my human life, my intellectual life, my solitude, my transcendence, my brains, and my fearful, fearful ambition? I failed miserably and thought it was my own fault. You can't unite woman and human any more than you can unite matter and anti-matter; they are designed not to be stable together and they make just as big an explosion inside the head of the unfortunate girl who believes in both.[27]

How, then, can the explosive polarity of encoded roles be reconciled? Russ answers this question in three ways, the first in a metaphysical symbol and the second and third in the plotting and the denouement. "To resolve contrarities," she explains, "unite them in your own person":

> This means: in all hopelessness, in terror of your life, without a future, in the sink of the worst despair that you can endure and will yet leave you the sanity to make a choice—take in your bare right hand one naked, severed end of a high-tension wire. Take the other in your left hand. Stand in a puddle. (Don't worry about letting go; you can't.) Electricity favors the prepared mind, and if you interfere in this avalanche by accident you will be knocked down dead, you will be charred like a cutlet, and your eyes will be turned to burst red jellies, but if those wires are your own wires—hang on. God will keep your eyes in your head and your joints knit one to the other. When She sends the high voltage along . . . you just shed it over your outside like a duck and it does nothing to you—but when She roars down in high voltage and high amperage both, She is after your marrow-bones; you are making yourself a conduit for holy terror and the ecstasy of Hell. But only that way can the wires heal themselves. Only in that way can they heal you . . . if you let yourself through yourself and into yourself and out of yourself, turn yourself inside out, give yourself the kiss of reconciliation, marry yourself, love yourself—[28]

The revolution of contraries involves, then, the synthesis of their dialectic in the fully developed self, the sheer force of the human personality seizing and molding polarities into something beyond the original pair of opposites. This is precisely the phenomenon that burned heroes alive in the mad-woman novels and that enabled those few women who could pass through the grid of traditional sexual "opposites" to achieve a new strength. The carpenter, in Arnold's *The Cook and the Carpenter*, undergoes such an experience in her love relationship with Three. The carpenter has been interested in the way her mind can give concrete form to chaos, in the achievement of structure through the application of intellect:

> I remember when my mind was structured, imprisoned in the time my body happened to be born, its thoughts impaled on the language of that structure-system. I was still wriggling too when the cook and I were together—we were people with histories, of a certain age. You know. Caught behind a jut of earth. Still seeing things in pros and cons, this or that, a versus b— opposites. But with you. . . . It's not at all that you are a third possibility, it's that you are all three at once—plus, minus, and other. You are three if three is a perfect circle of all possibilities.[29]

"Pros or cons," "this or that," "a versus b—" constitute the kind of thinking in polarities, either/or logic, that feminist theoreticians feel lies at the root of Western thought and gives rise to sex-role stereotyping. "By becoming whole persons," Daly argues, "women can generate a counterforce to the stereotype of the leader, challenging the artificial polarization of human characteristics into sex-role identification." These theoreticians consider the discarding of either/or thinking concerning sex roles and its replacement by both/and reasoning necessary to an androgynous (or "gynandrous") approach to life: "The becoming of androgynous human persons implies a radical change in the fabric of human consciousness and in styles of human behaviour."[30]

Women's fiction transforms such metaphysical thought structures into a posited new being. June Arnold's description of the relationship between the carpenter and Three constitutes a *Gedankenexperiment*, a concept given concrete expression in an imaginary world. These novels, as experimental stages of new gender possibilities, embody the implications of the dialectical process. Such narrative fiction both describes the conflicts between contrary worlds of gender freedom and gender rigidity, such as the Whileaway/Manland and commune/Texas town polarities in Russ and Arnold, and projects new modes of being that negate, absorb, and transcend the antitheses from which they spring. Whereas authors in the novel of heterosexual love satirize gender stereotyping and propose a more open world, the "new space" of lesbian fiction is based on the theory that women can be free from gender roles only by separating themselves from men, by breaking out of the patriarchal enclosure altogether. "Lesbians," writes Chesler, "particularly feminist lesbians who are trying to subdue their self-contempt, sexual timidity, and heterosexually modelled role-playing, feel that at this point in history only women can be midwife, mother, sister, daughter, and lover to the woman as *human being*."[31] "All women are lesbians except those who don't know it," writes Jill Johnston, "naturally they are but don't know it yet I am a woman who is a lesbian because I am a woman and a woman who loves herself naturally who is other women is a lesbian a woman who loves women loves herself naturally."[32] Through the experience of Eros with other women, in this understanding, women experience themselves for the first time not as others but as essences, reaching that place in their consciousness where they can tap the sources of their own libidinal energy.

# CHAPTER VII

# SINGLENESS AND SOLITUDE

I HAVE NOTED THAT IN FICTION DEALING WITH WOMEN'S LOVE FOR women, as well as in some science fiction and equal-marriage narratives, characters move away from the margins of patriarchal space and into a core of centralized being, a place of integrated selfhood that I have termed a new space or new cosmosis. The remarkable thing about such fiction is that it leads the reader away from the normative point of view and towards the antinormative one. The tension between society and the individual embodied in these narrative structures creates an implosion of consciousness, opening the way for a radical shift in vision. Lesbian heroes, precisely because of their marginal perspective, are able to illuminate the nature of patriarchal experience and to posit alternatives to it. This same insight radiates from much of what I define as odd-woman fiction. I use the term to describe fiction in which the hero tries to live on her own (whether or not she has been married or is involved in affairs); she is "odd" because she is not half of a couple and fulfills no set function within a nuclear family. She thus holds the same position as the "fallen woman" with regard to her society: "tainted" as her sexually active counterpart is "ruined," she is an "old maid," a target of much of the same scorn heaped upon the sexual renegade.

## GOING IT ALONE—ECONOMIC AUTHENTICITY

Historically, the situation of the single woman in society became "odd" only rather late in the nineteenth century, as the industrialization of such home trades as the cloth industry moved the locus of activity from the home to the factory and as the nuclear, rather than the extended, family became the norm. The term *spinster* originally defined a socioeconomic function: each household was glad to have an unmarried woman or two to clothe and feed in return for her part in the continuous spinning of flax, cotton, and wool necesary to the home weaving industry. Spinsters also helped with the domestic chores in large families and took the place of wives for their fathers and brothers in a period of high mortality for married women. These women were certainly not social anomalies in numbers, moreover: Nan Bauer Maglin has pointed out that in England during the Victorian era there were "about a half million more English women than men who would never be married," some of them leisured and middle class, some of them struggling for a living.[1] In America during the same period a similar surplus of unmarried women, particularly in small towns and rural areas, resulted from men's migrations westward to cities to seek employment, as well as from the death of men in the Civil War. In this way whole towns in New England became little matriarchies, run by single women, widows, and grass widows with the aid of the very young and the very old.

Judging from the popularity of fiction concerning her, the self-sufficient, autonomous woman who chooses not to be married, who happens to remain unmarried, or who finds herself out of the marriage market for a significant period of time fascinates the reading audience. Her early-nineteenth-century prototypes, as described by Papashvily, are the "indispensable women" and "the deserted wife." The former were exemplified by Mrs. Hannah F. S. Lee's *Elinor Fulton* (1837), in which the hero "fell to and supported the whole household, and contrived and planned and inspired and held the family together until her father recouped his fortune"; this situation was duplicated in Mrs. E. L. C. Follen's *Sketches of Married Life* (1838), in which Amy rose to a similar occasion, "supported the family and, if this were not enough, further defied society by going to the hospital and nursing her desperately ill fiancé back to health." The deserted wife, similarly, found it necessary to be economically self-sufficient and appeared as hero in nearly every one of Mrs. E. D. E. N. Southworth's enormously popular books: "For through ninety volumes Mrs. Southworth dreamed, and millions of women dreamed with her, the recurring dream: I loved him; I gave him everything—for what? I was ignored, scorned, betrayed, rejected, but he will come back and yearn for what he cast so lightly away."[2]

Novels depicting women supporting themselves were shocking to some and headily new to many: the theme of the author-hero, which we see in Alcott's depiction of Jo March, remained a fascinating one to women readers throughout the period.[3] It is no coincidence that the climax of Fanny Fern's (Sara Parton's) *Ruth Hall* (1853) occurs when the hero receives a facsimile reproduction of the certificate from the Seton Bank that she has earned with her writings and that represents, after a long and painful struggle, her economic liberation. Like Alcott's Jo, Ruth both fulfills her personal need for meaningful work and rescues her family because of hours spent potboiling in a garret. Thus we have the reverse of the new-woman-subdued plot pattern—namely, the doll-woman grows up. This novelist's novel mirrors the situation described by Stowe and Alcott, dealing with the economic liberation of earning one's own living and repudiating the vicious criticism of detractors.

The reading audience seems to have been fascinated not only by the success stories of woman writers but by tales of women supporting themselves in any fashion: even the eminently domestic novelist Charlotte Yonge created an independent hero for *The Daisy Chain* (1856). Ethel May, a thin, awkward, very intelligent young woman, uninterested in marriage, achieves her childhood ambition of founding a church in a neglected region. Stories of missionary adventures, similarly, were popular not merely for their pious content. The vocation of missionary was often chosen because of the fact that only in foreign countries (out of the context of Western patriarchy) could a woman develop her full potential. One woman doctor, Hyla Stowell Waters, has recently remarked that the only chance she had to practice as a surgeon after graduating from medical school as late as 1921 was to go to China as a medical missionary.[4] (It is interesting, in this regard, that the self-effacing Yonge donated the proceeds of *Daisy Chain* to the Melanesian Mission.)

Around the turn of the century what we might call the "businesswoman's novel" appeared, dealing with women who sought careers. This genre was to remain popular until the sexual counterrevolution overwhelmed it in the 1940s. Edna Ferber's Emma McChesney novels, which are about the adventures of a traveling saleswoman for T. A. Buck's Featherloom Petticoats, provide a semicomic example of the genre. *Roast Beef Medium* (1911) gets its title from the meal that Emma, distrusting all else, invariably orders in hotels. Emma supports her teenage son on her considerable earnings and, in the sequels, *The Business Adventures of Emma McChesney* (1913) and *Emma McChesney and Co.* (1915), rises to the top of her business. A less lighthearted treatment of the same theme can be found in the later novels of Charlotte Perkins Gilman, the great-niece of Stowe, who used her fiction to map out her theories of "domestic economy," complete with budgets. Her *What Diantha Did* (1910), which spoofs in its title Grant Allen's "feminist" best-seller, *The Woman Who Did* (1895), concerns the escape of Diantha Bell from a sedentary life of waiting around for her fiancé to make enough money to marry her. After being a maid herself, she establishes herself as an organizer of boarding houses and more efficient employment for domestic servants. Her hotel eventually makes her enough money to marry her lover, who will not have her because she won't give up her work and stay home like his conventional sisters, whom she has always deplored. The denouement consists of the revelation that it is through Diantha's efforts that he has been able to buy his ranch, and the novel ends with his condescension, after she marries him and achieves international fame, to let her discuss her business at home. "All This" is the title of the chapter detailing her business success; "And Heaven Beside" is the title of the denouement, where she at least earns the respect of her spouse.

The novel, then, at the close of the 1870–1920 period, expresses some hope that women will be able to find both gainful employment and the personal fulfillment of heterosexual relationships. Those who have chosen celibacy and made themselves "odd" in the eyes of society seem, moreover, less "unsexed" than might be expected. The times, unfortunately, were not going to remain favorable for the businesswoman or her working-class sister.

"One of the curious features of [Richardson's] portrait of Miriam Henderson," remarked an American critic in 1928, "is her insistence on the superiority of her heroine's mind—on its . . . richness and power and depth . . . as compared . . . with the minds of the men whom she meets." "There is," he concludes, "something a little pinched and sour and old-maidish in this."[5] This sentiment can be translated thus: a woman who sees herself as having more richness and power and depth than the men she meets is not a real (e.g., man's) woman; she is an inadequate sexual creature, wizened, ugly, and infertile. Dorothy Deegan, in *The Stereotype of the Single Woman in American Novels* (1951), surveys a sample of works by both men and women published between 1901 and 1935 and concludes that the following characteristics are true of the image of single women in American literature: when they have heterosexual relations, they are depicted as ridiculous; their interest in society and the community is usually at the level of gossip; they are both pitied and ridiculed by other men and women; they are apathetic and resigned about their place as outcasts from the married world; they do not discuss their singleness or reflect on it. When they are schoolteachers, they are poor ones; the dressmakers gossip; the genteel retainers both gossip and are parasitically dependent; the maiden sisters live in an old house after their parents' death and act eccentric. To Deegan, moreover, such responses stem logically from the single woman's choice to "live her life apart from the traditional pattern of marriage," which is the "very current of life itself." To swim outside this current is to "deliberately evade the responsibilities of living," to "guard too closely their own way of life." "To live a self-centered life," she concludes, "is the direct antithesis of the giving and sharing required in successful marriage and parenthood, and perhaps society is reluctant to realize that the single life can be anything but a selfish existence."[6] If the only avenue for "responsibility," for "giving and sharing," is marriage and domesticity, and if singlehood is postulated as antithetical to these qualities, then to choose to remain single is suspect, heretical, and "eccentric"—and the self-sufficient single woman becomes a social pariah.

Women authors writing about single women thus chronicle episode after episode of "female difficulties," including the self-imposed punishments of internalized societal opprobrium. In modern British fiction Jean Rhys spends her oeuvre exploring such figures. Julia Martin, in *After Leaving Mr. Mackenzie* (1931), is left alone as a middle-aged woman after a poor marriage and after losing a baby, entirely dependent on what her "face" can do to bring her the attention and donations of her male friends. These old lovers and acquaintances despise her for her poverty and for her aging, pathos, and importunity.[7] As her complexion, or sexual "face," fades with age, Julia becomes colder and more tired and finally, in defeat, goes back to Mr. Mackenzie, the circular plot in this novel paralleling the back-to-the-fold accommodationism typical of the novel of marital rebellion.

Whereas pathos characterizes the tone of Rhys's fiction, which depicts heroes who are powerless against the economic realities of modern life, a number of novels portray the economic struggles of women less sympathetically. Stella Dallas, in Olive Higgins Prouty's 1923 bestseller of that title, is a distastefully self-centered divorcée who blights the lives of husband and daughter alike; this novel is a reminder of early attitudes toward divorced women. Tempering an otherwise negative attitude towards such heroes, Sheila Kaye-Smith, in *Mrs. Gailey* (1951), uses the woman on the make as a 1950s version of the emancipated woman of the 1920s. Mrs. Gailey is trying to take advantage of the class confusion after World War II to get a leg up in British society for the laudable purpose of supporting her retarded son, whom she has left behind in London. Although her problems are sympathetically depicted, she is a victim of economic scarcity who associates with "bounders" and semicriminal characters in order to improve her social position. In this regard she is very much like Jean Rhys's heroes, women who must struggle to "cope" at the barest level of existence, single women who must fawn on men or die. They meet the same fates, thus, as the apparently intrepid Lulu Bett in Zona Gale's 1920 best-seller, who, for all her ability as the strong spinster in her family,

must marry in order to survive in the world. The deadlocked characterizations of the women in this category of single-woman fiction seem
to derive from the ironic discrepancy between the high hopes of the
turn of the century and the economic realities of life in the modern
patriarchy. They are also heir to a more generalized distaste for the
social pariah that is quite similar to that for the "old maid."

## SINGLE WOMEN AND SEX

The deteriorating fortunes of the single-woman hero who indulges
in sexuality parallel the situation of the woman struggling for economic survival. Although novels that deal with single women engaged
in heterosexual affairs overlap to a degree with novels of punishment,
puzzlement, and passion, considered in chapter 5, those which I will
study in this section are characterized by a focus on the woman hero
as a single person who emerges from the entanglements of passion
with her singlehood intact, a modern sister of the prepatriarchal virgin.
Typical heroes of this type early in the modern period were the self-
sufficient country women and farm women in Atherton, Sinclair, Cather, and Glasgow. In Glasgow's *Barren Ground,* as we saw in chapter 2,
the hero battles the elements and her lover, creates a farm for herself,
transcends love, and survives. In that she experiences passion and a
passionless but convenient marriage and triumphs nonetheless over
the gynophobic scorn of her fellow farmers, Dorinda violates a whole
series of sexual codes. She is rewarded richly, nonetheless, for all of
her deviations.

Sheila Kaye-Smith's *Joanna Godden* (1921), like *Barren Ground,*
deals with a strong, self-satisfied farm woman who pits herself against
the men of her Sussex village to make a success of her land. Joanna is
a big, boisterous, and flamboyantly dressed woman who decides to
manage her own sheep farm after her father's death. She runs the
farm her own way, orders her men about, transgresses every local
rule of sexual politics, and is still considered a "fine woman," although
the men also describe her as an unbroken mare. After the death of her
fiancé, Joanna, unwilling to put her sexuality to one side, pursues a
caddish city clerk named Albert and conceives an illegitimate baby.
Out of fear of the embarrassment that will accrue to her spoiled, ultra-
feminine sister, Ellen, Joanna is forced to choose between keeping the
baby and keeping the farm. The novel ends as, at the age of forty, she
decides to sell Ansdore and go off alone to have the baby. Although
at the denouement Joanna is punished for her passion, she pursues her
own idea of happiness, namely, raising her baby. The strong, young,

androgynous woman hero does not survive intact in another of Kaye-Smith's treatments of her, however: in *Superstition Corner* (1934), a historical novel dealing with "Galloping Kate," a twenty-eight-year-old Catholic of the sixteenth century, the hero becomes entangled in her contradictory desires to be self-sufficient, on the one hand, and married, on the other.[8]

When a single woman has an adequate career and is no longer beset by the basic necessities for physical survival, she still remains limited in the world of love. Jane Clifford, the thirty-two-year-old professor of women's studies in Gail Godwin's *The Odd Woman* (1974), untroubled by overt societal scorn for her "old maidhood," experiences emotional and sexual restrictions in her quest for authentic eroticism. A single woman who seeks to model her partnerships on George Eliot's twenty-five-year-long relationship with Lewes, Jane will not settle for anything less than Eros on this long-term, mutually esteeming basis.

Jane is not content to accept either her friend Gerda's man hating (which is a caricature of "women's lib") or the solution of Ellen Glasgow, "whose favorite theme," she reflects, "was men's inhumanity, men's inferiority to women. Glasgow created a heroine in *Barren Ground* who could live without love, a heroine whom Sonia Marks's students could not identify with because they were not ready to live without love."[9] In spite of the only partially satisfying elements in her affair with Gabriel, her sexual relationship enables Jane to achieve self-enhancement. As in Oates and Lessing, Eros brings a personal development that stops short of an equitable exchange with a partner, and the hero's brief moments of epiphanic passion give way to separation and return to singlehood. Unlike Drabble's heroes of *The Waterfall* and *The Realms of Gold*, who use their "true loneliness" as a space in which heterosexual Eros may flower, Godwin, Oates, and Lessing, like Porter, Richardson, and Kaye-Smith, portray romantic love and personal self-sufficiency as incompatible.

## "OLD MAIDS"

Women who make their own decisions about their sexuality, whether those decisions are for Eros or celibacy, participate in Harding's "true virginity" but, at the same time, reject social acceptance. In a society that associates feminine sexuality with subordination to a male, both women who refuse permanent heterosexual relationships and women who choose celibacy are outcasts. The fact that freely undertaken sexual choices of any kind contradict patriarchal expectations for women accounts for the scorn heaped upon women who do *and* women who don't, sexually active and sexually celibate women alike. Popular Freudianism, with its attitude that women who are not sexually active are likely to be mentally ill, added to the vilification of celibate women already enforced in British and American society.[10] Although to some extent infected by this attitude, women novelists often depict the strengths of celibate, as of sexual, singlehood, engaging their fiction in a debate about whether society should view the independent, celibate hero as "happy."

An interesting early case of this single-woman-debate genre was *The Whole Family, A Novel by Twelve Authors* (1908); those authors included William Dean Howells, Mary Wilkins Freeman, Henry James, Elizabeth Stuart Phelps, and Alice Brown.[11] Each one takes the point of view of a member of a small-town family caught in an entanglement over the youngest daughter's engagement, and, despite the multiple authorship and one lost suitor, the novel is for the most part unified and consistently witty. In one crucial aspect, however, it is ambivalent in the extreme: in the disparity between the chapter presenting the perpetrator of all the mix-ups, the "Old Maid Aunt," and all of the other chapters. After an innocuous introduction to the action by William Dean Howells, Mary Wilkins Freeman tries to set the tone for the character of Aunt Elizabeth (as she is known in Eastbridge), or Lily Talbert (as she is known elsewhere). In a skillfully written interior monologue, Freeman sets up the complexity involved in Lily's being, to everyone around her, an "old maid" while, in her own estimation, she is a fully authentic person, perhaps, she even admits, too "womanly" for the good of those around her, a thirty-six-year-old single woman constantly and to her own embarrassment (and titillation) having one young man after another fall in love with her. When she tries to warn Peggy's fiancé away from her and to tell the rest of the family to watch out for his fickleness, they laugh it off, blaming it on her old-maid fancies. Although, in Freeman's chapter, Lily acts sensibly and with compassion, not one of the authors in the rest of the book comes wholeheartedly to her defense. The men recognize her sexuality; the women decry her as a man-stealing old vampire. Freeman's well-rounded and complex portrait of the ironic discrepancy between Lily's authenticity and the stereotype of the old maid is swallowed up in hostile points of view: Henry James has "the Married Son" describe her as "the prowling Eliza," Mary Stewart Cutting agrees that "she is trying to take Mr. Goward's affections away from Peggy," and John Kendrick Bangs, writing as "The Son-in-Law," proposes "a Bill for the Protection of Boys, and the Suppression of Old Maids Who Don't Mean Anything By It." In the last chapter Lily is banished from society: cut off from the family, her great New York society friends exposed as a bunch of charlatans, she goes away in a maidenly black dress to begin a career as a mesmerizer.

The debate over the relative happiness of the married woman and the single one is nowhere more prominent than in Virginia Woolf's total work, as evidenced by her tendency to counterpoint married women with unmarried ones. These women study each other's state of mind, envy each other's position, and live contrasting life-styles. The debate begins with dialogues between Rachel Vinrace and a group of single women in *The Voyage Out* (1915), it occupies the central dialectic between Mary Datchet and Katharine Hilbery in *Night and Day*, it crops up in *Mrs. Dalloway* (1925) in the stereotypically negative figure of Miss Kilman, it is developed to its greatest metaphysical ramifications in the thematic counterpointing of Lily to Mrs. Ramsay in *To the Lighthouse* (1927), it informs the characterization of Eleanor Pargiter in her relationship to a series of couples in *The Years* (1937) and of Rhoda in comparison to Susan in *The Waves* (1931), and it has its final ramifications in the contrasting characters of Ida and Miss La Trobe in *Between the Acts* (1941). In Woolf's characterizations of the single woman we find some of the either/or philosophy manifested in Sarton's *The Small Room*: Rachel Vinrace and Mary Datchet choose death and a celibate singlehood over the alternative of marriage, a fate also implicit for Miss Kilman; Miss La Trobe is creative at the expense of continuous misery, and Rhoda kills herself, leaving only Eleanor Pargiter and Lily Briscoe engaged in continuing self-analysis over whether they can permit themselves to be happy outside marriage.

May Sarton, similarly, spends a considerable amount of time in her novels debating the alternatives of singlehood and matrimony. Her most striking contributions to the old-maid-or-wife debate, however, are her two old-maid novels proper, in which, like Mary Wilkins Freeman in "A New England Nun" and Sarah Orne Jewett in *The Country of the Pointed Firs*, she stands the stereotype on its head. She takes the large-bonedness, eccentricity, and "prickliness" in Miss Pickthorn (*Miss Pickthorn and Mr. Hare*, 1966) and shows that they represent aspects not of a silly, unfulfilled neurotic but of a self-dependent character who is able to hold her own in a village full of gossips who call her the "Maiden Porcupine." In *Joanna and Ulysses* (1963), similarly, Sarton plays upon the stereotype of the old maid's love for animals to develop a rebirth narrative in which the hero comes to terms with the wounds of the past (her mother's death by torture at the hands of the Nazis) through healing a wounded donkey that becomes, in turn, the mediator for the return of her artistic creativity. Joanna, like Miss Pickthorn, achieves her individuation surrounded by the jeers of an old-maid-hating village, in this case the inhabitants of a Greek island. Although she has done nothing but paint alone, wear striped slacks, and cure the donkey, a little boy tells Joanna that "some say you are queer, a witch, they say. They say you are proud, an Athenian woman with her nose in the air." The patriarchal islanders, clearly, fear Joanna's self-sufficient "pride" and ability to choose to remain single: "a woman alone," remarks Sarton, "and who seems happy to be alone arouses mixed emotions; she threatens something people do not talk about, and if she is not very lucky indeed she will be punished in one way or another for being a threat."[12]

Other woman authors also carry on a debate about nonmarriage much like the marriage debate of the 1870–1910 period. On the one hand we have the cruel and stereotyped portrait of Miss Hobchick in Pamela Hansford Johnson's *Blessed above Women* (1936) or of the two old-maid sisters in Esther Forbes's *Miss Marvell* (1934); on the other hand there are well-rounded portraits, such as that in Mary Ellen Chase's *Mary Peters* (1934) and Carson McCullers's Amelia Evans in *The Ballad of the Sad Café* (1944). If there are smears of strong spinster figures, like Fannie Hurst's description of Charlotte Ames in *Lonely Parade* (1942), who looks "like a cross between a Tamany alderman, a baby-elephant, and a Buddha . . . having missed the supreme carnal satisfactions,"[13] there is also Edith Wharton's skillful manipulation of the stereotype in *The Old Maid* (1924), where it turns out that the supposedly spinsterish hero is raising a daughter out of wedlock.

## SINGLE WOMEN AND WITCHCRAFT

The accusation of "witch," as we can see in Sarton's *Joanna and Ulysses*, springs from an intense societal fear of a powerful, untrammeled woman who, by daring to *enjoy* her unmarried state, defies social norms. In the past, of course, it was the label of witch that had brought nine million women to violent deaths in Western Europe, very often midwives who eased the pain of childbirth and who were the only source of safe abortions. "The role of witch," remarks Mary Daly,

> was often ascribed to social deviants whose power was feared. All women are deviants from the male norm of humanity (a point emphasized by the "misbegotten male" theory of Aristotle and Aquinas, the "penis-envy" dogma of the Freudians, and other psychological theories such as the "inner space" doctrine of Erikson and the "ani-

ma" theory of Jung). However, those singled out as witches were frequently characterized by the fact that they had or were believed to have power arising from a particular kind of knowledge, as in the case of "wise women" who knew the curative powers of herbs and to whom people went for counsel and help. Defined as evil, they became the scapegoats of society, and in this process, the dominant ethos was reinforced.[14]

The old maid is frequently associated in popular culture with the witch, the two stereotypes springing from a common gynophobic fear of self-determined women. Thus Mary Wilkins Freeman, in an unpublished manuscript, "Jane Lenox," has a single-woman hero declare herself perfectly contented with a status that she recognizes as "monstrous" to the normal point of view:

> I am a rebel and what is worse than a rebel against the over-government of all creation . . . I even dare to think that, infinitesimal as I am . . . I, through my rebellion, have power. I, Jane Lenox, spinster, . . . living quietly, and apparently harmlessly in the old Lenox homestead in Baywater, am a power.

> And another thing which was my birthright: the character of the usual woman. I am a graft on the tree of womanhood. I am a hybrid. Sometimes I think I am a monster, and the worst of it is, I certainly take pleasure in it.[15]

I will speak in "witches incantations, poetry, old women's mutterings," declared poet Robin Morgan one hundred years later. "I/am/a/monster. I am/a/monster./I am a monster./And I am proud."[16] Like Pamela Hansford Johnson and Rosamond Lehmann, such authors recognize that the being they relish is necessarily transformational, a new gender beyond maleness and femaleness.

Two novels, Esther Forbes's historical novel *A Mirror for Witches* (1928) and Sylvia Townsend Warner's *Lolly Willowes* (1926), make an interesting pair, taking opposite sides in extending the old-maid debate to cover the subject of witches. In Forbes's novel the author condemns the central character from the very beginning. Doll Bilby is dragged away from the pyre where her parents are being burned to death to be adopted by a kindly New England sea captain, against whose family she gradually works her inherited evil. "Bewitched," she will "bewitch" others, and the novel merely shows how the inevitable results of her evil blood unfold. *Lolly Willowes*, in contrast, is a carefully balanced portrait of an unmarried woman who becomes a witch, dealing first with her old-maid situation and then with her quest towards a completely satisfying and self-determined status as a member of a coven.

From her childhood Laura has known that to "come out" and marry will be to dwarf her personality. Townsend Warner describes her as a young girl:

> [her] legs were very slim and frisky, they liked climbing trees and jumping over haycocks, they had no wish to retire from the world and belong to a young lady. . . . Sooner or later she must be subdued into young-ladyhood; and it seemed befitting that the change should come gravely, rather than with the conventional polite uproar and fuss of "coming-out"—which odd term meant as far as she could see, and when once the champagne bottles were emptied and the flimsy ball-dress lifted off the thin shoulders, going in.[17]

Here we have the eventual old maid as a young tomboy who, in refusing to "grow up grotesque," becomes "odd" from the point of view of a society whose norms the hero dislikes. Laura remains on her parents' estate, which is a brewery (brewsters in England were originally women wise in herbs, we learn) until she gives in, after her parents' death, to her brother's demand that she live with him and his wife. There she stays for twenty years, suffering the full opprobrium of an old-maid relative as "Lolly," until one day she takes it into her mind to go and live by herself at "Great Mop."

The brother's reaction expresses the civil status of the unmarried female in a capsule: " 'Lolly! I cannot allow this. You are my sister. I consider you my charge,' " but when it turns out that he has lost half of her money in stupid investments, she takes what remains and goes. At first she works with a henwife and "felt wise and potent. She remembered the henwife in the fairytales. . . . She was sister to the spaewife, and close cousin to the witch." She gradually realizes that all of the villagers are members of a coven and goes with them to the all-night dance, hardly the evil conclave described in Forbes:

> These depressing thoughts were interrupted by red-haired Emily, who came spinning from her partner's arms, seized hold of Laura and carried her back into the dance. Laura liked dancing with Emily; the pasty-faced and anaemic young slattern whom she had seen dawdling about the village danced wth a fervour that annihilated every misgiving. They whirled faster and faster, fused together like two suns that whirl and blaze in a single destruction. A strand of the red hair came undone and brushed across Laura's face. The contact made her tingle from head to foot. She shut her eyes and dived into obliviousness—with Emily for a partner she could dance until the gunpowder ran out of the heels of her boots.[18]

Like the "five-pointed flower" of June Arnold's lesbian collective, the energy of the dancing women generates from a communal acceptance and solidarity and redeems them from the "normal" frustrations of the patriarchy. The dance transforms "Lolly" back into Laura, her true self, the witch experience becoming a redemptive one for the woman who has been thwarted from development by a couple-filled world.

Townsend Warner thus redefines the negative old-maid/witch stereotype, developing not a "cute" portrait of a "good coven" for its fantasy effect but a picture of a mutually supportive community. " 'When I think of witches,' " remarks Laura to the devil,

> "I seem to see all over England, all over Europe, women living and growing old, as common as blackberries, and as unregarded. I see them, wives and sisters of respectable men, chapel members, and blacksmiths . . . listening to men talking together in a way that men talk and women liisten. Quite different to the way women talk, and men listen, if they listen at all. . . . Is it true that you can poke the fire with a stick of dynamite in perfect safety? . . . Anyhow, even if it isn't true of dynamite, it's true of women. But they know they are dynamite, and long for the concussion that may justify them. Some may get religion, then they're all right, I expect. But for the others, for so many, what can there be but witchcraft? That strikes them real."[19]

Reacting to partriarchal bonds, which make them "outsiders" in their own world, knowing themselves to be full of spunk and rage, these women long for a space where they can bond with like-minded spirits and "be natural" without censure.

### THE GREEN WORLD AND THE SINGLE WOMAN

Witchcraft, a Stone Age religion in which the priestess plays the role of the goddess and in which the sun and moon, seasonal cycles, birth, fertility, and vegetation are the focus of the rituals, belongs to the green-world archetype; it is a set of practices and beliefs linking women to nature.[20] Even when authors are not explicitly (or perhaps even consciously) dealing with witches as such, fiction in which heroes draw power for self-sufficiency from nature has perennially delighted the reading audience. Under the guise of local-color fiction, or regionalism, and of popular "romance" fiction, women heroes are described as laws unto themselves in their solitude, happy among the animals and plants, sometimes in the company of other women but essentially alone. Sarah Orne Jewett's heroes, for example, convey an infectious gaiety and sense of selfhood in their wanderings about New England. The two girlfriends, Nelly (the narrator) and Kate, whose summer adventures in Maine constitute the short stories in her first book, *Deephaven*, haven't a thought for young men but are hardly nonpersons as a result: they wander over the country making friends and asking questions; they ride, hike, and explore, their exploits providing a liberated tone that undoubtedly accounted for Jewett's popularity among women readers. The narrator of a later collection, *The Country of the Pointed Firs*, is equally happy with her occupation. Almira Todd, the widow and herbologist who intrigues the narrator, introduces her to a series of other "odd women" who are supporting themselves on the difficult terrain of the northern Maine coast: there is Almira's mother, old Mrs. Blackett, who, at eighty-six, lives on Green Island by herself winter and summer alike, and there is the story of "poor Joanna," a hermit woman who, disappointed in love, subsisted for years before her death on an even more remote island off the Maine coast. The picture of the narrator writing her tales in a rented schoolhouse suggests a companion portrait of self-dependency to Mrs. Todd, gathering tansy in the field outside.

I have noted how lirelong allegiance to the green world enables a few heroes, like Cather's Alexandra, Glasgow's Dorinda, and Kaye-Smith's Joanna, to pass through and beyond Eros, absorbing its beneficence for the personality and yet remaining self-sufficient. In such fiction the hero, by refusing to abandon her ties with nature, avoids the usual fate of the heroes in the novel of development. She is able, thus, to achieve selfhood through a creative solitude. Such best-selling romances as those of Elizabeth Goudge may derive their popularity from the appeal that the archetypal figure of the woman at home in nature holds for the reading audience. The heroes of two Goudge novels with quite different settings, for example—Froniga in *The White Witch* (1958), which is set in seventeenth-century England, and Mary Lindsay in *The Scent of Water* (1963), set in England in the 1950s—have specific green-world locales. Froniga, a half-gypsy like Mary Webb's Hazel, centers her life around a cottage in the Chilterns, and Goudge devotes pages to each herb in her garden and Froniga's recipes for healing. "The creatures never feared her," she remarks in a manner identical to Jewett's in "A White Heron." "One of her unordinary powers, and the only one that gave her nothing but joy, was her power over them."[21] In primitive iconography, as Joseph Campbell has noted, we frequently find the figure of "the lady of the beasts," a powerful goddess at home with wild animals perhaps best known through the unicorn tapestries hanging in Paris's Musée de Cluny. In Froniga we seem to have a rendition of this powerful green-world archetype, known to England through such Celtic divinities as Dana and Brigit. Mary Lindsay, though not explicitly tied to witchcraft traditions, inherits her namesake's cottage and there discovers the power of the green world to alleviate pain and loss. As in witchcraft's transmission from generation to generation, she takes the child Edith as understudy. The green world is thus the primary agent of the hero's quest for authenticity. Whereas from a patriarchal perspective one would expect the single, eccentric, old woman, or old maid, to be a figure of derision and social ostracism, in much of women's fiction she becomes a hero representing the possibilities of growth and survival.

## TRANSFORMATIONAL SOLITUDE

In literature dealing with single women, as in lesbian fiction, authors seem to be clearing out a new space that is in actuality an old, or archetypal, landscape of the psyche, a place that, essentially apatriarchal, contains once-forgotten possibilities of personal development. Rekindling old images, buried archetypes, and discarded choices, such fiction brings its heroes through quests towards personal transformation or rebirth. This achievement does not occur only in middle and old age. In two novels from the sixties, we have young British women achieving a significant degree of autonomy through the isolating experience of childbirth out of wedlock. Jane Graham, in Lynne Banks's *The L-Shaped Room* (1961), and Rosamund Stacey, in Drabble's *The Millstone* (the American version was *Thank You All Very Much*, 1965), choose singleness rather than marriage in spite of their pregnancies out of a desire to "go it alone." Jane Graham remarks to Toby, a young friend who lives in the same building, that his protests about her dragging him away from his writing are an illustration of the weakening effects of marriage:

> This was what one person's needs could do, if inflicted on another person. "You don't have to make money for me. I'm not your responsibility. I'm not anybody's but mine. And you're not anybody's but yours. I won't take the responsibility for you losing the will to write, or for shackling your motives, or anything else. We've no right to wish our problems on each other. That's the difference between being married and single and we're single."[22]

Jane ultimately gives in to interpersonal dependency, however, in that she comes to think of her pregnancy as the "dark months" and returns to keep house for her drunken father. Rosamund, on the other hand, achieves true privacy, control over her own destiny, and love, the last in her deep feeling for her daughter, Octavia. She can "do for herself," as her feminist mother has urged. Jane returns from the "dark world" of feminine space to the paternal enclosure; Rosamund accepts her childbirth and her daughter as positive, beneficent experiences, giving birth to her self.

As Nancy Hardin has noted, Rosamund's pregnancy and childbirth make her *more* intellectual rather than the opposite, better able to conduct her research and get ahead in the scholarly world than before. She learns about her connection to other human beings both through her experiences with other women in the prenatal clinic and in the discovery of her own openness and vulnerability when Octavia is ill. "I suddenly thought that perhaps I could take it and survive. . . . But then, however fleetingly, I felt that I could take what I had been given to take. I felt, for the first time since Octavia's birth, a sense of adequacy. Like Job, I had been threatened by the worst and, like Job, I had kept my shape."[23] Giving birth to Octavia is thus a vehicle for her coming to herself, her personal rebirth, an integration of individual feeling and intellect with social relationships that is the paradoxical essence of true solitude. "Keeping your shape" seems to be easier in the single state than in marriage, in spite of the barrages of fortune, the anxiety of loneliness and of worrying about the "other" woman, and the scorn of the coupled world. Modern single women heroes, I should repeat, do not always achieve this state by avoiding personal relationships but, more often, by seeing them as a step towards the ultimate goal of selfhood.

This is the case in the classic modern odd-woman bildungsroman, the immensely detailed and complex *Pilgrimage*, by Dorothy Richardson, and in Godwin's *The Odd Woman* in that both Miriam and Jane are likely to continue in their quests for love and for human relationships while protecting their solitary selves from excessive ravishment. This is also the case in odd-woman literature in which women are involved in emotional and spiritual growth well into their later years. "I woke in tears this morning," writes May Sarton in her *Journal of a Solitude*, "I wonder whether it is possible at nearly sixty to change oneself radically. Can I learn to control resentment and hostility, the ambivalence, born somewhere far below the conscious level? If I cannot, I shall lose the person I love. There is nothing to be done but go ahead with life moment by moment. . . ."[24] Similarly, Sarton's widowed Mrs. Stevens struggles with the ghosts of her several deep, intense love affairs, not in a regressive nostalgia but in the attempt to move forward in her development and understanding. The novel's epigraph reads, appropriately, "From love one can only escape at the price of life itself; and no lessening of sorrow is worth exile from that stream of all things human and divine."[25]

Other women heroes in this genre, long married, discover that they are born raw and naked all over again after widowhood, finding themselves shedding their secondary identities. Joanna Roux, in Gillian

Tindall's *Someone Else* (1969), emerges from wifehood and tries romance, sex, old friendships, but she winds up having to face the difficulty of creating a life for herself when she has belonged to somebody else for years.[26] The widowed, sixty-year-old hero of Pamela Hansford Johnson's *An Avenue of Stone* (1947) is demoralized by her new entanglements, and Kate in Lessing's *The Summer Before the Dark* (1973) is faced with a similar dilemma when her husband and children outgrow their need for her. She tries a romantic affair, which turns sour, and gets a prestigious job with a national food company but finds that it replicates her wife-and-mother role.

For all these older women heroes the road towards self-understanding that they had previously pursued—namely, relationships with other people—becomes increasingly secondary, giving way to a puzzling over the nature of the cosmos itself rather than over human entanglements. "But what is becoming tiresome now in the American ethos is the emphasis on sex, and especially on orgasm as an end in itself," writes Sarton. "Let us think more about flowers and animals in a new way. . . . [Sex] will have its day and its hour and the orgasm, should it occur, will come not as a little trick cleverly performed, but as a wave of union with the whole universe. The emphasis on orgasm per se is just another example of the devaluation of all that is human."[27] Sarton's satisfaction in her "natural" human sensuality is similar to the attitude of many women authors as they progress through works dealing with sexual politics towards a concern with nature and the natural universe. Thus Alice Brown, Josephine Herbst, Ellen Glasgow, Rosamond Lehmann, Doris Lessing, Mary Ellen Chase, and Zona Gale all develop in their later work a new attitude, not a turning away from sensuality and relationships as much as an acceptance of a dialectic between these relationships and a wider world for the human mind to explore. In 1925 Zona Gale wrote to her father:

> Heavenly things are happening. Literally heavenly. I mean in dreams, and in awakening with a sense of mother, or her nearness . . . I feel so sure that the time of the first stirring of life in the earth, in the trees, the movement of sap and the ripening warmth of the sun is more than physical. That more than matter is attuned to the quickening of life in the spring. That the whole phenomenon is profoundly spiritual, and that what we see around us, in reviving beauty, is merely an earthly manifestation of something which takes place in infinitely greater measure, within and about us. Why should not the spirit have its rhythm as do the stars.[28]

The quality of solitude in women's fiction often involves these images of inverted Platonic mysticism—journeys to the earth rather than escapes to an abstract empyrean. At the same time, the quest for the pulse of nature is attuned to something "spiritual," the beloved green world providing a bridge to the wider universe.

Ellen Glasgow wrote about her lover, Gerald, in much the same language with which Gale treated her mother's death. When Gerald died, she said,

> I sank into an effortless peace. Lying there, in that Golden August light, I knew, or felt, or beheld, a union deeper than knowledge, deeper than sense, deeper than vision. Light streamed through me, after anguish, and for one instant of awareness, if but for that one instant, I felt pure ecstasy. In a single blinding flash of illumination, I knew blessedness. I was a part of the spirit that moved in the light and the wind and the grass.[29]

The vision of this woman novelist seems to turn toward the earth, toward an alliance with the organic universe. The epiphanic visions that occur in Lessing and Woolf take on precisely this same quality of naturism *through* Eros, of a mystical vision gained not by rejecting nature but by incorporating it.

In Woolf's *The Years*, for example, Eleanor Pargiter develops an interest in love in her later years, which parallels her curiosity about the nature of the universe as expressed in various Eastern philosophies. Her final epiphanic vision in the novel occurs as she watches the gestures of a young couple whom she does not know helping each other lovingly into a cab. The mixture of concern with personal relationships and sudden, solitary revelations that characterizes so much of Woolf's fiction is also found in individual novels by Vita Sackville-West, Mary Ellen Chase, and May Sarton. Lady Slane, in Sackville-West's *All Passion Spent* (1931), turns eighty-eight before she can freely pursue the solitude that she has desired:

> Only in a wordless trance did any true apprehension become possible, a wordless trance of sheer feeling, an extra-physical state, in which nothing but the tingling of the finger tips recalled the existence of the body, and a series of images floated across the mind, unnamed, unrelated to language. That state, she supposed, was the state she approached most closely to the self concealed within her, but it was a state having nothing to do with Henry.[30]

Mrs. Ramsay, in Woolf's *To the Lighthouse*, achieves precisely this kind of wordless epiphany when sitting alone for a moment, at rest from the demands of her husband and children, in a state so self-enhancing that she prefers it to life itself.[31] Sara Holt, similarly, in Mary Ellen Chase's *Edge of Darkness*, shares with her friend Lucy

Norton the ability to achieve moments of overwhelming insight: "She had lost all identity, all consciousness of herself. She had become blotted out, erased, lost, in what seemed to be succeeding waves of understanding, engulfing waves of surprise and wonder, of pity, hope, and faith, and one final overwhelming wave of gratitude. . . . [Then] the circle of light had gone."[32]

The older women who experience this apotheosis, I must reiterate, are escaping from the moil and toil of female roles and duties but not from the stream of life itself: they participate in an organic mode of mysticism shared with the single women, widows, and women wise in herbs pictured by the regionalist traditions and shared, too, with those few women in our sample who achieve the equitable passion of erotic authenticity. These older women, moreover, can be understood within the context of my definition of virgin as the woman who is whole unto herself, in tune with her own instincts, able to give, receive, or withhold sexuality as she sees fit. The women heroes who seek and are transformed by solitude have come to terms with the "shadow," the "self-hater," in Lessing's terms, of woman's psyche and have transmuted polar "male" and "female" attributes into a new, androgynous consciousness.

"The fact that a middle-aged, single woman, without any vestige of family left, lives in this house in a silent village and is responsible only to her own soul means something," writes May Sarton in her *Journal of a Solitude*. "The fact that she is a writer and can tell where she is and what it is like on the pilgrimage inward can be of comfort."[33] Only in the silence of withdrawal from relationships does Sarton feel free to break away from gender roles to revitalize herself for new relationships, new works of art, new stages in the process of maturation. "Has it really happened at last?" she asks herself as she nears her sixtieth birthday. "I feel released from the rack, set free, in touch with the deep source that is only *good*, where poetry lives."[34] The two streams of thought about singlehood that come together in Sarton's journal are those manifested in odd-woman fiction throughout its history: on the one hand, a recognition of societal opprobrium for not being part of a couple or family; on the other hand, a sense of energy springing precisely from this ability to release oneself from relationships, to allow oneself authentic individuality. This is not, as Sarton acknowledges, the *only* way a woman can achieve maturity, but it is *a* way, with its own set of problems and adventures.

In his description of the youthful quest for adulthood Carl Jung identifies two figures that occur as archetypal guides for the soul: the "wise old man" and the "young maiden." A man must come to terms with both the paternal guide figure and his own undeveloped "femininity" in order to take his place in the world: these figures thus are taken to represent facets of the selfhood that need to be used. In women's literature the figure of the wise old woman often replaces the figure of the wise old man. This replacement explains the prominent role of the wise woman in a young hero's education: Lucy Norton is apprenticed to Sara Holt, Jenny to Froniga, Peggy to Eleanor Pargiter, Lily to Mrs. Ramsay, the interviewer Jenny to Mrs. Stevens, Jane Clifford to her mother and grandmother. The reader, in turn, is apprenticed, looking to the older women as figures of repose and energy, individuality and strength, figures illustrating the eventual goal of her own quest for selfhood. Eccentric to the patriarchy but at home in her "own shape," surrounded by beneficent plants and animals and willing to teach a chosen disciple her knowledge of herbs and of the human heart, the mature odd woman seems to echo an archetypal figure long buried in women's collective memory—the earth goddess as "lady of the beasts" surrounded by bird, beast, and flower. I shall explore further dimensions of such archetypal figures in the following chapter, in which I study texts in women's fiction specifically concerned with the feminine power inherent in women's archetypal inheritance.

# PART IV

# TRANSFORMATION OF THE SELF

*And now we who are writing women and strange monsters*
*Still search our hearts to find the difficult answers,*

*Still hope that we may learn to lay our hands*
*More gently and more subtly on the burning sands.*

*To be through what we make more simply human,*
*To come to the deep place where poet becomes woman,*

*Where nothing has to be renounced or given over*
*In the pure light that shines out from the lover,*

*In the pure light that brings forth fruit and flower*
*And that great sanity, that sun, the feminine power.*

MAY SARTON, *"My Sisters, O My Sisters"*

# CHAPTER VIII

# NOVELS OF REBIRTH
# AND TRANSFORMATION

BY ALLOWING MATURE, AUTHENTIC VOICES TO BREAK THROUGH THE MASKS of "old maid," "single woman," "old woman," and even "witch," authors of the single-woman novel subvert long-standing gender stereotypes. Stereotypes differ from archetypes, I feel, in representing clusters of symbols that have become rigid and hence restrictive to full personal development. Archetypes, conversely, are fluid and dynamic, empowering women's personalities to grow and develop. Some feminist theoreticians take stereotype and archetype as synonymous. Mary Daly, for example, sees both as part of a "trap designed by society's physicians of the soul" and creating a false " 'paradise' of archetypes and repetition."[1] I am suggesting, however, that archetypes are both projective and "repetitious," futuristic and rooted in women's history, means by which Daly's "new space" and "cosmosis of sisterhood" may be attained. Although there are *underlying* narrative and symbolic patterns perceivable as archetypes in women's literature, certain twentieth-century authors have made more self-conscious use of archetypal patterns. In order to study the role of archetypes in women's fiction in depth, I will examine four novels structured according to one recurrent narrative archetype, that of the rebirth journey, or quest into the unconscious.

As I noted in the previous chapter, a number of older women, having lived through various feminine and masculine roles and having rejected a good many social expectations, attain a state of unity with the green world and with the universe. These heroes have experienced a transformation of the personality, a centering upon personal, rather than patriarchal, space, that differentiates them from the younger heroes of the novel of development. Theologian Carol Christ makes a distinction between the "social quest" and the "spiritual quest" by defining the social quest (corresponding in function to the bildungsroman) as a "search for self in which the protagonist begins in alienation and seeks integration into a human community where he or she can develop more fully" and the spiritual quest as the "self's journey in relation to cosmic power or powers. Often interior, it may also have communal dimensions."[2] In women's fiction social quests are usually found in the bildungsroman and spiritual quests in novels whose heroes are over thirty, most often in middle or old age. If the purpose of the novel of development is to integrate the individual into her society, its generic function is frequently aborted by society's unwillingness to assimilate her. The older woman hero, in contrast, has "been through all that"; her goal is to integrate her self with herself and not with a society she has found inimical to her desires. The distinction between the young hero's quest for social integration and the older woman's quest for selfhood can best be illustrated in those multiple-volumed novels that contain both types. In Lessing's *Children of Violence*, for example, the first four volumes constitute a social quest in which Martha is pushed about by social and economic forces, but in the fifth volume, *The Four-Gated City* (1969), she becomes fully conscious of her victimization by society and, through a quest for spiritual rebirth, becomes master of her self. For Richardson's Miriam in volume 7 of *Pilgrimage*, as for Martha, earlier epiphanies recur and consummate a rebirth experience that results in a renovation of her personality.

Carl Jung's descriptions of this transformation, or "individuation" process, are helpful in coming to terms with women's rebirth fiction. Insofar as it applies to the individual life span (in contrast to rebirth experiences of reincarnation and metempsychosis) Jung defines *Wiedergeburt* as involving either renovation or transformation of an individual so that all of his or her faculties are brought into conscious play. This may involve a "renewal without any change of being, inasmuch as the personality which is renewed is not changed in its essential nature, but only its functions, or parts of the personality, are subjected to healing, strengthening, or improvement." Moreover, it may take the form of a transformation of personality in that the individual undergoes an "essential transformation" or "total rebirth" by taking on the characteristics of a suprahuman figure to whom he or she is initiated in mystery, rite, or dream.[3]

Jung and his followers felt that understanding the process by which an individual journeyed into the unconscious was essential if such destructive phenomena as violence and war were to be eradicated from the human experience. When unconscious materials are repressed, divided off from day-to-day experience, and not assimilated by the conscious mind, they lead to mass eruptions like Nazism. "When instincts and chaotic images and urges arise from the unconscious in flood proportions," explains M. Esther Harding, "they break up human or individual bounds. One thing only can stand against this power of the un-conscious and this, paradoxical as it may sound, is the power of the individuality." The rebirth journey and similar experiences

> bring to consciousness the lost values of the psyche, which lie so largely in the realm of Eros, and by this means the human being be-comes more complete. In the terms of the ancient religions it would be said that through participating in the various stages of the mys-tery initiations man is born again and becomes a "twice-born" spirit. For when a man or woman submits to the laws or principles of his own being and gives up the personal orientation of the ego he grad-ually defines the limits of his own nature and the individuality crys-tallizes within him.[4]

Individuality, which I have identified in this study with authenticity and totality of self, transcends social roles, thus differing from "the personal orientation of the Ego," and goes beyond personhood as a *merely* social function. Through breaking with day-to-day behavior, paradoxically, the "reborn" hero can battle those forces likely to dis-rupt society. The rebirth journey takes the hero beyond social boun-daries and back again, its goal the renewal of society.

Among the elements of the personality that Jung and Harding find potentially dangerous to society are those values traditionally clus-tered around the concepts of "masculinity" and "femininity," or, in Jung's terms, the *animus* and the *anima*. Although, as I have pointed out in the Introduction, this polarization according to gender ap-proaches stereotyping, Jung's recognition that unassimilated gender norms constitute social dangers places him in a conceptual framework not unfriendly to feminist scholarship. The "superordinate personality," the elixir or goal of the rebirth journey, is androgynous, nonsexist, in tune with both inner being and the natural world in the same manner as those singularly "centered" odd-women heroes I have described.

Such a crystallization of the personality comes about when the ego, which Jung differentiates from the self, leaves the narrow bounds of its persona, or social mask, and plunges into the unconscious. The ego, as Jung defines it, "extends only as far as the conscious mind," whereas the self comprises "the *whole* of the personality, which includes the unconscious as well as the conscious component. The Ego is thus re-lated to the self as part of the whole."[5] Whatever is experienced in the inner journey must be understood as at one and the same time indi-vidual and collective, the materials of the unconscious deriving from the repository that Jung spent his lifetime codifying according to what he termed its intrinsic organization in "definite recognizable patterns."

The problem that he himself acknowledged, however, was that since so much of women's experience is socially marginal, there was not as frequent a correlation between unconscious and "recognizable patterns" in women's social experience as in men's.

In Jung's schema, as in much of Western theory, ego, or consciousness, is symbolically identified with "the masculine" and the world of the unconscious with "the feminine." The realm of personal dreams and memories, which I would term the subconscious, reflects these daily experiences. To the degree that women are alienated from full participation in society, they are also alienated from these "upper" realms of the ego and the subconscious. In addition, women find it hard to translate the contents of their unconscious into recognizable symbols and myths. Since in Jung's schema the unconscious consists largely of "the feminine"—a quality translated into male religions, myths, and cult practices as alien and fearful—women must come to terms with unconscious materials distorted by cultural bias. It is important to be very careful in considering such figures as the "earth mother" and "goddess" since an archetype can vary from gynophobic to celebratory according to the critic's views on femininity. Northrop Frye, for example, in his analysis of the rebirth pattern, describes the feminine figure as a "typical agent of cunning," a source of destruction who rules the underworld of "violence and trickery." Uniting in her being the polar forces of Ares and Eros, war and love, she is "Venus, whose alternative form is Diana of the triple will, the white goddess who always kills, and whose rebirth is for herself."[6] The archetype of the goddess may appear, thus, in Frye's schema, but the perspective is radically different when a woman writes about her. Such an erotically independent, self-regenerative, and organically powerful archetype is far more likely to appear beneficent than destructive to the woman writer.

The fact that one can create an outline of women's quest for rebirth that seems to parallel in its figures and sequence such formulae as Jung's quest for individuation, Campbell's adventures of the hero, and Frye's romance journey should not lead one to assume fundamental analogies between the way that these archetypalists perceive their material and the way women authors present similar archetypes. The difference between the way that men and women writers and scholars perceive archetypes derives, as I have indicated throughout this study, from their different experiences in society. The radical otherness of women's experience is borne out in the eccentricity, apatriarchal outcome, and arcane symbolism that characterize fiction dealing with women heroes who complete the ultimate quest for human adulthood.

## PHASE I: SPLITTING OFF FROM FAMILY, HUSBANDS, LOVERS

This first aspect of the journey inwards takes the form of an acute consciousness of the world of the ego and of a consequent turning away from societal norms that the author often graphically and specifically details. In this sense the novels of marital rebellion (in which marriage is portrayed as "that hideous institution") and of social protest (in which the economic enclosure is excruciatingly detailed) herald, although they rarely undertake, the inward plunge away from patriarchal experience. In a novel like Oates's *Do With Me What You Will*, this rejection of the normative occurs in an intricately detailed assessment of the world of law, politics, and crime that prompts Elena's abandonment of her husband and lover. Beth sets out on her social quest in *Small Changes* after being galvanized into action by a particularly awful evening with her husband, and the narrator of Atwood's *Surfacing* is shown driving away from the city where she has had a traumatic experience with her lover. In Woolf's *To The Lighthouse* Mrs. Ramsay is precipitated into an inward plunge after a particularly trying day with her husband, and in Lessing's *The Four-Gated City* the hero leaves two husbands behind in Africa, journeying forth on a new life in England.

## PHASE II: THE GREEN-WORLD GUIDE OR TOKEN

As in the epiphanic visions of childhood and adolescence, the hero is helped to cross the threshold of her adventure by some ordinary phenomenon that suddenly takes on extraordinary portent. These green-world guides and tokens crop up in such esoteric forms as witches' familiars, as the puddle that takes Rhoda, in *The Waves*, over the threshold of reality, as some innocent fruit jars in *Lolly Willowes* that set Laura off on her quest for a coven. Beth conjures up an imaginary turtle to help her escape her marriage, and Kate, in Lessing's *The Summer Before the Dark*, turns to dreams of a seal as a vehicle for her plunge into the inner journey. A prototypical case, in which the first and second phases are combined, occurs in volume 4 of *Pilgrimage* (*Clear Horizons*), in which Miriam makes use of a flute song and a landscape to turn away from society. Miriam hears the melody "coming punctually as she turned to seek help from Michael who would not give it" and undertakes a rebirth experience through an epiphanic vision. As Shirley Rose comments, it is in response to the discrepancy between her inner needs and what her lover offers that Miriam turns toward an inward path: "The birth-thrust is into the self. The physical organs of birth have been translated into the imagery of nature. . . . the birth canal is through 'the gap in a low hedge, between two dewy lawns.' "[7]

## PHASE III: THE GREEN-WORLD LOVER

Whether as an actual figure or a revery one, an ideal, nonpatriarchal lover sometimes appears as an initiatory guide and often aids at difficult points in the quest. He (sometimes she or it) does not constitute the turning point or goal of the rebirth journey, as does the goddess or anima in the male rebirth journey. Whereas in the novels that I treated in chapter 2 this figure leads the hero towards social development, as in the case of the Corn God in *O Pioneers!*, who becomes a vehicle bringing Alexandra to marriage, in rebirth novels this figure leads the hero away from society and towards her own unconscious depths. In this sense I would include *Wuthering Heights* as a rebirth novel since the path that Catherine takes is away from society and into a love consummated in tragedy and death. Such a figure, it is important to note, is less likely to dominate the hero than to constitute a phase through which she must pass. This is the case with Three in *The Cook and the Carpenter*, her lovemaking a catalyst in the integration of the carpenter's personality, and with Joe in Atwood's *Surfacing*, a real lover who nonetheless seems semianimal, archaic, like a furry buffalo. Sometimes the green-world lover is actually an animal: a heron in Sarah Orne Jewett's story, a fox in *Gone to Earth*, a donkey in *Joanna and Ulysses*, a stag in the witchcraft rituals, a bull in the Cretan mysteries of Minos, and the unicorn that appears in women's poetry and needlework.[8] The hero may love it, pretend to be it (as in Jo March's identification with a horse), or follow it. In the modern novel, it seems to me, the figure represents a combination of the Native American animal guide, or spirit, and an incorporation into the personality of one's sexual and natural forces, one's Pan, as it were, or one's own internal Adonis.

## PHASE IV: CONFRONTATION WITH PARENTAL FIGURES

In women's rebirth fiction the fourth phase is most often a confrontation with figures in the memory, from the past, rather than the actual battle undergone by the young hero of the novel of development. Even if the older woman hero has turned away from society because of disenchantment with her past, she must still come to terms once more with the father and mother figures resident in what I have described as the subconscious, her repository of personal memories. Woolf's *To the Lighthouse,* as she herself acknowledged, represented her coming to terms with the relationship between her father and mother. In *The Children of Violence* Martha reconciles herself to her father in an earlier volume and to her mother in *The Four-Gated City* before she can proceed to unlock her own unconscious resources. Elena's self-reconciliation can take place only within the framework of her memories of father and mother, and Sarton's Mrs. Stevens must bring to mind the way that her father had actually treated her mother, much in the manner of the Ramsay marriage, before she can complete her quest for renewal.

## PHASE V: THE PLUNGE INTO THE UNCONSCIOUS

After the hero confronts the figures of the subconscious, she can journey toward the unconscious proper, the realm from which the green-world lover and the guide or token have summoned her. These two figures, as we have seen, seem matrilinear in the general sense of suggesting a realm of inherited feminine power quite different from patriarchal culture. In Jung's description of the rebirth journey one must come to terms, in this phase of plunging into the unconscious, with one's "shadow," the self-destructive potential manifest in the personal realm as social rebellion, which, in the unconscious, accretes the power of the sexual opposite. These figures constellate into a powerful "autonomous complex," capable, if unassimilated, of throwing up disturbing figures in both dream and, through projection, real life.

It is at precisely this point that Jung's model warps in its fit with the experience women manifest in much of their fiction. The personal (subconscious) content of the shadow, in Jung's schema, would be antisocial, rebellious against gender among other societal norms. In women's fiction, quite the contrary, the shadow seems to bring with it from the social world the opprobrium for womanhood associated with sexism, infusing characters with self-loathing. Women heroes often blame themselves for their own normal human desires, warping their quests for Eros, for example, by internalizing patriarchal norms about feminine sexuality. For women, the shadow of self-hatred is tremendously strengthened by complicity with society. In the male psyche the merging of shadow and anima gives rise to the "dual mother," feared and loathed as an archetype of maternal creation and destruction. Shadow and animus, in women's fiction, constellate into figures combining gynophobia with such "masculine" impulses as logic, aggression, and power struggles. Far from meaningless as a pattern in women's fiction,

Jung's animus/shadow complex seems responsible for those monsters of male logic, ego, and destructiveness so much more frequent than their matrilinear counterpart, the green-world lover.

Because men's rebirth journeys so frequently provide them with images and symbols that have analogues in known mythological and religious material, even androgyny (the incorporation of their "feminine" components) may serve as a boon to the societies to which they return. Women's rebirth journeys, in contrast, create transformed, androgynous, and powerful human personalities out of socially devalued beings and are therefore more likely to involve denouements punishing the quester for succeeding in her perilous, revolutionary journey.

Although Jung admits the shadow's originally social origin, he overlooks the loathing for women that the shadow's cultural origin contributes. This same loathing, nonetheless, may inform his own description of the "anima" as "dual mother," split by his masculine perspective into two parts, one destructive and the other creative. This bifurcated figure derives its dualistic nature, I am suggesting, more from the fact that women are "other" to men than from an essentially binary quality. There is a similar "split" in the shadow/animus figures as they appear in women's fiction, accounting for the unreasoning attraction that keeps heroes submissive to them and derived, similarly, from their essential quality of "otherness" to the female hero. Whereas the encounter with the anima is supposed to be the crucial experience leading the male back to society as a superordinate or reborn person, women encounter the animus as a block to full development. They must penetrate beyond this male temptation of self-destructive complicity to that "deep place," as May Sarton puts it, "where poet becomes woman," a place of "great sanity" that can be derived, for women, only from "feminine power." In far more novels than otherwise, however, such an outcome is blocked by the hero's inability to come to terms with her feelings about the "perfectly nice horrible husband" figure; this fact may account for the greater number of novels in which women are done to death or driven mad by their socially acceptable consorts than of novels in which they achieve rebirth.

The rebirth journey entails risk and psychological danger, as likely to lead to madness as to renewal. Reflecting this fact, fictional heroes often experience surreal images and symbols, disassociated fantasies, and chaotic noises that mimic clinical madness. The experience of this level, which I have termed "literary insanity" in contrast to the objective horrors of genuine madness, can either finish the hero off entirely or provide the turning point in her quest. The problem, as we have seen, is that "insanity," whether literary or clinical, is often a perfect mirror of the feminine persona's place within society, an image of the enclosure and of its victims, and thus the transformed hero who has survived this layer of her unconscious is unlikely to be able to reintegrate herself fully into "normal" society.

## FOUR INNER JOURNEYS COMPLETED

### Mrs. Ramsay and the Androgynous Elixir

During the half century since the publication of Virginia Woolf's *To the Lighthouse* (1927) critics have taken account of the importance of sex roles to the characterization: some have understood the Ramsay marriage as an anatomy of complementary "masculine" and "feminine" attributes, but a good number have taken it as a description of sexual warfare.[9] New insights into the way women authors build characterization out of the destructive aspects of gender norms and an understanding of the inner journey should be helpful in a new look at the structure of the novel. The nineteen numbered sections of "The Window," the first part of the triadic structure, consist of a dialectical alternation between material devoted mainly to Mrs. Ramsay (sections 1–3, 5, 7, 10, 11, 16), material concerned with the way Mr. Ramsay's mind works (sections 6, 8), and syntheses revealing the way that others view the marriage (sections 12, 17, 19). In addition, sections 4, 9, 13–15, and 18 disperse the focus onto the perspective of the children and the houseguests.

Woolf's portrait of Mr. Ramsay's mind is not unsympathetic, although she uses the satiric devices of parody and buffoonery of Victorian male norms in order to deride his aspirations. "Who shall blame him?" she asks, rhetorically, after a hilarious portrait of his attempts to get from "Q" to "R" in his mind: "Who will not secretly rejoice when the hero puts his armour off, and halts by the window and gazes at his wife and son. . . . who will blame him if he does homage to the beauty of the world?"[10] Woolf uses "the hero" and "the beauty of the world" with tongue in cheek in this omniscient passage and goes on to portray precisely how such gender stereotypes lead husband and wife into difficulties.

Section 7, a key text, seems to open with the "blame" for the marriage squarely placed upon Mr. Ramsay, at least from the perspective of his youngest son: "But his son hated him." James resents his father's interruption of his time with his mother: "he hated him for the magnificence of his head; for his exactingness and egotism." From the initial paragraph of the novel we know that James's feelings are deep and violent; when he thinks of his father, he imagines knives, scimitars, pokers, representing both his father's power and weapons that he would like to use against him: "Had there been an axe handy, a poker, or any weapon that would have gashed a hole in his father's breast and killed him, there and then, James would have seized it." To the extent that James resents, fears, and would like to expropriate his father's apparent potency, we have the stock Oedipal situation and images correspondingly phallic in the Freudian manner. James, in this interpretation, is an envious understudy who wants to usurp his father's power. He eventually does so in part 3 by properly handling the tiller of the boat in which he, his father, and Cam are sailing to the lighthouse.

There is another dimension to James's behavior, however, which carries it beyond the small boy's hatred for his mother's lover characterized by Freudianism. "But most of all," Woolf informs us, "he hated the twang and twitter of his father's emotion which, vibrating round them, disturbed the perfect simplicity and good sense of his relations with his mother." If James were reacting to a conventional sexual relation, we would not expect him to allocate emotionalism to the father and "good sense" to the mother but more likely the reverse. This suggestion of a turnabout from the usual male-female pattern introduces a striking use of genital and kinesthetic imagery in the succeeding paragraphs of section 7:

> Mrs. Ramsay, who had been sitting loosely, folding her son in her arm, braced herself, and, half turning, seemed to raise herself with an effort, and at once to pour erect into the air a rain of energy, a column of spray, looking at the same time animated and alive as if all her energies were being fused into force, burning and illuminating (quietly though she sat, taking up her stocking again), and into this delicious fecundity, this fountain and spray of life, the fatal sterility of the male plunged itself, like a beak of brass, barren and bare. He wanted sympathy . . . to be taken within the circle of life, warmed and soothed, to have his senses restored to him, his barrenness made fertile, and all the rooms of the house made full of life. . . ."[11]

The extraordinary eroticism of the imagery is not unusual in Woolf, who is given to writing of the human psyche as an integer of body and mind. It is not surprising, either, that she should use such forceful models of genital imagery since she was, after all, Freud's English publisher and as early as 1919 had dedicated her fiction to "the dark places of modern psychology."[12] What is strikingly original here is the use to which Woolf puts such imagery. Like Karen Horney, her contemporary and a Freudian psychoanalyst, Woolf perceives that penis envy has less to do with infantile attitudes than the role of both girls and women in society, "that it is a secondary formation embodying all that has miscarried in the development toward womanhood."[13] What Woolf does in this key passage is to develop three interrelated sets of sexual images to portray a psychosexual adaption forced upon Mrs. Ramsay by the circumstances of her marriage and times.

The three sets of images can roughly be described as: first, pouring of life fluids upwards; second, the reception of the male in a widening out, an unfolding or circling motion that encloses him; and third, the motion of plunging, of the "arid beak" sucking at both erection and circle. On one level we might take Woolf's use of the term to "pour erect" in the general sense of erecting the mind and spirits, denoting a totality of alertness, a complete focusing of the personality with all of its faculties upon one object. Clearly, however, Woolf's usage is heavily dependent upon the sexual undertone. The "rain of energy" and the "column of spray" are analogous to ejaculation. The fluid imagery is linked to light imagery ("burning and illuminating") through still another submerged metaphor between the "column of spray" and the biblical pillar of cloud by day and of fire by night. This, in turn, links Mrs. Ramsay's fountainhead experience to the core symbol of the novel, the lighthouse, which, as we shall see in our analysis of section 11, is her *animus* figure.

James is also associated with the lighthouse-column-penis figure to the extent that he himself, in the classical Freudian sense, is a penis substitute, "standing between her knees, very stiff." The child and the doll, in Freud's understanding, are penis replacements for the little girl, who, in her dismay at finding the organ missing, must vainly look ahead to the faraway consummation of motherhood. James is involved in something not strictly usual in sexual configurations, however, since he is experiencing his mother's performance of both male and female functions: "as he stood stiff between her knees [he] felt her rise in a rosy-flowered fruit tree laid with leaves and dancing boughs into which the beak of brass, the arid scimitar of his father, the egotistical man, plunged and smote, demanding sympathy." Here we come upon the second set of kinesthetic images, which, like those of the fountainhead, become thematic to both "The Window" and the novel as a whole. The flowers in the novel are not static but in the motion of unfolding, as in time-lapse photography, the petals uncurling, the leaves dancing, encircling the male and the children and the houseguests. The flowering, or unfolding, imagery continues to be associated (as a pun, perhaps, on "rose") with lovely things that rise: the smell of the *Boeuf en Daube*, for example, rising out of the pot full of a "confusion of savoury brown and yellow meats, and its bay leaves and its wine," which celebrates the occasion of Minta and Paul's engagement, an event also figured forth in garlands of flowers. Similarly, the child Rose creates a pyramid of fruit to add to the festivity, an occasion that makes Lily Briscoe suspect Mrs. Ramsay of, priestesslike, leading "her victims to the altar."

The engagement, like the Ramsay marriage, is a cause for both celebration and sadness, at once a consummation and a sacrifice. This negative aspect of the relationship between the Ramsays is brought out in the third set of sexual-kinesthetic images, closely associated with the flowering and circling images in that the linear figure of the "beak of brass," "arid," "sterile," plunges into the center of them, destroying, devouring. In striking contrast to the organic figures that they invade, metallic, sharp figures of beaks, knives (James sees his father as "lean as a knife"), scimitars, and weapons recur throughout the novel, always in association with a sterile but destructive element. Mr. Bankes, for example, stabs at Lily's painting with a "bone handled knife," breaking up her moment of concentration; Mr. Ramsay, walking in Mrs. Ramsay's garden in the evening, perceives her flowers not as organic but as "spear-like" and "red-hot pokers"; Paul Rayley is perceived as a "crowbar"; and Mary and Joseph, the black rooks, are described in their marital battles as cutting the air into "exquisite scimitar shapes."

There is certainly a strange reversal of the standard masculine and feminine patterns in section 7: although the "delicious fecundity" and "circle of life" into which the male plunges might be the usual feminine configuration, it is the man who is thought of as the one who brings fecundity to the one who is barren, an adjective with connotations of childlessness in the woman. At the conclusion of the section, however, we have Mr., rather than Mrs., Ramsay filled with the fluid of creation: "Filled with her words, like a child who drops off satisfied, he said, at last, looking at her with humble gratitude, restored, renewed, he would take a turn. . . ." It is Mrs. Ramsay who is to "fill" the rooms of the house with life, and after her death they contain an empty space, reminiscent of a stillness in beauty in the sense that she has chosen to go down into the shadow, to retreat into solitude and death, rather than continue her exhausting relationship to her husband and children.

Mrs. Ramsay's response to the experience of section 7 is ambivalent: she feels throbbing through her "the rapture of successful creation," but, unlike Mr. Ramsay, she also "felt not only exhausted in body . . . but there also tinged her physical fatigue some faintly disagreeable sensation with another origin." As she reads James the story of the fisherman and his domineering wife, she recognizes the source of her malaise: "she did not like, even for a second, to feel finer than her husband; and further, could not bear not being entirely sure, when she spoke to him, of the truth of what he said." She is responding, here, to an uncomfortable sensation of superiority but also to the destructive effect of sexual politics upon her psyche.

It seems clear from Virginia Woolf's total work that in the Ramsays she portrays a particular type of incomplete relationship, that between an intellectual whose emotional side is underdeveloped and the woman to whom he turns for mothering. In a number of other instances, of which Terence Hewit in *The Voyage Out*, Ralph Denham in *Night and Day*, and Bernard in *The Waves* come most immediately to mind, she develops male figures whose emotional lives are in some degree of harmony with their intellectual development. In *To the Lighthouse*, in contrast, she carefully underlines the disharmonies, the discordant element, of the Ramsays' marital relationship, depicting what happens to a woman who chooses to love a childish spouse.

Since the fountainhead experience described in section 7 is linked consistently with the lighthouse through imagery of rising, illumination, circling, and stroking, it seems imperative to arrive at a clearer understanding of the connection between this experience and the thematic symbol of the lighthouse. The description, like a number of other strongly erotic passages in Woolf's novels, represents a deliberate portrait of the processes of the psyche as described through sexual imagery. We are cognizant enough of the flaws in Freud's theory of penis envy to discard any shallow interpretations of Mrs. Ramsay's "erections" as a way of "getting back at" Mr. Ramsay, particularly since the action is undertaken in concern and love. Because of the accompanying imagery of fluidity, light, flowers, and encircling, we do not have any sense of violence or rape, interpretations more appropriate to the scimitar-brass-beak imagery describing Mr. Ramsay. Rather, the column, in its erection and life-giving powers, suggests a quest into the innermost reaches of Mrs. Ramsay's psyche along the path of Eros, leading to a consummation by her assuming androgynous characteristics in reponse to Mr. Ramsay's infantile asexuality.

We might consider Mrs. Ramsay's experience, then, as an act of androgynous creativity in which the hero calls upon the greatest reach of her internal nature—including motions and forces usually allocated to men alone—to respond to her marital situation. In a second key text, section 11, Woolf depicts Mrs. Ramsay turning away from her marriage to plunge into an inner journey where the *animus* figure is no longer projected upon her husband but has become a crucial element in her own quest for individuation. "When the libido leaves the bright upper world," writes Jung of the rebirth experience,

> whether from choice, or from inertia, or from fate, it sinks back into its own depths, into the source from which it originally flowed. Whenever some great work is to be accomplished, before which a man recoils, doubtful of his strength, his libido streams back to the fountainhead—and that is the dangerous moment when the issue hangs between annihilation and new life. For if the libido gets stuck in the wonderland of this inner world, then for the upper world man is nothing but a shadow, he is already moribund or at least seriously ill. But if the libido manages to tear itself loose and force its way up again, something like a miracle happens: the journey to the underworld was a plunge into the fountain of youth, and the libido, apparently dead, wakes to renewed fruitfulness.[14]

Mrs. Ramsay undertakes such a journey to the underworld in section 11 of "The Window," a return along the path of the libido to the fountainhead, or core, of her personality, involving the assimilation of her *animus*, or internal "manly" attribute. Whether she actually ever returns to the upper world, however, is problematic: her death soon after suggests that she is victimized by the process rather than saved to enjoy her transformation. The process of rebirth, however, occurs in both "Time Passes," in terms of the distintegration and reintegration of the empty house, and "The Lighthouse," in Lily's absorption of the powers that Mrs. Ramsay has won.

In section 7, as we have noted, Mrs. Ramsay's experience is tinged by exhaustion and discontent with her role: it is in section 11, in contrast, that she replenishes her "fountainhead" by turning away from her family and placing herself under the power of the lighthouse. With her husband and children momentarily out of sight, she relishes her solitude, pondering how beneath the surface of her personality "it is all dark, it is all spreading, it is unfathomably deep; but now and again we rise to the surface and that is what you see us by." The persona, which in Jung's terms is that aspect of the personality visible to the world, is subsumed by the superordinate self, which surfaces in Mrs. Ramsay in section 11 with encircling, erect, and flowering motions, a "summoning together" and "resting on a platform of stability." As in other Woolf novels, the moment of being contains both illumination and shadow, both blazing light and a "wedge of darkness":

> Losing personality, one lost the fret, the hurry, the stir; and there rose to her lips always some exclamation of triumph over life when things came together in this peace, this rest, this eternity; and pausing there she looked out to meet the stroke of the Lighthouse, the

long steady stroke, the last of the three, which was her stroke. . . . She looked up over her knitting and met the third stroke and it seemed to her like her own eyes meeting her own eyes, searching as she alone could search into her mind and her heart, purifying out of existence that lie, any lie. . . . it was odd, she thought, how if one was alone, one leant to things, inanimate things; trees, streams, flowers; felt they expressed one; felt they knew one, in a sense were one; felt an irrational tenderness thus (she looked at that long steady light) as for oneself. There rose, and she looked and looked with her needles suspended, there curled up off the floor of the mind, rose from the lake of one's being a mist, a bride to meet her lover.

With some irony in her interrogation, for when one woke at all, one's relations changed, she looked at the steady light, the pitiless, the remorseless, which was so much her, yet so little her, which had her at its beck and call (she woke in the night and saw it bent across their bed, stroking the floor), but for all that she thought, watching it with fascination, hypnotised, as if it were stroking with its silver fingers some sealed vessel in her brain whose bursting would flood her with delight, she had known happiness, exquisite happiness, intense happiness, and it silvered the rough waves a little more brightly, as daylight faded, and the blue went out of the sea and it rolled in waves of pure lemon which curved and swelled and broke upon the beach and the ecstasy burst in her eyes and waves of pure delight raced over the floor of her mind and she felt, It is enough! It is enough![15]

The strokes of the silver fingers, of the lighthouse rays, are opposite in effect, though parallel in motion, to the inorganic, metallic "beak" of Mr. Ramsay, and the lighthouse thus becomes a fantasy lover pulled up out of Mrs. Ramsay's unsatisfied inner world. The description of this process enables Woolf to answer the question posed by Lily in section 9: "What art was there, known to love or cunning, by which one pressed through into those secret chambers?" What Lily does not know the reader has learned from the descriptions of both the exhausting epiphany of section 7 and the replenishing one of section 11.

The sexual overtones of silver fingers and strokes of light associated with the lighthouse make it loverlike but not necessarily masculine. Although the lighthouse is shaped like a phallus, its rays enter the room in circling, as well as probing, motions, corresponding to the combination of circular and surging kinesthetic imagery of section 7. Jung's concept of the animus, the source of libido resident in the feminine unconscious, and my archetype of the green-world lover do not precisely fit this archetypal symbol. The goddesslike power of combined feminine sensuality and androgynous strength that Mrs. Ramsay displays throughout the book depends upon this inanimate object as her guide or totem, perhaps even as her familiar. There is a marked split between the world of the lighthouse and that of Mrs. Ramsay's persona: the lighthouse provides her with a solitary, antisocial ectasy, "something real, something private, which she shared neither with her children nor with her husband." Thus, like numerous other Woolf characters (Rachel Vinrace, Rhoda, and Clarissa, for example), Mrs. Ramsay turns away from gender norms to an inner and gender-transcendent essence that she finds more valid than social roles, preferring tranquility in solitude to a world that impinges excessively upon her autonomy.

Because there is no range for Mrs. Ramsay to exercise this inner or androgynous elixir, for society has no place for women of her strength and gender complexity, her rebirth journey aborts. Jung warns of cases where the psyche becomes entranced in the inner world and unable to return; as feminist archetypalists, we must call attention to the unentrancing aspects of the alternative. Thus it seems that Mrs. Ramsay indeed "loses herself," dying of "a stroke" soon after the summer scene on the island. She lives on, in the subsequent sections of the book, through objects as inanimate and powerful as the lighthouse. She becomes embodied in the "ebb and flow" of objects, which, after her death, have permission to take over the abandoned house at their will, arranging themselves in time and space according to not human needs but their own inner essences as "things as they are." The process by which the house and its contents settle into a "thisness" and are rehumanized only at the last moment by the return of the family constitutes a rebirth experience paralleling Mrs. Ramsay's experience in "The Window" and Lily's in "The Lighthouse." "Time passes," a tour de force of lyric prose, executed upon a setting without human beings, provides a variation on the personless and tranquil state of mind that is Mrs. Ramsay's elixir.

Lily's role as understudy or apprentice to Mrs. Ramsay is a study in the creative solitude of the odd woman, troubled by the constant temptation of giving up her shape to the demands of sexual politics. A perusal of the images that Woolf uses to describe Lily suggests that her role of understudy is applicable even in minute particulars, and the archetypal motifs of the Demeter/Persephone narrative underlying the final section place this apprentice/master relationship in the realm of a prototypical rebirth journey. In sections 1–3 of "The Lighthouse" Lily is in the same posture vis-à-vis Mr. Ramsay as was his wife in 7 and 11 of "The Window": that is, she is trying, on the one hand, to give something to him and, on the other, to draw her solitude around her so as to protect her psyche from his ravishings. Whereas in section 7 of "The Window" his beak had plunged into Mrs. Ramsay, here Lily also has to tolerate his "bearing down on her," "greedy," "distraught," groaning, and sighing. "His immense self-pity, his demand for sympathy poured and spread itself in pools at her feet, and all she did, miserable sinner that she was, was to draw her skirts a little closer round her ankles, lest she should get wet. In complete silence she stood there, grasping her paint brush." One must admit for Mr. Ramsay an increase in fluidity at least, even if he seems, like Alice in Wonderland, to be about to drown in his own tears. Whereas Mrs. Ramsay turned to the lighthouse, Lily turns to her brush, a small but parallel vehicle for her creative endeavors:

> With a curious physical sensation, as if she were urged forward and at the same time must hold herself back, she made her first quick decisive stroke. The brush descended. . . . A second time she did it—a third time. And so pausing and so flickering, she attained a dancing rhythmical movement, as if the pauses were one part of the rhythm and the strokes together, and all were related; and so, lightly and swiftly pausing, striking, she scored her canvas with brown running nervous lines which had no sooner settled there than they enclosed (she felt it looming out at her) a space. Down in the hollow of one wave she saw the next wave towering higher and higher above her.[16]

The three rhythmic strokes, the sense of fluidity, the use of the brush in the creative act are parallel to Mrs. Ramsay's lighthouse epiphanies, and, like her mentor, Lily "lost consciousness of outer things, and her name and her personality and her appearance" while "her mind kept throwing up from its depths, scenes, and names, and sayings, and memories and ideas, like a fountain spurting over that glaring, hideously difficult white space, while she modelled it with greens and blues."

Just as Mrs. Ramsay finally achieved her moment of ecstasy in section 11, not through her husband but through the figure of the lighthouse, Lily reached her vision under the aegis of a semimythical, seminaturistic figure springing out of the unlikely presence of Mr. Carmichael:

> Then, surging up, puffing slightly, old Mr. Carmichael stood beside her, looking like an old pagan God, shaggy, with weeds in his hair and the trident (it was only a French novel) in his hand. . . . he stood there spreading his hands over all the weakness and suffering of mankind. . . . now he has crowned the occasion, she thought, when his hand slowly fell, as if she had seen him let fall from his great height a wreath of violets and asphodels which, fluttering slowly, lay at length upon the earth.[17]

She is enabled, through this vision of a Neptune or Poseidon, to add the final line to her picture; whether the line represents his trident, the lighthouse, the paintbrush, or her own *animus* is not explicit. For James, just reaching the lighthouse, the tiller has performed the same function as Lily's brush: he has achieved his creativity and, at last, embodied his father's phallic attributes.

"If one is a man," Woolf writes, "still the woman part of the brain must have effect, and a woman also must have intercourse with the man in her. Coleridge perhaps meant this when he said that a great mind is androgynous. It is when this fusion takes place that the mind is fully fertilized and uses all its faculties."[18] This is essentially what Jung was saying when he described the integrated psyche as the one that assimilates *animus* and *anima* in bringing the creative powers of Eros, or the libido, into full play.

This state of mind is not only experienced by Mrs. Ramsay but is passed on from initiate to initiate. The purpose of feminine mysteries of initiation in African tribes, writes Mircea Eliade, is for the older women to introduce the younger to the "mystery of childbearing," not merely for its fertility powers but also for a "discovery that she is a creator on the plane of life [that] constitutes a religious experience that cannot be translated into masculine terms." Eliade comprehends the sexual components of such rituals as vehicles of spiritual mysteries: "It is not the natural phenomenon of giving birth that constitutes the mystery; it is the revelation of the feminine sacredness; that is, of the mystic unity between life, woman, nature, and the divinity. This revelation is of a transpersonal order, for which reason it is expressed in symbols and actualized in rites."[19] *To the Lighthouse* is structured according to a passage of power from Mrs. Ramsay to Lily. Woolf, who was convinced that women could come to know themselves only through an incorporation of the lives of their mothers, grandmothers, and great-grandmothers, began writing the novel as a way of understanding her relationship as daughter to her parents. She blends this subconscious, personal material with the rebirth archetype by incorporating motifs derived from one of the oldest mother/daughter narratives of all, the Demeter/Kore archetype.

Brooding over her painting and over Mrs. Ramsay's import on her life in "The Lighthouse," Lily, in a trance, sees Mrs. Ramsay as Persephone, letting her

> flowers fall from her basket, scattered and tumbled them on to the grass and, reluctantly and hesitatingly, but without question or complaint—had she not the faculty of obedience to perfection?—went

too. Down fields, across valleys, white, flower-strewn—that was how she would have painted it. The hills were austere. It was rocky; it was steep. The waves sounded hoarse on the stones beneath. They went, the three of them together, Mrs. Ramsay walking rather fast in front, as if she expected to meet some one round the corner.[20]

At the subconscious level, the "three" may be Mrs. Ramsay and her two deceased children, Prue and Andrew. Archetypally, Woolf may be representing the two goddesses, mother and daughter, accompanied by Persephone's son, Triptolemos. The field corresponds to the Rharian plain at Thria that Demeter replenished after the restoration of Kore, and the basket that Mrs. Ramsay spills may refer either to Kore's basket full of flowers that she dropped when raped, to the *Cista Mystica*, the basket in which Demeter keeps the sacred symbols of masculinity and femininity used in the Eleusinian mysteries, or to both. Mr. Carmichael's apotheosis as Neptune suggests an empowering appearance of Poseidon, lover of Demeter and father of Persephone. However, though in the Demeter/Kore narrative and in the rites based upon it the mother grieves after the traumatic rape of her daughter and quests through heaven and earth to restore her, in *To the Lighthouse* the daughter figure, Lily, seeks out the mother in Mrs. Ramsay. Lily's entire role in the novel is one of inquiry into the source and nature of Mrs. Ramsay's unique elixir, corresponding to the quest of the Eleusinian initiate for an understanding and assimilation of the power of the goddess Demeter. She learns, in the course of the novel, that such a power is to be gained by a careful preservation of the self in the face of such demands as Mrs. Ramsay's, and through coming to terms with her memories she is able to assimilate the elixir and use it in her own creative endeavor.

### Seduction of the Minotaur and the Hieroglyphic Elixir

Anaïs Nin's *Seduction of the Minotaur* is the last novel in the five-volume *Cities of the Interior* (1961), a multivolumed work that differs from *Pilgrimage* and *The Children of Violence* in being less sequential than cyclical, dealing with the development of one hero but with the interaction of three—Lillian, Sabina, and Djuana. The first and last volumes, nonetheless, are concerned chiefly with Lillian's quest for selfhood, the final volume structured as a rebirth journey toward both the land of "Golconda" and her unconscious. Lillian's descent into the underworld parallels Mrs. Ramsay's in some ways, but the denouements form an interesting contrast: whereas Mrs. Ramsay's power is explicit and is absorbed as such by Lily, Lillian does not achieve a full understanding of what she has experienced because the quest's goal remains undecipherable.

Lillian's quest follows the pattern of a turning away from her lover, Jay, after she had left her husband, Larry, in America. She crosses the threshold of consciousness during her ocean voyage to the fictional Golconda, which has elements of the Mexico where she spent her childhood. Jung based his description of the transformation of the personality in part upon the "night sea journey" described by Frobenius as analogous to the apparent undersea journey of the sun from dusk to dawn. In this version of the rebirth archetype the hero is swallowed up by an undersea monster but by wile and luck emerges cast up into a new land. Although at first Lillian refers to the boat that takes her to Golconda as a "solar barque," she soon realizes that she cannot proceed through mythological (unconscious) adventures until she comes to terms with personal material. She must confront her memories of her mother and father, come to terms with the difference between her authentic personality and the person they thought her to be. "Already," she muses, "she regretted having come. This was not a journey in her solar barque. It was a night journey into the past, and the thread that had pulled her was one of accidental resemblances, familiarity, the past. She had been unable to live for three months a new life, in a new city, without being caught by an umbilical cord and brought back to the figure of her father."[21]

The reference to the "thread" pulling the hero down into her unconscious may be a leitmotif drawn from the Theseus legend, in which Ariadne provided the hero with a ball of string to guide him through the labyrinth of the minotaur. Lillian's experience remains personal at this level, however, and subconscious rather than unconscious: "Lillian had never seen herself with her own eyes. Children do not possess eyes of their own. You retained as upon a delicate retina, your mother's image of you, as the first and the only authentic one, her judgement of your acts."[22] In order to grow Lillian needs to develop a sense of her self as her primary source of being, in spite of, or in contrast to, the way husband/lover/mother/father have previously assessed her personality. Though she recognizes both her "masculinity" and her "femininity," Lillian conforms to gender expectations in her love affair, marriage, and family life. As a womanly woman endowed with qualities normatively considered "unwomanly," she has been unable to integrate her faculties fully.

In *Ladders to Fire* (1946), the first volume in the sequence, Nin describes Lillian's adolescence, when she thought of herself as a Joan of

Arc who "rushes forward" to ask boys to dance rather than wait passively to be asked, and later she falls in love with passive men who don't know how to handle her "aggression" except to identify her as a "mother." For "a man it is natural to be the aggressor and he takes defeat well," remarks Nin. "For a woman it is a transgression, and she assumes the defeat is caused by the aggression. How long will woman be ashamed of her strength?" Although Nin tends to discuss the "aggressive" side of Lillian as "manly" and her self-doubt as "femininity," she sees her as one unity, a woman: "She had two voices, one which fell deep like the voice of a man, and another light and innocent. Two women disputing inside of her."[23]

Lillian carries her green world about with her in the form of an "inner chamber," containing

> the mother madonna holding the child and nourishing it. The haunting mother image forever holding a small child.
> Then there was the child itself, the child inhabiting a world of peaceful, laughing animals, rich trees, in valleys of festive color. The child in her eyes appeared with its eyes closed. It was dreaming the fertile valleys, the small warm house, the Byzantine flowers, the tender animals and the abundance. It was dreaming and afraid to awaken. It was dreaming the lightness of the sky, the warmth of the earth, the fecundity of the colors.
> It was afraid to awaken.[24]

As in the Demeter/Kore materials, in which the mother and daughter goddesses mingle identities, Lillian, in this passage, is at one and the same time madonna and child. In the subconscious realm, she has left her own children behind with her husband, Larry; in the realm of the unconscious, she has been unable to realize either her internal mother or her internal child. She has been unable to assimilate her experiences as mother because her family has enclosed her to the point that she is alienated from her own being. There has been a split between her true self and the expected gender roles of wife and mother. "Who had made the marriage?" she asks herself in retrospect.

> Who had desired the children? She could not remember the first impetus, the first choice, the first desire for these, nor how they came to be. It was as if it had happened in her sleep. Lillian, guided by her background, her mother, her sisters, her habits, her home as a child, her blindness in regard to her own desires, had made all of this and then lived in it, but it had not been made out of the deeper elements of her nature, and she was a stranger in it.[25]

Eventually, the house/children/husband became stifling and cut her off from the green world itself. Another character complains that her husband's presence

> killed the life in me so completely that I could hardly feel the birth of my children. I became afraid of nature, of being swallowed by the mountains, stifled by the forest, absorbed by the sea. I rebelled so violently against my married life that in one day I destroyed everything and ran away, abandoning my children, my home and my native country. But I never attained the life I had struggled to reach. My escape brought me no liberation. Every night I dream the same dream of prisons and struggles to escape. It is as if only my body escaped, and not my feelings.[26]

In her love affair with Jay, Lillian is turned into the mother of a petulant child. Husband or Parisian artist, six of one or half a dozen of the other, she must escape both of them and begin to birth, to recreate, herself.

The world to which she turns in *Seduction of the Minotaur* is the green, tropical land of Golconda, where she tries to reverse her alienation from nature by incorporating it into herself ("Once or twice, her mouth full of fruit, she stopped. She had the feeling she was eating the dawn"); to overcome her fear of being absorbed by the sea she immerses herself willfully in the waters several times a day. During this reimmersion into the plant-and-animal world the memories of her mother and father appear. She takes as *animus* figure and guide Dr. Hernandez, a strangely melancholy man of whom she finally decides to ask the compassionate question "What ails you?" Her decision comes too late, however, and he dies before she can ask the question. Hers is thus a failure shared with Parzival in his first visit to the grail castle: like Parzival and the Fisher King, she has been curious about what ails Dr. Hernandez but has not voiced her compassionate question aloud. Having failed him, she has failed herself: "If only they had gone down together, down the caverns of the soul with picks, lanterns, cords, oxygen, x-ray, food, following the blueprints of all the message of the geological depths where lay hidden the imprisoned self."

Because of her lack of compassionate curiosity and also, perhaps, because she still wants to be guided by a fatherly, male doctor into her own unconscious (Nin's own analysis with the Jungian Allende was problematic in this regard), Lillian fails in a quest for the life she "had struggled to reach," the life of the deepest selfhood where it merges with the unconscious of the race:

> She was now like those French speleologists who had descended thousands of feet into the earth and found ancient caves covered

with paintings and carvings. But Lillian carried no searchlight and no nourishment. Nothing but the wafer granted to those who believe in symbolism, a wafer in place of bread. And all she had to follow were the inscriptions of her dreams, half-effaced hieroglyphs on half-broken statues. And no guide in the darkness but a scream through the eyes of a statue.[27]

The "bread" that Lillian seeks is sacramental, an inner sign of universal power, perhaps corresponding to the sacred food eaten in the Eleusinian ceremonies, the mass, and the grail narratives. As a "wafer" in place of bread it is one level removed from true substance, a symbolic and ritual vehicle unclear in its referent. Like the hieroglyphs in her caves and the inscriptions in her dreams, the purport of the elixir is "half-faced," inscrutable. Lillian's failure perhaps results from projecting her *animus* onto Dr. Hernandez rather than seeking it within herself. Without having achieved androgyny or having resolved her own inner puzzlement she returns to her husband.

On her flight back to America Lillian sees "the minotaur" as her reflection in the airplane window. "It was not a monster, It was a reflection upon a Mirror, a masked woman, Lillian herself, the hidden masked part of herself unknown to her, who had ruled her acts." In pre-Hellenic Cretan religion the minotaur was the animal-lover of the queens, the "bull of Minos" corresponding to the horned god of the witches. He thus represents both *animus* and green-world lover to the queen, who participates in a *Hieros gamos*, or lovemaking ritual, with him in order to reestablish her erotic, political, and religious hegemony. Queen and minotaur, like lady and unicorn, are powerful figures of feminine autonomy and power. For Lillian, however, the minotaur remains a "mask" covering her true self, an archetypal symbol that she cannot assimilate. At the denouement her persona remains alienated from its own unconscious materials, the symbols containing her power and identity remain encoded, and her rebirth journey remains uncompleted.

### Margaret Atwood and the Elixir of Maternity

Whereas the outcome of Lillian's quest is problematical, that of Atwood's hero's quest in *Surfacing* (1972) is as definite and precise as Mrs. Ramsay's. Among other things in this novel, the author deals with what Carol Christ identifies as a quest in which "spiritual insight surfaces through attention to the body," leading to the hero's "achievement of authentic selfhood and power [which] depends on understanding one's grounding in nature and natural energies."[28] As in so many cases in women's fiction, *Surfacing* describes an immanent naturism achieved by a hero who turns away from society and towards the universe as a whole, reconciling the spiritual to the physical through the vehicle of a green-world Eros. As in Woolf and Nin, moreover, the quest penetrates a world of unconscious materials that is at one and the same time a wholly new space and, in terms of motifs from ancient mythoreligious materials, a wholly old one.

"The lake was the entrance for me," remarks Atwood's narrator about the Canadian lake where she journeys away from the city to search for her father, who has disappeared from the island where the family had spent summers during her childhood. This island in a lake constitutes both the green world of childhood remembered and a locus of transformation, or rebirth. Central to the hero's quest is her coming to terms with her missing father and with the memory of her deceased mother. She brings her own animus/shadow, or patriarchal enclosure, with her in the form of David and Anna, a couple deeply involved in a "hideous-institution" variety of marriage, and she also brings Joe, her green-world lover. She tries to understand her recent, shattering affair with a married man who had compelled her to have an abortion. Imagery of knives, plastic blood containers, and city mechanisms, as in *To the Lighthouse*, are contrasted to organic, or natural, imagery. Even the natural processes of sex and birth have been transformed by "civilization," Anna's orgasmic screams sounded to the hero in the next room "like an animal's at the moment the trap closes."

Besides the lake itself, the narrator finds a guide for her quest in her father's scribbled notes, which at first seem to be executed in madness but which she learns are sketches of ancient Indian cave drawings and hieroglyphics. Whether he is dead, mad, or returned from the dead are all one to the hero, who seeks the power latent within these symbols insofar as it has drawn him into a world that she also desires. Having found the site of the drawings and having dived down to them from her canoe, she comes upon a "dark oval, trailing limbs. It was blurred but it had eyes, they were open, it was something I knew about, a dead thing, it was dead." In actuality her drowned father, the figure represents the memory of her aborted fetus and of the frogs and snakes that her brother had killed in closed jars, "evil grails." In trying to translate the hieroglyphs that had preoccupied her father and led to his death and in diving down to their site and finding his dead body, she absorbs into her own experience the transformation that he has achieved. This consists of his turning from the world of logic to that of mysticism: "He had discovered new places, new oracles, they were things he was seeing the way I had seen, true vision; at the end, after the failure of logic. When it happened the first time he must have been terrified, it would be like stepping through a usual door and finding yourself in a different galaxy, purple trees and red moons and a green sun."[29] The "new places" found by her father are repositories of power that find expression in the new/old language of "hieroglyphs," the power of an ancient people who respected natural energies and, the hero suspects, would be profoundly hostile to modern technology.

"It would be right for my mother to have left something for me also, a legacy," remarks the hero. "His was complicated, tangled, but hers would be simple as a hand, it would be final." She finds some scrapbooks that her mother has saved and in them her own childhood drawings, which she takes as her mother's legacy. One is of "a woman with a round moon stomach: the baby was sitting up inside her and gazing out. Opposite her was a man with horns on his head and a barbed tail." At first glance these figures seem stereotypically masculine and feminine, the horns of the male suggesting "the gods of the head, antlers rooted in the brain," and the womb of the feminine figure representing pregnancy and fertility. The dual symbol, however, suggests the myth of the Cretan queen married to the minotaur, a green-world lover analogous to the hero's lover Joe, whom she associates with furry things and with a buffalo. This horned lover, or the devil in Christian symbology, plays an important role in Tammuz/Adonis and witchcraft materials, which I consider in the concluding chapter. The father figure, moreover, had balanced out his "logic" with mystery, and the hero's mother, as the hero remembers her, had been a strong woman who had chased away bears, saved her brother from drowning, and tamed the wild birds.

The parental figures thus transcend the personal and familial and become universal, or archetypal. The hero, having absorbed her personal history, transforms it into a phase of her rebirth journey. She deplores the split in herself between head and body, mind and nature, and wants to rejoin or integrate them as parts of her selfhood. Her transformation consists, then, in her internalization of faculties that she has projected upon others rather than brought to life within herself. Thus her decision to get pregnant by Joe, which at first glance seems to be one that will precipitate her as passive woman back into the enclosure, is a self-actualizing choice. She initiates herself into the mysteries of femininity through her mother and into those of the power of nature through both her mother and her father and induces Joe to impregnate her as part of a process of creative solitude:

> He trembles and I can feel my lost child surfacing within me, forgiving me, rising from the lake where it has been prisoned for so long, its eyes and teeth phosphorescent; the two halves clasp, interlocking like fingers, it buds, it sends out fronds. This time I will do

it by myself, squatting, on old newspapers in a corner alone; or on leaves, dry leaves, a heap of them, that's cleaner. The baby will slip out easily as an egg, a kitten, and I'll lick it off and bite the cord, the blood returning to the ground where it belongs; the moon will be full, pulling. In the morning I will be able to see it: it will be covered with shining fur, a god, I will never teach it any words.[30]

The lost child only partially represents the aborted fetus: it also represents the hero's lost childhood and her lost inner self.

The reunion of selfhood and the natural world places her, like in Mrs. Ramsay's trance, in an alinguistic or prespeech world. Earlier in the novel she experienced the pine woods as "sight flowing ahead of me over the ground, eyes filtering the shapes, the names of things fading but their forms and uses remaining, the animals learned what to eat without nouns. Six leaves, three leaves, the root of this is crisp." "First I had to immerse myself in the other language," she remarks; this process consists of her conceiving a child by Joe and then of withdrawing from human beings and submerging herself in the wilderness:

> My back is on the sand, my head rests against the rock, innocent as plankton; my hair spreads out, moving and fluid in the water. The earth rotates, holding my body down to it as it holds the moon; the sun pounds in the sky, red flames and rays pulsing from it, searing away the wrong form that encases me, dry rain soaking through me, warming the blood egg I carry. I dip beneath the water, washing my eyes.[31]

In Atwood's narration, as in Harding's definition of "Virgin," we can perceive a woman who is fully "feminine" but in a forceful and autonomous way, a giver of birth independent of partiarchal institutions. By making herself "crazy," Atwood's hero assumes, in Daly's terms, "the role of witch and madwoman . . . tantamount to a declaration of identity beyond the good and evil of patriarchy's world, and beyond sanity and insanity."[32] "She hates men," David remarks to Joe and Anna. "Either that or she wants to be one. Right?" None of the three can recognize that the hero has achieved an androgynous synthesis beyond male and female but perceive her, rather, as a deviant: she senses that they are forming a "ring of eyes, a tribunal; in a minute they would join hands and dance around me, and after that the rope and the pyre, cure for heresy." Her breakthrough as independent mother makes her achievement more far-reaching than Mrs. Ramsay's and Lillian's, whose maternity has been part of their alienation rather than a power for transformation. In affirming the power of birth as one among other attributes of a self reborn through the assimilation of green-world potency, Atwood creates a hero in a tradition shockingly new precisely because it is radically old.

### The Four-Gated City and the Collective Vision

The fifth volume of *Children of Violence*, as I have indicated, constitutes a marked shift from a social quest dealing with Martha's political and socioeconomic life in Africa to a spiritual quest, or rebirth journey, leading to her transformaton into a superordinate personality. This quest follows the broad outlines with which we are familiar: her crossing of the threshold consists first of her journey to England and then of her crossing from one side of the Thames to the other, where she will live out most of her life. Her "guide," or "watcher," is a "lit space" that comes to her as a trancelike state of mind not unlike Mrs. Ramsay's lighthouse epiphany and that is a "high stretch of herself," timeless in that it combines new visions and recurrent epiphanies remembered from her African childhood:

> No use to say: remember the lit space and its marvellous brother, the turn of the spiral above it when one had gone through the band of noise. Because, having left them behind, having sunk away, one was in a place with its own memories, its own knowledge. You could, perhaps, during the long day of work, responsibility, people, noise, have a flash of reminder: *These places exist*, but that was because the day had lifted you towards them, like a wave, for just a brief moment. . . . Because for some reason the walls of the place you were in now had become thinned, and light came in from the other.[33]

Martha's development depends upon a dialectic between the "band of noise" filled with everyday distractions and the state of mind in which she dwells in this inner world. Like all the rest of Lessing's fiction *The Four-Gated City* ( 1969 ) is encyclopedically social, filled with details of life in the sixties and seventies, through which Martha moves in a series of self-initiatory stages. First, she experiences Eros in her love affairs with Jack and Mark, which recall in their intensity her earlier affair with Thomas. She does not, when making love to Jack, "think of her two husbands, Knowell and Hesse," but of this lover with whom the green world and the world of Eros had been most deeply interfused. During sex with Jack, Martha is lifted up into a world of vision, Eros becoming a vehicle for epiphanic transcendence. Her vision, like that of the golden city in the first volume of *Children of Violence*, is of a specific locus, an archetypal city of equity and beneficence where she "saw in front of her eyelids a picture of a man and a woman, walking in a high place under a blue sky holding children by the hand, and with them all kinds of wild animals, but they were not wild at all: a lion, a leopard, a tiger, deer, lambs, all as tame as housepets, walking with the man and the woman and the lovely children, and she wanted to cry out with loss."[34] She comprehends Eros, in that it leads to such vision, as a fountainhead of spiritual, as well as physical, energy, that although "people regarded sex as the drainer, the emptier," it is in truth, "the maker of energy." Immediately after the beneficent vision, as always in Lessing, the converse of the archetypal city appears in the form of a place where all the faces are "tortured and hurt," and Martha herself appears as but "a middle-aged woman, thickened and slowed."

Eros, or the central drive of the self called up from the depths of the unconscious, thus creates both a world of love and a world of hate, archetypal cities that Frye would term apocalyptic and demonic. The dual visions that Martha experiences with Jack are recapitulated in *City in the Desert*, a novel that she helps Mark to write and that turns out to be similar to Thomas's scribbled notes left when he went mad and died in Africa. Mark projects in his novel an ideal city formed around "a kind of centre" with roads approaching it from the four quarters, a city in which people pursue their responsibilities from inner and organic, rather than forced and external, dictates. It is a "gardened city" in which "even the trees and plants were known for their properties and qualities and grown exactly, in relation to other plants, and to people and buildings." In this way it resembles the planet Annarres in Ursula Le Guin's *The Dispossessed*, in which the anarchic principle of government according to the naturally communal desires of the citizens is contrasted to the technological dictatorship of the planet Urras.

Mark's ideal, mandalic city revolves around a center where "hidden People" dwell whose personal harmony, or self-collection, provides its sustenance. Around it, at Martha's suggestion, Mark depicts a "shadowy city" of poverty and envy filled with people who want to seize the secret of the inner city. The fulcrum of the novel within a novel is the trauma of invasion and destruction, the loss of a beneficent green world to one of violence and greed. The novel thus recapitulates the plot structure of *The Four-Gated City*, in which the dark, satanic mills of technology destroy England's green and pleasant land.

Meanwhile, during the twenty years that she forms the center of the Radlett Street household, Martha absorbs all of the feminine roles that she thought she had left behind in Africa along with her two marriages and her daughter. She also confronts her dying mother and eventually

experiences a substitute reconciliation with her daughter by befriend-
ing her contemporary Rita and by stepping to one side when Rita
woos and marries Mark. Like Atwood's hero she makes herself a locus
of power through assimilating maternal roles, not only as mother and
counsellor to the young but also as lover to Mark and deep friend to
his "mad" wife Lynda, in whose insanity she fully participates. "Martha and Lynda are guide and teacher to each other," remarks Christ.
"It is as though two separated parts of woman's experience, mother
and witch or madwoman, are joined. From the integration of the separated [*sic*] comes a new power."[35]

Martha can complete her inner journey only by moving away for
three months to an apartment by herself, where she carves out a place
for a terrifying if creative solitude. Her guide to this inner world is a
figure she calls "the Devil," whose teachings are the contrary, or negative "shadow," of the "lit space." The principal occupant of Martha's
unconscious is a figure she calls her "self-hater," who keeps her in
anguished loathing of herself and her life. Her "perfect solitude" thus
leads not to an epiphanic and beneficent vision but to her own shadow
side, to her life "turned inside out, so that she looked at it in reverse."
She realizes that Lynda is arrested in this place of self-hate, living
always in the mad jabbering and chattering of the punitive "band of
noise." Martha recognizes the existence of this self-hater within her
own consciousness and confronts it but does not overcome it. Considering Lessing's impatience with feminism and her insistence that relationships between men and women are only one in a long series of
divisive social forces, I would suggest that Martha's failure to overcome her own "self-hater" may have something to do with Lessing's
devaluation of sexual politics as a radical cause of contemporary spiritual malaise. One recalls the hideous, androgynous dwarfs dancing
their litany of self-loathing in *The Golden Notebook* as further em-
blems of Lessing's distaste for solving spiritual problems through
transcending gender norms. Recently she has probed more deeply into
the relationship between sexual politics and the health of civilizations,
in *The Marriage between Zones Three, Four and Five* (1980) in her
*Canopus in Argos: Archives* series, but in the final volume of *Children
of Violence*, relationships between men and women are subsumed in
the general crises preceding a worldwide holocaust.

Martha holds firm against the "band of noise" within her head by
accepting her own responsibility for evils she had blamed on society
and by maintaining conscious control over herself as she moves through
the surreal spaces that she terms "Bosch country," "Dali landscape."

She is able to use her wits to "chart the country of the soul," and "the Devil" conducts her through the "stations of the cross"; on this enigmatic experience Lessing does not elaborate.

Martha's assuming responsibility for the good and evil of her world enables her to complete her quest. "Whatever she initially experiences as alien to herself," remarks Christ, "is gradually understood to be as much internal as external, and conversely as much external as internal. For Martha there is no radical duality between self and world."[36] She perceives the relationship between the individual and the collective much as did Blake, who saw the "human form divine" and England as interchangeable. Like Blake, who described the progression necessary for human life as based on "contraries," antithetical forces held in balance by the power of Los, or the creative imagination, Lessing shows Martha learning to forge a new life from the contraries of "love, hate, black, white, good, bad, man, woman." Although the precise nature of Martha's power, of her ability to keep her mind together in the "band of noise" and territory of madness, is not explicit, her successful rebirth journey enables her to "listen" to the voices heralding the holocaust of 1977 and give directions on how to survive it. Martha has become a citizen of the "hidden city," her "secret," or elixir, enabling her to rescue enough people to begin a new collective on an island off the Scottish coast.

The reconciliation, or synthesis, of the "masculine" and the "feminine" into an androgynous personality explicit in Woolf, Nin, and Atwood is simply assumed by Lessing, who makes Martha and Mark nonrigid in their sex roles and implicitly androgynous in their expectations of each other. The pairs of opposites that Martha must transcend include "male" and "female" among other contraries, divisive social forces that must be transformed. Lessing pairs Martha and Mark's garden city, or utopia, similarly, with the dystopic shadow city, both constituting collective archetypes that are more generally human than specifically feminine. Most significant about Martha's rebirth journey, it seems to me, is its profoundly political outcome: unlike those of the other heroes of this archetypal narrative, Martha's elixir has specific external, or social, effects, and, through her transformation, she becomes a builder of a new society upon the ashes of society as known.

The reconciliation of the psychological and the political as illustrated in Martha's experience may help to counter objections that a number of feminist scholars have made not only to fiction structured upon the rebirth journey, or "spiritual quest," but also to the world of archetypes that informs women's fiction. Such criticisms revolve around the asocial nature of these journeys, which so frequently take the form of a hero's turning her back upon society and seeking powers that seem wholly inward or individualistic. This quality makes Miriam's epiphanies seem a "featureless freedom" to Kaplan and leads Showalter to remark of Schreiner, Egerton, and Grand that "given the freedom to explore their experience, they rejected it, or at least tried to deny it. The private rooms that symbolize their professionalism and autonomy are fantastic sanctuaries, closely linked to their own defensive womanhood." "For Mrs. Ramsay," Showalter remarks, "death is a mode of self-assertion. Refined to its essences, abstracted from its physicality and anger, denied any action, Woolf's vision of womanhood is as deadly as it is disembodied. The ultimate room of one's own is the grave."[37]

I would argue that the sanctuaries and rooms into which women withdraw from society are indeed "fantastic," but in a positive sense. As fantasies they are projections of an ideal world desired by author, hero, and reader, realistically depicted in their dialectical relationship to society as known. To journey down into such a world, paradoxically, is to go outward as one goes inward, or, as Jean Pickering describes the process of *The Four-Gated City*, "Martha opens new rooms in herself only by first going through a region of conflict. . . . And the outer life is parallel to the inner life: in the last analysis, Martha's experience seems to tell us, they are the same thing, for the further one goes into one's own rooms, the more one discovers that they are inhabited by all humanity." Carol Christ offers a resolution of the apparent dichotomy between "spiritual" and "social" quests in her recognition that "the novels of female quest may be seen . . . as fundamental stories which may have the power to create new ways of being for women in new worlds," and another feminist theologian, Judith Plaskow, feels that such formerly stereotypical figures as the "earth mother" may be transformed by such fiction into vehicles of feminine power.[38]

Writers like Woolf, Nin, Atwood, and Lessing have often been described as being excessively inward, personalistic to the point of urging retreat upon women rather than engagement with social forces. Although the narratives I have studied in this chapter indeed portray a radical disjunction between the hero's immediate society and the universal visiion to which she aspires, I see that disjunction as a reflection of the fact that she has not been recognized as having a meaningful role in society since before the advent of the patriarchy. Her pulling back and away from partriarchal experience in this sense constitutes a healthy action, a *reculant pour mieux sauter*, or a gathering up of her powers to enable her to leap forward more effectively, a process like that which Daly defines as the "qualitative leap" beyond the "male maya" empowered by "the light of those flames of spiritual imagination and cerebral fantasy [that] can be a new dawn."[39]

Women's fiction originates from and guides us toward a world of archetypes, a repository of symbolic and narrative patterns, that reflects women's desire for a fully feminine and yet fully human authenticity. In the concluding chapter I will review the manner in which the structures of women's novels adapt to such archetypal patterns and briefly restate my own hypotheses about the relationship between women's fiction and patriarchal culture.

# CHAPTER IX

# ARCHETYPAL PATTERNS
# IN WOMEN'S FICTION

"THE GREAT THEME OF THE EUROPEAN NOVEL," WRITES WALTER ALLEN, "and perhaps especially of the English novel, has been man's life in society; more precisely, the education of men and women, in the sense of their learning to distinguish, through their inescapable involvement in society, the true from the false both in themselves and in the world about them; and this applies no less to the fiction of a rebel like D. H. Lawrence, whose work is as much about society as about sex, than to that of Jane Austen."[1] We have seen that both in rebellion and accommodation women's fiction shares the inextricable social involvement that Allen finds characteristic of the genre as a whole; truth of self for the woman hero, however, involves a particularly acute and in many ways unique rebellion against social norms, her authenticity continually challenged by prescribed gender roles. Thus, although one can bring to mind parallel rebellions on the part of many alienated male heroes, women's shared experience *as women* endows their fiction with a degree of continuity, abundance of analogue, and uniformity of concern sufficient to elucidate a single work by reference to the field of the woman's novel as a whole. Not only does this tradition span nearly three centuries in Britain and America; its narrative and symbolic structures reflect an even more ancient, unresolved tension between feminine power and feminine powerlessness in the history of human culture. We have surveyed the relationship between aspects of women's fiction and various descriptions of the role of women in primitive and prehistoric societies. With the field as a whole in mind, it is also possible to see a relationship between the rise of women's fiction in the last several centuries and three interrelated repositories of archetypal materials: the Demeter/Kore and Ishtar/Tammuz rebirth narratives, the grail legends of the later Middle Ages, and the cluster of archetypal and ritual materials constituting the Craft of the Wise, or witchcraft. After summarizing the structural continuities in women's novels I have surveyed, I will suggest their relationship to these ancient archetypal complexes.

Allen's definition of the novel presupposes an orderly sequence by which men and women are led into the socially accepted truths and falsehoods in a progression from childhood immaturity to adulthood. My organization of materials suggests such a sequential pattern in that I have dealt with categories of novels arranged according to the aspect of human development that they depict: initiation into adulthood in the bildungsroman, entry into marriage and social involvement in novels of the enclosure, and the quest for sexuality in novels of Eros and for personal transformation, usually in middle and old age, in the novels of rebirth. At each phase, however, the orderly pattern of development is disrupted by social norms dictating powerlessness for women: young girls grow down rather than up, the socially festive denouements appropriate to courtship and marriage fiction are often subverted by madness and death, Eros and celibacy alike are punished with tragic denouements, and when a rebirth journey is attempted, the reward of personal power makes the conquering hero a cultural deviant.

Of all women's novels except those dealing with older single women and with rebirth, the novel of development seems most informed by desires alien to the patriarchy. The young girl, who derives a sense of power from the green world or from her green-world lover, is drawn into the enclosure, her mood shifting from happiness to terror as she submits to marriage and atrophy. Only in the fantasy cultures of science fiction does she retain freedom to control her own body and to fulfill an adult social function.

By satirizing "masculinity" and "femininity," women authors subvert the usual intent of novels of courtship and of marriage; through treating gender roles in the institution of marriage as abnormal, they indicate apatriarchal alternatives. Novels of social protest and of marriage display far more resemblances in structure and tone to each other than one might expect as a result of their conformity to gender norms. Even in novels dealing with the Black and proletarian experience social critiques do not lead to new societies, and although rebellions are clearly articulated, society controls the heroes in the end. It is as if the branch of women's fiction that deals most specifically with society were incapable of either fully rejecting it or fully accommodating to it, the result being the disjunctions of narrative structure, ambivalences of tone, and inconclusive characterizations typical of this category. The novels of Eros, in contrast, involve characters who commit the crime of feminine sexuality, becoming outcast or deviant as a punishment. Novels of successful heterosexual, lesbian, and solitary Eros, along with the small category of equal-marriage novels, transcend "masculinity" and "femininity" in projecting the possibility of a relationship between fully authentic human beings.

In women's fiction the expected sequence of life phases is disrupted at every step by the tension inherent in women's experience. My material depicts a circle rather than an evolution, the older and transformed women heroes having far more in common with the uninitiated young women than with the characters most integrated with the social enclosure. The greater the personal development of a hero, the more true she is to herself and the more eccentric her relationship to the patriarchy. A quality of consciousness that is essentially antisocial characterizes the most admirable heroes. Other critics besides myself have noted this alinear, cyclical, timeless consciousness: Sydney Kaplan, for example, in her book on Richardson, Sinclair, Woolf, Lehmann, and Lessing, notes a simultaneity in chronology in which a character's consciousness is suspended in several time periods at once, a tendency towards spatial relativity, and a patterning of objects and images according to arrangements that seem "illogical" to the normative perspective.[2] Women heroes turn away from a culture hostile to their development, entering a timeless achronological world appropriate to their rejection by history, a spaceless world appropriate to rebellion against placelessness in the patriarchy. Even Freud, asserts Juliet Mitchell, thought that "the power of women ('the matriarchy') is pre-civilization, pre-Oedipal."[3] "The tool for representing, for objectifying one's experience in order to deal with it, culture," agrees Firestone, "is so saturated with male bias that women almost never have a chance to see themselves culturally through their own eyes. So that finally, signals from their direct experience that conflict with prevailing (male) culture are denied and repressed."[4] The marginality of the woman hero derives from her attempts at adherence to antisocial signals, and the uniqueness of women's fiction derives from feminine eccentricity, which has characterized human culture since long before the first woman author sat down to write.

The archetypal patterns that we have seen in women's fiction constitute signals from a buried feminine tradition that conflict with cultural norms and influence narrative structures. One of the difficulties that women writers experience is the fact that woman's ego, or persona, her social being, exists from day to day in a world not only deaf to such buried messages but filled with contrary materials. An author's normative values derive from the subconscious realm, where memories and dreams of day-to-day life are engendered; when she wants to describe her unconscious world, she cannot adapt material from culture but must delve into a region whose patterns are less likely to conform to socially available myths, religions, and rituals than to seem puzzling, encoded, and hieroglyphic. Rarely brought to consciousness in any socially acceptable form, these materials are, to use Laura Willowes's term, "dynamite in one's boots," full of potential for celebration and growth but also, because they are so strongly repressed, for explosion.

My first inkling that women's fiction contained links to archetypal systems from the ancient past was based on apparently random coincidences between isolated textual and mythological motifs. I wondered why Harding's definitions of virginity, mature Eros, and androgyny should correspond so closely to desirable qualities described in novels of Eros and rebirth; why, when Woolf dealt with the unconscious, she used so many leitmotifs from grail legends; and why so many images, motifs, and symbols analogous to witchcraft appeared in stories and novels by women. It gradually became clear that women's fiction could be read as a mutually illuminative or interrelated field of texts reflecting a preliterary repository of feminine archetypes, including three particularly important archetypal systems—the Demeter/Kore and Ishtar/Tammuz rebirth myths, Arthurian grail narratives, and the Craft of the Wise, or witchcraft.

The principal archetypes that recur in women's fiction—the green-world epiphany, the green-world lover, the rape trauma, enclosure, and rebirth—find counterparts in these three complexes of ritual and narrative, which Carl Jung, Emma Jung, Jean Markale, Jane Ellen Harrison, Margaret Alice Murray, and Joseph Campbell all perceive as archetypal repositories of uniquely feminine and androgynous import. The Demeter/Kore narrative, as we saw in the previous chapter, is of particular importance to women, uniting the feminine generations. The psychological effect of participating in the Eleusinian mysteries, suggests Carl Jung, is to "extend the feminine consciousness. . . . An experience of this kind gives the individual a place and meaning in the life of the generations, so that all unnecessary obstacles are cleared out of the way of the life-stream that is to flow through her. At the same time the individual is rescued from her isolation and restored to wholeness. All ritual preoccupation with archetypes ultimately has this aim and this result."[5] Jung's understanding of the personal enhancement resulting from formalized reenactment of such archetypes suggests a parallel theory of the effect of women's fiction upon an audience, a subject that I shall briefly touch upon in concluding this study. His recognition that the Demeter/Kore narratives have particular appeal to women also extends to a suggestion that they derive from feminine materials alien to the patriarchy: "In fact, the psychology of the Demeter cult has all the features of a matriarchal order of society, where the man is an indispensable but on the whole disturbing factor."[6] The disturbing element in this archetype, as in women's fiction informed by the rape-trauma pattern, is Pluto's abduction and rape of Persephone; Demeter overcomes this disturbance, however, in rescuing her daughter.

The archetypes of the green world and the green-world lover so characteristic of women's fiction may derive from two sets of ancient rituals celebrating the death and rebirth of the seasonal year. Both the Demeter/Persephone and the Ishtar/Tammuz narratives (also the Aphrodite/Adonis and Isis/Osiris stories) underlie ancient feminine rituals celebrated in preclassical and classical times. Both sets of narratives have uniquely feminine overtones, and the rites that derive from them have had a perennial appeal to women. Jane Ellen Harrison remarks that the Demeter/Kore (Persephone) celebrations at the end of September were "almost uncontaminated by Olympian [patriarchal] usage," deriving from pre-Hellenic practices in Thrace and Crete.[7] Carl Jung concurs that "in the formation of the Demeter/Kore myth the feminine influence so far outweighed the masculine that the latter had practically no significance. The man's role in the Demeter myth is really only that of seducer or conqueror."[8] With other scholars allocating the origin of rape narratives to the conquering of pre-Hellenic villages by the invading Aryan and Semitic tribes,[9] it seems clear that such rituals deal with a widespread usurpation of feminine power. The story of the abduction of Persephone by Pluto, of her mother's grief (Demeter herself was tricked and raped twice, once by Poseidon and another time by Zeus), Demeter's devastation of vegetation, her quest for her daughter, and the triumphant rebirth of both Persephone and the green world make up the Eleusinian rites.[10] (These rites are part of secret oral traditions, and thus our understanding of them is pieced together from a medley of contemporary and historical accounts.)

The ritual of following the road that Demeter took in her grief and her triumph creates a transformation or rebirth of the personality in the participant; although male initiates existed, the transformational power derived from the relationship of women to each other. In the four rebirth texts that I considered in the previous chapter the reuniting of daughter with mother plays a similar role in the transformation of the hero's personality: Lily discovers and absorbs the power of Mrs.

Ramsay, Lillian attempts to reconcile her inner "Madonna" and child, Atwood's hero is able to assimilate the green-world figure of her dead mother into her own powers of maternity and rebirth, and Martha Quest becomes a beneficent and life-saving woman after her mother's final visit and death. In other novels the quest of the mother for the daughter leads to the rebirth of the mother: the plot of Kay Boyle's *The Underground Woman* (1973), for example, is based on the loss, locating, and letting go of a daughter, an experience that brings the hero to herself at the denouement; Lessing's *Memoirs of a Survivor* (1975) uses a similar pattern, that of an older woman coming to terms with a girl who is left in her care and who is taken away in a kind of interplanetary apotheosis; and E. M. Broner's *Her Mothers* (1975) is structured on the hero's quest back into her own daughterhood and forward through Europe, Israel, and California in search of her missing daughter.

The mothers and daughters in women's fiction seem also to be enacting the various aspects of the triple goddess, who was virgin, maternal figure, and old woman at one and the same time. The third figure in the triad, who has often been gynophobically perceived as "devouring mother" or "crone," represents the wise older mother's knowledge of the best moment to fledge or let go of her children, a moment that, if precipitous or delayed, can lead the maternal element to become destructive. She also controls death and rebirth. The fully matured feminine personality comprehends all three elements and can bring any one of them into play at any time. A novel that is structured according to the Demeter/Kore archetype, like the Eleusinian mysteries, comprises a story of the rejuvenation of the mother in the personality of the daughter and of the daughter in the personality of the mother.

The archetype of the green-world lover seems related to the dying god in the stories of Aphrodite and Adonis, Ishtar and Tammuz, Isis and Osiris. These goddesses have lovers who die and whom they restore to life: Ishtar (as in the parallel case of Isis and Osiris) through a perilous journey and Aphrodite through the mediation of Zeus. In both cases, the goddess's love for her consort gives her the power of rebirth, his return celebrated in rituals appealing primarily to women. Jessie Weston notes of the Tammuz and Adonis figures that the hero can be released from death only through feminine power and that in many of the rituals based on these stories women accompany a figure of their god, tearing their hair in their grief for him and celebrating his return with wild dances. "The most noticeable feature of the ritual was the prominence assigned to women," remarks Weston. "It is the women who weep for him and accompany him to his tomb. They sob wildly all night long; this is their god more than any other, and they alone wish to lament his death and sing of his resurrection."[11] Other feminist scholars have pointed out that cults of Isis and of Dionysus were not only openly permitted to women throughout Greek and Roman history but were considered a proper feminine activity, however wild and ecstatic the celebrations. They provided an outlet for women to celebrate their eroticism, power, pride, and joy, an outlet that also typifies both grail and witchcraft narratives. Although such figures as Charlotte Brontë's Heathcliff and Rochester contain elements of the dying-god archetype, he is more often an imaginary figure projected from within the hero's psyche, like Willa Cather's Corn God in *O Pioneers!* or the lovers dreamt of but never brought to life in Woolf's *Night and Day* and Chopin's *The Awakening*. In women's fiction the hero herself is more likely to become a "dying god" of feminine eroticism, punished by madness, death or ostracism, or to fall victim sexually to his opposite, the gothic rapist, hideous husband, or unsuitable suitor.

Jessie Weston suggests a number of links between the dying-god narratives and rituals and the popular grail legends of the High Middle Ages, and one need not go at length into the scholarship explaining such a continuity to recognize in the Celtic Breton culture from which the grail legends derive many elements of feminine authenticity. The feminine eroticism evident in the cults of Osiris, Tammuz, Adonis, and Dionysus provided women with a chance to celebrate with each other a licensed rebellion against marital fidelity. Celtic women, according to Jean Markale, enjoyed a higher degree of freedom over their own bodies than women in patriarchal systems, a freedom based on their ability to control segments of the communally owned property and cattle. Among the Celtic peoples settled in Britain, Ireland, and Wales at the time of the Anglo-Saxon invasions (and who later joined with the Normans to defeat them) infidelity was condoned, divorce easy, women warriors and queens powerful, and a number of goddesses revered and worshipped.

Both Emma Jung and Jean Markale argue that the grail legends contain rebellions against the institution of matrimony and other patrilinear norms. "Mythologically," remarks Markale, "the Quest for the Grail is an attempt to re-establish a disciplined sovereignty, usurped by the masculine violence of the despoiling knight, while the kingdom rots and the king, the head of the family . . . is impotent." Restoration can be achieved only by "the appointed successor, the nephew of the wounded king."[12] His qualities, in Emma Jung's description, are less rigidly "masculine" than androgynous: he must achieve compassion, the ability to ask the wounded king what ails him; this impotent king, whose lands have been laid waste by the Rape of the Maidens of Logres (see above, p. 25), is that key figure in all matrilinear systems, Perceval's mother's brother.[13] We are dealing, clearly, with the rape-trauma archetype and with an archetypal quest to restore a kingdom punished for violating women. The Breton materials are full of stories of women exiled to islands, "submerged princesses" forced underwater or into underground "fairy grottoes" or castles by usurping males.[14] Typical narratives of this type are those involving the island of Avalon, where Arthur was taken after his death, and islands of immortal women sought by the hero in the medieval prose poem "Voyage of Bran." Ladies of the lake, fairy queens, elf maidens, and mermaids are all archetypes expressing the repression of powerful women. "In the ever more prevalent symbolism of a magical Beyond and land of the dead," remarks Emma Jung, "there is a psychological expression of an extraordinary stirring of the unconscious, such as does happen from time to time, especially in periods when the religious values of a culture are beginning to change."[15] The grail as container of beneficence, feeder of the tribe, and locus of rebirth predominates in this material as still another archetype of feminine power. As "mother pot," "magic cauldron" (with which Persephone can regenerate the dead heroes and heal the sick), golden bowl of healing, etc., this archetype expresses women's generative and regenerative powers and corresponds to the sacred vessels of the vestal virgins and to Demeter's *Cista Mystica*, or magic basket.[16]

The disruptively feminist element in the grail material may have been responsible for the gradual denigration of women in the Arthurian legend. Whereas in much of folklore, fairy tales, and earlier accounts Morgan la Fée was an admirable warrior-goddess or -priestess and Guinevere a respected queen indulging in socially accepted extramarital behavior, by the fifteenth century writers like Malory were interpreting them as figures of horror, treachery, and adultery. Some of the Celtic standards for feminine eroticism seem to have found their way into the courtly love tradition under the patronage of Eleanor of Acquitaine, who tried the cases of true lovers at her court and forbade them to be married, but even within her lifetime her teachings were invaded by mysogynistic repudiations. Perhaps the veneration of the Virgin Mary—who, as Magna Mater, Stella Maris, Our Lady of the Vineyards, Our Lady of the Barley, Our Lady of the Caves, etc., amalgamated qualities of pre-Christian virgins alien to the Roman Catholic conception of chastity—represents a weakened survival of the goddess into the Middle Ages. "Apart from a tendency to restore the ancient mother goddess in the guise of the Virgin Mary," writes Markale, "there have been a great number of heresies within Christianity itself that have sought to implement the female rebellion."[17] Scholars of witchcraft like Trevor-Roper, Gerald Gardner, and Mary Alice Murray have noted the correspondence between places where large numbers of witches were tried and loci of heresies—places like Wales, Cornwall, the Channel Islands, the Isle of Man, and Ireland in the British Isles and the Pyrenees, Vosges, and Ardennes on the continent, marginal to the centers of patriarchal power.[18]

The Craft of the Wise, or witchcraft, in its herbal lore and healing, fertility dances around a horned god, and belief in reincarnation, "mother pots," or cauldrons, seems to constitute a variation on the dying-god, Celtic, and grail archetypal repositories. The witches acted as midwives, advisors, and healers to their villages, gathered in colleges located on islands or in the mountains, controlled considerable property, and were particularly concerned with the feminine reproductive cycle. The witch cult persisted in England throughout the Roman occupation and was popular in Norman England during the eleventh through the thirteenth centuries (some think that most Normans, and all of the Plantagenets, were members of covens),[19] and only with the "Renaissance" and "Age of Reason" was it subjected to a patriarchal backlash so virulent that between the fourteenth and the eighteenth centuries churchmen and scholars, undoubtedly motivated by its subversive feminine element, killed perhaps as many as nine million individuals.

> This death took the forms of burning at the stake, strangulation, crushing with stones, whipping, hanging, drowning, and unspeakable and vile tortures. . . .
> It was an example of insanity and womanhating for which there can be no reparation. The majority of those put to death were women; women as young as ten and eleven; women so far into pregnancy that they gave birth in the flame of their funeral pyre and saw their infants perish before they themselves did; women who were burned "quick," that is to say *alive* while their male counterparts were mercifully strangled before being put to the torch; women who were old, alone, lonely, and senile and who talked to themselves and their pets; women who enflamed lust in the groins of their celibate priest-confessors; women who miscarried after having been beaten by their husbands, and who knew that their husbands walked free as they screamed in agony on the rack for their crime against God-Jehovah.[20]

As a result, "secrecy and fear of discovery necessarily wiped out the open scholarship of the ancient matriarchal colleges and sacred islands. . . . Those who were herbalists let their gardens go to seed. Those who kept the ancient matrifocal law did so within the confines of their homes, but publicly joined the throngs of enslaved female chattel and swaggering masters."[21] Contemporary witches and scholars of witchcraft have suggested that the testimonies exacted under torture reflect less of the witch cult itself than the phallocentric and rabidly gynophobic imaginations of the "witch doctors" and judges.[22] The true Craft of the Wise, meanwhile, was passed down orally through the generations to the present.

Clearly, there are some very interesting links between the classical women's rites represented by the Demeter/Kore and Ishtar/Tammuz archetypes, the feminine and androgynous elements in the Celtic grail legends, and the witch cult in Western Europe. All three archetypal repositories express the desire of women for erotic autonomy, meaningful social roles, and celebration of femininity, which we have seen emerge in women's fiction as that cluster of values constituting totality of self. The rise of the novel, notes Carolyn Heilbrun, "coincided with the denigration of women among the social classes that were its public." Heilbrun is referring to the new wave of repression during the rise of the industrial era, ironically converse to its progressive technological advances. The tension between men and women in modern Western history, as we have seen, creates the discrepancy between expectations and reality underlying women's fiction. Thus, "it became necessary," Heilbrun believes, "that the feminine impulse seize upon some new and hitherto unknown outlet. No doubt this is an oversimplification; it is perhaps sufficient to say that the rise of power of the novel and the beginning of the most absolute fall in the power of woman occurred at the same time."[23] As Laurence Stone has suggested, the increasing volume of novels by women after the eighteenth century attests to rebellion against this new wave of patriarchal repression (see above, p. 41). The "hitherto unknown outlet" of prose fiction, in my hypothesis, drew upon archetypal narratives that had been known to women since ancient times.

I believe that the novel performs the same role in women's lives as do the Eleusinian, dying-god, and witchcraft rituals—a restoration through remembering, crucial to our survival. "If women say again and again that society denies them clear paths to fulfillment," writes Patricia Meyer Spacks, ". . . they also affirm in far reaching ways the significance of their inner freedom. . . . That escape through writing declared possible by Anaïs Nin and Anna Wulf emblemized an even larger kind of escape, through imagination."[24] Women's "escape through imagination" is not escapist but strategic, a withdrawal into the unconscious for the purpose of personal transformation. The deadlocks in women's fiction that many feminist critics deplore result from women's powerlessness in Western culture, but women authors present them in such a way that their novels become vehicles for social change.

Without pretending to survey the field of the reader/text relationship, which is central to much modern critical theory, I would like to suggest that the restorative power of women's fiction consists in a dialectical relationship between novel and audience. Women's fiction may indeed be suspended between two poles of desire, deadlocked between contrary forces rarely resolved within an individual text, and hence polar or dichotomous rather than dialectical. The process that dialecticians characterize as *aufheben*—to negate, absorb, and transcend—is rarely completed in an individual novel; even in those few instances when heroes emerge as fully developed personalities, their social future is uncertain. I perceive the woman's novel as a symbolic vehicle indicating a meaning or import that it does not itself contain. In negating gender behavior, absorbing or integrating "masculine" and "feminine" roles into those few fully mature characters, it points towards transcendence or synthesis. The woman's novel asks questions, poses riddles, cries out for restitution, but remains in itself merely rhetorical, an artifact or idea rather than an action. As in the archetypal rituals of Demeter and Kore and of the dying god, Persephone is always being raped and restored, the god always dying and being reborn. The synthesis, or final element, of the dichotomy between loss and restoration does not occur within the individual novel or even in the field as a whole but in the mind of the reader, who, having participated in the narrative reenactment, must put its message into effect in her own life.

The synthesis, or new space, indicated in women's fiction describes a world so alien to the patriarchy as to be invisible or, in Mary Daly's description, unhearable, an "intersubjective silence, the vibrations of which are too high for the patriarchal hearing mechanism. It is, then, ultrasonic."[25] As a group women writers are so threatened by punishment for the "abnormality" of subverting the cultural weapon of language to their own ends that they have found it necessary to find wavelengths upon which to communicate such "sounds of silence." Many women writers are themselves subservient to gender norms that they have internalized as their own values. Nonetheless, sometimes deliberately, but often unconsciously, they have developed tactics of diversion, modes of communicating feminist messages through media jammed with static. As a result, much of women's fiction constitutes a "vibration" available only to the consciousness of those men and women already at odds with the strictures of gender. Nevertheless, as Hélène Cixous puts it, women's writing constitutes "the *possibility* of change itself . . . the movement which precedes the transformation of social and cultural structures."[26]

It seems to me, then, that the archetypal patterns in women's fiction provide a ritual experience for the reader containing the potential for personal transformation and that women's novels constitute literary variations on preliterary folk practices that are available in the realm of the imagination even when they have long been absent from day-to-day life. A woman knitter once wanted to learn to spin her own wool and found the directions in the handbook on spinning hard to follow. When she actually picked up her spindle and began to wind the threads through it and to twirl it in rhythm, she found that her fingers already seemed to know how to perform motions arcane to her conscious mind. She coined the term *unventing* for this rediscovery of a lost skill through intuition, a bringing of latent knowledge out of oneself in contrast to "invention" from scratch.[27] Following this model, I would term the writing and reading of women's fiction a form of "unvention," the tapping of a repository of knowledge lost from Western culture but still available to the author and recognizable to the reader as deriving from a world with which she, at some level of her imagination, is already familiar.

To put it another way, for three centuries women novelists have been gathering us around campfires where they have warned us with tales of patriarchal horror and encouraged us with stories of heroes undertaking quests that we may emulate. They have given us maps of the patriarchal battlefield and of the landscape of our ruined culture, and they have resurrected for our use codes and symbols of our potential power. They have exaggerated the worst attributes of the "male" and the "female" enemy so that they become laughable, paper dragons. They have provided us moments of epiphany, of vision, when we can feel rising from our depths a quality that altogether transcends the gender polarities destructive to human life. They have dug the goddess out of the ruins and cleansed the debris from her face, casting aside the gynophobic masks that have obscured her beauty, her power, and her beneficence. In so doing, they have made of the woman's novel a pathway to the authentic self, to the roots of our selves beneath consciousness of self, and to our innermost being.

# Notes

## 1. INTRODUCTION

1. "The particular problem faced by Zeus in that period," writes Joseph Campbell of the period of Iron Age invasions into Bronze Age Greece, "was simply that wherever the Greeks came, in every valley, every isle, and every cove, there was a local manifestation of the goddess-mother of the world whom he, as the great god of the patriarchal order, had to master in a patriarchal way." *The Masks of God: Occidental Mythology*, Viking, 1964, p. 149.

2. C. G. Jung, introduction to M. Esther Harding, *The Way of All Women*, G. P. Putnam, 1970, p. xv.

3. See my "Archetypal Approaches to the New Feminist Criticism," *Bucknell Review* 21, no. 1 (Spring 1973), pp. 3–14. See also Naomi R. Goldenberg, "Jungian Psychology and Religion," chapter 5 in *The Changing of the Gods: Feminism and the End of Traditional Religions*, Beacon Press, 1979, pp. 46–72.

4. "For woman stands just where man's shadow falls," writes Jung in this same vein, "so that he is only too liable to confuse her with his own shadow. Then, when he wishes to repair his misunderstanding, he tends to overvalue the woman and believe in her desiderata." *Psychological Reflections*, ed. Jolande Jacobi, Pantheon, 1953, p. 97. See also C. G. Jung, *Psyche and Symbol*, ed. Violent Staub de Laszlo, Anchor, 1958, pp. 11–12; *The Basic Writings of C. G. Jung*, ed. Laszlo, Modern Library, 1959, pp. 311–13; and C. G. Jung, *The Development of Personality*, trans. R. F. C. Hull, Pantheon, 1954, p. 198.

5. Joseph Campbell, *Hero With a Thousand Faces*, Princeton, 1949, p. 116.

6. *Occidental Mythology*, pp. 26–27. See also pp. 163–64.

7. M. Esther Harding, *Woman's Mysteries, Ancient and Modern*, Bantam, 1973, p. 121. In *When God Was a Woman*, Merlin Stone documents "evidence from Sumer, Babylon, Canaan, Anatolia, Cyprus, Greece and even the Bible [revealing] that despite the fact the concept of marriage was known in the earliest written records, married women, as well as single, continued to live for periods of time within the temple complex and to follow the ancient sexual customs of the Goddess. The Bible itself reveals that these women were free to come and go as they pleased." Harvest, 1976, p. 155.

8. *Woman's Mysteries*, pp. 8, 123.

9. See, for example, Claude Lévi-Strauss, *Structural Anthropology*, trans. Claire Jacobson and Brooke Gundfest Schoepf, Penguin, 1968, pp. 61–62, as quoted by Juliet Mitchell, *Psychoanalysis and Feminism*, Vintage, 1974, p. 371.

## 2. THE NOVEL OF DEVELOPMENT
### (with Barbara White)

1. Hannah More, *Coelebs in Search of a Wife*, Caddell and Davies, 1808, p. 186.
2. Jane Austen, *Northanger Abbey*, Dent, 1910, p. 199.
3. Patricia Meyer Spacks, *The Female Imagination*, Avon, 1975, p. 200.
4. Simone de Beauvoir, *The Second Sex*, Knopf, 1953, p. 362.
5. Ibid., pp. 710–11.
6. Sarah Orne Jewett, *Deephaven*, J. R. Osgood, 1877, p. 203.
7. Sarah Orne Jewett, *The Country of the Pointed Firs*, Doubleday, 1956, pp. 166–67.
8. Ellen Glasgow, *Barren Ground*, Doubleday, 1933, p. 684.
9. Ibid., p. 239.
10. Ibid., p. 244.
11. May Sinclair, *Mary Olivier, A Life*, Macmillan, 1919, p. 93.
12. Ibid., p. 379.
13. Dorothy Richardson, *Pilgrimage*, Knopf, 1967, vol. 4, p. 72.
14. Maud Bodkin, in *Archetypal Patterns in Poetry*, was one of the first theoreticians to wonder whether "one could find in the poetry of woman writers any imaginative representation of man, related to the distinctive inner life of a woman in the same manner as an image of woman appearing in poetry shows relation to the emotional life of a man." She suggests Brontë's Heathcliff as a fictional variation on such an archetypal figure. Oxford, 1963, pp. 290–91, 305.
15. Virginia Woolf, *Night and Day*, Harcourt, Brace & Co., 1948, pp. 107–8.
16. Willa Cather, *O Pioneers!*, Houghton, 1954, p. 206.
17. Ibid., pp. 239–40.
18. "Elucidation," quoted by Emma Jung and Marie-Louise von Franz, *The Grail Legend*, trans. Andrea Dykes, Putnam's Sons, 1970, p. 202. See also Jessie Weston, *From Ritual to Romance*, Doubleday, 1957, p. 172.
19. Hazel Mews, *Frail Vessels: Woman's Role in Woman's Novels from Fanny Burney to George Eliot*, Athlone Press, 1969, p. 25.
20. For a further analysis of norms for women in America see Patricia Jewell McAlexander, "Sexual Morality in the Fiction of Charles Brockden Brown: Index to a Personal and Cultural Debate Regarding Passion and Reason," Ph.D. dissertation, University of Wisconsin, 1973, and "The Creation of the American Eve: The Culture Dialogue on Nature and Role of Women in Late-Eighteenth Century America," *Early American Literature* 9, no. 3 (Winter 1975), pp. 252–66.
21. Florence Hilbish, "Charlotte Smith, Poet and Novelist, 1749–1806," Ph. D. dissertation, University of Pennsylvania, 1941, p. 59, n. 218.
22. Mrs. Charlotte Smith, *Emmeline, The Orphan of the Castle*, J. Robins, n.d., p. 171.
23. Ann Radcliffe, *The Mysteries of Udolpho*, E. P. Dutton, 1931, vol. 1, pp. 266, 267, 275.
24. Fanny Burney [Madame Frances D'Arblay], *The Wanderer, or Female Difficulties*, Longman, 1814, vol. 1, pp. 36, 50.
25. Mary Webb, *Gone to Earth*, Butler and Tanner, 1952, p. 14.
26. See, for example, Mrs. Opie, *Adeline Mowbray, or Mother and Daughter*, Crissy, 1841, and Mary Wollstonecraft, *The Wrongs of Woman, or Maria: A Fragment*, W. W. Norton, 1975.

27. Charlotte Brontë, *Shirley*, Allan Wingate, 1949, p. 381.

28. Harriet Beecher Stowe, *Oldtown Folks*, Houghton Mifflin, 1882, pp. 510–11.

29. Louisa May Alcott, *Little Women*, Grosset and Dunlop, 1947, p. 6.

30. Olive Schreiner, *The Story of an African Farm*, Fawcett, 1968, p. 166.

31. Ellen Moers, *Literary Women*, Doubleday, 1976, p. 108.

32. See also Claire Katz, "Flannery O'Connor's Rage of Vision," *American Literature* 46, no. 1 (March 1974), pp. 54–67.

33. Agnes Smedley, *Daughter of Earth*, The Feminist Press, 1973, p. 107.

34. Margaret Walker, *Jubilee!*, Bantam, 1966, p. 45.

35. This hypothesis and other materials in this chapter can be found in Barbara White, "Growing Up Female: Adolescent Girlhood in American Literature," Ph.D. dissertation, University of Wisconsin, 1974.

36. Joyce Carol Oates, *Wonderland*, Vanguard, 1971, pp. 268–69.

37. Rose Macaulay, *Dangerous Ages*, Liveright, 1921, p. 10.

38. Phyllis Chesler, *Women and Madness*, Avon, 1973, p. 39. See also Barbara Hill Rigney, *Madness and Sexual Politics in the Feminist Novel*, University of Wisconsin Press, 1978.

39. Ursula K. Le Guin, "Is Gender Necessary?" in *Aurora: Beyond Sexuality*, ed. Vonda McIntyre and Susan Janice Anderson, Fawcett, 1976, p. 132. See also James Warren Bittner, "Approaches to the Fiction of Ursula K. Le Guin," Ph.D. dissertation, University of Wisconsin, 1979.

40. Northrop Frye, *The Secular Scripture: A Study of the Structure of Romance*, Harvard, 1976, p. 83.

### 3. NOVELS OF MARRIAGE

1. Laurence Stone, *The Family, Sex and Marriage in England, 1500–1800*, Harper and Row, 1977, pp. 271–72, 668.

2. "Measured against a criterion of womanliness which states that the pure feminine mind must, even theoretically or imaginatively, know no sin, no evil, no sexual passion, all the three Brontes could not but seem unwomanly." Ewbank quotes Miss Rigby (of the *Quarterly*) as saying that if the novel was by a woman, it was by one who had " 'long forfeited the society of her own sex.' " When Mrs. Oliphant found out that *Jane Eyre* was by a woman author, similarly she announced that its particular brand of " 'grossness' " was of " 'a degree of refined indelicacy possible to a woman, which no man can reach.' " These reactions surprised Charlotte Brontë, particularly when she read in *The Christian Remembrancer* that her "love-scenes glowed with a fire as fierce as that of Sappho, and somewhat more fulginous." Upon consulting Miss Martineau, Charlotte learned that what she had done was describe an "uncommon" type of love, not commonly described in fiction (Inga-Stina Ewbank, *Their Proper Sphere: A Study of the Bronte Sisters as Early-Victorian Female Novelists*, Cambridge, 1966, p. 43).

Quoting a letter written about *Villette* by Matthew Arnold to Clough, Walter Houghton notes that Arnold considered it a disagreeable book " 'because the writer's mind contains nothing but hunger, rebellion, and rage' " (*Letters, 1848–1888*, 2 vols., ed. G. W. E. Russell, London and New York, 1901 [no publisher given in Houghton], quoted in Walter E. Houghton, *The Victorian Frame of Mind*, Yale University Press, 1957, p. 117).

3. Houghton, *Victorian Frame*, p. 117.

4. Jane Austen, letter quoted in Mona Wilson, *Jane Austen and Some Contemporaries*, Cresset, 1938, p. 37.

5. Charlotte Brontë, letter to Ellen Nussey, quoted in May Sinclair, *The Three Brontes*, Kennikat, 1967, p. 76.

6. Alternative ending (first edition) to George Eliot, *Middlemarch*, quoted from B. W. J. Harvey, "Criticism of the Novel," by critic Barbara Hardy, ed., *Middlemarch: Critical Approaches to the Novel*, Oxford University Press, 1967, p. 133.

7. Katherine Anne Porter, "The Necessary Enemy," *The Collected Essays and Occasional Writings of Katherine Anne Porter*, Delta, 1973, pp. 184–85.

8. *Literary Women*, p. 67.

9. Jane Austen, *Pride and Prejudice*, Random House, 1950, p. 104.

10. Elizabeth Stuart Phelps, *The Story of Avis*, Osgood, 1877, p. 192.

11. Ruth Suckow, *Cora*, Knopf, 1929, p. 53.

12. *The Collected Essays*, pp. 184–85.

13. Christina Stead, *The Man Who Loved Children*, Avon, 1940, p. 472.

14. Mary McCarthy, *A Charmed Life*, Harcourt, 1954, p. 115. See also the characters of John Roberts in Margaret Forster's *The Bogeyman* (1965) and Oliver in Fay Weldon's *Female Friends* (1974). In collusion with other family members such characters play a similar role in Kay Boyle's family novels, in Ellen Glasgow's *In This Our Life* (1941) and *The Sheltered Life* (1932), and in a wide variety of popular family novels like Rose Franken's *Young Claudia* (1946) and Mildred Walker's *Unless the World Turns* (1941).

15. Joyce Carol Oates, *Wonderland*, Vanguard, 1971, pp. 154–55 (italics hers). " 'I'm Helene Cady!' " she shouts at her doctor. " 'What has happened to me? I was supposed to grow up into a certain person, but where is that person? I've waited for years and nothing has happened, marriage hasn't made any difference' " (p. 304).

16. See Kaufman's *Diary of a Mad Housewife* (1967), Drabble's *The Garrick Year* (1964) and *The Needle's Eye* (1972), Lessing's *The Summer Before the Dark* (1973), and Erica Jong's *Fear of Flying* (1973).

17. John Oliver Hobbes, *The Dream and the Business*, Unwin, 1906, pp. 107–8, 279.

18. *Dangerous Ages*, p. 19.

19. Elizabeth Taylor, *At Mrs. Lippincote's*, Knopf, 1946, p. 122.

20. Charlotte Perkins Gilman, "The Yellow Wallpaper," ed. Elaine R. Hedges, The Feminist Press, 1973, pp. 19, 26.

21. Joan Didion, *Play It As It Lays*, Bantam, 1972, pp. 202, 213.

22. Gertrude Atherton, *Immortal Marriage*, Liveright, 1927, p. 311.

23. Dorothy Canfield Fisher, *The Home-Maker*, Harcourt, 1924, p. 222.

24. Ibid., p. 309.

25. Margaret Culkin Banning, *Spellbinders*, Doran, 1922, p. 180.

26. Pamela Hansford Johnson, *Catherine Carter*, Knopf, 1952, p. 476.

27. Mary Daly, *Beyond God the Father: Toward a Philosophy of Women's Liberation*, Beacon Press, 1973, p. 172.

## 4. THE NOVEL OF SOCIAL PROTEST

1. Vineta Colby, *Yesterday's Woman: Domestic Realism in the English Novel*, Princeton, 1934, p. 155.

2. Elizabeth Gaskell, *Mary Barton, A Tale of Manchester Life*, vol. 1 in *The Works of Mrs. Gaskell*, Penguin, 1970, p. 460.

3. Charlotte Elizabeth Tonna, "The Forsaken Home," *Wrongs of Women*, in *Works*, vol. 3, p. 445, as quoted in Ivanka Kovacevic and S. Barbara Kanner, "Blue Book into Novel: The Forgotten Industrial Fiction of Char-

lotte Elizabeth Tonna," *Nineteenth Century* 25, no. 2 (September 1970), p. 157. Of *Helen Fleetwood* Louis Cazamian remarks: "C'est une dissertation, non une oeuvre d'art; c'est un traité d'apologétique Chrétienne, où Satan prend la forme du manufacturier." (It is a dissertation, not a work of art; it is a treaty of Christian apologetics, in which Satan takes the form of the industrialist.) *Le roman social en Angleterre*, Librairie Georges Bellais, 1904, p. 432.

4. Phyllis Bentley, *A Modern Tragedy*, Macmillan, 1934, p. 435.

5. Elizabeth Stuart Phelps, *The Silent Partner*, Gregg Press, 1967, p. 68.

6. Sheila Rowbotham, *Women, Resistance, and Revolution*, Vintage, 1974, p. 21.

7. Josephine Herbst, *Rope of Gold*, Harcourt Brace, 1939, pp. 230, 148.

8. Agnes Smedley herself went into exile from America to become a prominent and beloved figure in the Chinese Revolution. See Paul Lauter, afterword to *Daughter of Earth*, The Feminist Press, 1973.

9. Sarah Wright, *This Child's Gonna Live*, Delacorte, 1969, pp. 6, 8.

10. See Shulamith Firestone, *The Dialectic of Sex*, Bantam, 1972, pp. 1–14.

11. Virginia Woolf, *Three Guineas*, Harbinger, 1963, p. 108. During the First World War Woolf had outraged her friends by her recognition of the relationship between militarism and masculinity and her refusal to take the war as a serious humanistic endeavor. "She was convinced," asserted E. M. Forster, "that society is man-made, that the chief occupations of men are the shedding of blood, the making of money, the giving of orders, and the wearing of uniforms, and that none of these occupations is admirable." E. M. Forster, quoted from Rede Lectures, 1942, in Nigel Nicolson, ed., *The Collected Letters of Virginia Woolf II*, Harcourt, 1976, p. xvii.

12. Toni Morrison, *Sula*, Knopf, 1973, pp. 142–43.

13. Jean Rhys, *Quartet*, Vintage, 1974, p. 97, pp. 159–60.

14. See also *After Leaving Mr. Mackenzie*, Harper and Row, 1931, and *Wide Sargasso Sea*, Deutsch, 1967.

15. Fay Weldon, *Female Friends*, St. Martin's, 1974, p. 249.

16. Fay Weldon, *Down Among the Women*, Warner, 1972, pp. 125, 122, 222.

## 5. LOVE BETWEEN MEN AND WOMEN

1. *Woman's Mysteries*, p. 122. See also Sarah B. Pomeroy, *Goddesses, Whores, Wives and Slaves: Women in Classical Antiquity*, Schocken, 1975, pp. 4–6, 211.

2. Rollo May, *Love and Will*, Norton, 1969, pp. 73–74.

3. Helen Waite Papashvily, *All the Happy Endings*, Kennikat, 1972, pp. 31–32.

4. Vineta Colby, *The Singular Anomaly: Women Novelists of the Nineteenth Century*, New York University Press, 1970, p. 70.

5. Copy of a letter in the Brotherton Library quoted by Aina Rubenius, *The Woman Question in Mrs. Gaskell's Life and Works*, Harvard, 1950, p. 212. See also pp. 204, 213–16.

6. *The Dialectic of Sex*, chapters 3 and 6, and Kate Millett, *Sexual Politics*, Doubleday, 1970, pp. 176–89.

7. *The Dialectic of Sex*, p. 132. See also Ann Barr Snitow, "The Front Line: Notes on Novels by Women, 1969–1979," *Signs* 5 (Summer 1980), pp. 702–18.

8. Olivia Manning, *The Doves of Venus*, Windmill, 1955, p. 156.

9. See Marilyn Campbell, "Some Literary Images of American Working Women from the Turn of the Century to the Depression," student paper, University of Wisconsin, 1973, p. 40.

10. Quoted by Edward Garnett, preface to Norah James, *Sleeveless Errand*, Babau, 1929, p. 2.

11. Ruth Suckow, "Literary Soubrettes," *The Bookman* 63 (July 1927), pp. 517–21.

12. Pamela Hansford Johnson, preface to *This Bed Thy Centre*, Macmillan, 1962, p. iii.

13. See "The Fog of War," *The London Times Literary Supplement* (27 April 1972), p. 280; Elizabeth Peer, "Sex and the Woman Writer," *Newsweek* (5 May 1975), p. 76; and Peter S. Prescott, "Women on Women," *Newsweek* (14 February 1972), p. 94.

14. Carol Ohmann, "Emily Brontë in the Hands of Male Critics," *College English* (May 1971), p. 912.

15. Elaine Showalter, *A Literature of Their Own*, Princeton, 1977, p. 212.

16. Glass's narrator, the hero's son, maintains the ambivalence in attitude towards his mother's love affair typical of the authorial persona in this genre: on the one hand, he finds his mother's behavior distasteful but, on the other hand, remarks that "it seemed odd to me that Mother should be condemned for her *one* Fish, while father had access to the whole Ocean." Joanna Glass, *Reflections on a Summer Mountain*, Knopf, 1974, p. 257.

17. Doris Lessing, *The Temptation of Jack Orkney and Other Stories*, Knopf, 1972, p. 156.

18. Doris Lessing, "Play with a Tiger," in *Plays By and About Women*, ed. Victoria Sulivan and James Hatch, Random, 1974, p. 261.

19. Joyce Carol Oates, *Marriages and Infidelities*, Fawcett, 1972, p. 52.

20. Doris Lessing, *Briefing for a Descent into Hell*, Knopf, 1971, p. 255.

21. Mary McCarthy, *The Company She Keeps*, Harcourt, 1942, pp. 303–4.

22. Rosamond Lehmann, *Dusty Answer*, Reynal and Hitchcock, 1927, p. 375.

23. Rosamond Lehmann, *Invitation to the Waltz*, Reynal and Hitchcock, 1932, p. 81.

24. Rosamond Lehmann, *The Weather in the Streets*, Reynal and Hitchcock, 1936, p. 55.

25. Rosamond Lehmann, *The Ballad and the Source*, Reynal and Hitchcock, 1945, p. 97.

26. Rosamond Lehmann, *The Echoing Grove*, Harcourt, 1953, p. 104.

27. Ibid., p. 363.

28. E. D. Pendry, *The New Feminism of English Fiction*, Kenkyusha, 1956, p. 168. See Sydney Kaplan, *Feminine Consciousness in the Modern British Novel*, Illinois, 1975, chapter 4.

29. Doris Lessing, *The Golden Notebook*, McGraw, 1963, p. 508.

30. Joyce Carol Oates, *Do With Me What You Will*, Fawcett Crest, 1973, p. 525.

31. Margaret Drabble, *The Waterfall*, Signet, 1969, p. 79.

32. Nancy Hardin, "An Interview with Margaret Drabble," *Contemporary Literature* 14, no. 3 (Summer 1973), p. 292.

33. Margaret Drabble, *The Realms of Gold*, Popular Library, 1977, p. 24.

34. Ti-Grace Atkinson, *Amazon Odyssey*, Link Books, 1974, p. 43.

35. *The Waterfall*, p. 164.

36. *Amazon Odyssey*, p. 43.

## 6. LOVE AND FRIENDSHIP BETWEEN WOMEN
### (*with Andrea Loewenstein*)

1. Virginia Woolf, *A Room of One's Own*, pp. 123, 125–26.
2. *The Singular Anomaly*, p. 122. For a thoroughgoing study of the relationships between women in women's fiction see Janet Todd, *Women's Friendship in Literature*, Columbia University Press, 1980.
3. May Sarton, *Journal of a Solitude*, Norton, 1973, pp. 90–91.
4. May Sarton, *The Small Room*, Norton, 1961, p. 75.
5. May Sarton, *Plant Dreaming Deep*, Norton, 1968, p. 90.
6. May Sarton, *Mrs. Stevens Hears the Mermaids Singing*, Norton, 1965, pp. 24–25.
7. Ibid., p. 129.
8. Ibid., pp. 98, 105.
9. Marge Piercy, *Small Changes*, Doubleday, 1973, p. 418.
10. Phyllis Chesler, *Women and Madness*, Avon, 1973, p. 184.
11. See Marie Kuda, ed., *Women Loving Women: A Select and Annotated Bibliography of Women Loving Women in Literature*, Lavender, 1974, p. 10.
12. Bettie Wysor, *Lesbian Myth: Insights and Conversations*, Random House, 1974, p. 192.
13. Radclyffe Hall, *The Well of Loneliness*, Sun Dial Press, 1928, p. 177.
14. Ibid., p. 447.
15. See review by Robert Cantwell in the *New Republic* (2 October 1935).
16. See Jeanette H. Foster, *Sex Variant Women in Literature*, Vantage Press, 1956, for a further bibliography.
17. Del Martin and Phyllis Lyon, *Lesbian/Woman*, Glide, 1972, p. 280.
18. Jane Rule, *The Desert of the Heart*, Macmillan of Canada, 1964, p. 125.
19. Jill Johnston, *Lesbian Nation*, Simon and Schuster, 1973, pp. 151–54.
20. Rita Mae Brown, *Rubyfruit Jungle*, Daughters, 1974, pp. 94, 113.
21. Gertrude Stein, *Things As They Are*, Bunyan, 1950, p. 32.
22. Elana Nachman, *Riverfinger Woman*, Daughters, 1974, pp. 101, 116.
23. June Arnold, *The Cook and the Carpenter*, Daughters, 1974, p. 50.
24. Ibid., p. 10.
25. Ibid., pp. 140–41.
26. Ibid., p. 79.
27. Joanna Russ, *The Female Man*, Bantam, 1975, p. 151.
28. Ibid., pp. 138–39.
29. *The Cook and the Carpenter*, p. 87.
30. *Beyond God the Father*, p. 15.
31. *Women and Madness*, p. 190.
32. *Lesbian Nation*, p. 266.

## 7. SINGLENESS AND SOLITUDE

1. Nan Bauer Maglin, "Fictional Feminists in *The Bostonians* and *The Odd Women*," in *Images of Women in Fiction*, ed. Susan Koppelman Cornillon, Bowling Green, 1972, p. 225.
2. *All the Happy Endings*, pp. 44, 116.
3. See Susan Gorsky, "Old Maids and New Women, Alternatives to Marriage in Englishwomen's Novels, 1847–1915," *The Journal of Popular Cul-*

*ture* 7, no. 1 (Summer 1973), pp. 68–86; "The Gentle Doubters, Images of Women in Englishwomen's Novels, 1840–1970," in *Images of Women in Fiction*, pp. 28–54; and Hazel Mews, chapter 1, "Women Standing Alone," in *Frail Vessels*.

4. Remark made to Jacqueline Van Voris during the course of an interview for *College: A Smith Mosaic*, Smith, 1975.

5. Quoted from an anonymous "American Critic" by Walter Allen in his preface to *Pilgrimage*, vol. 4, p. 6.

6. Dorothy Yost Deegan, *The Stereotype of the Single Woman in American Novels: A Social Study with Implications for the Education of Women*, King's Crown, 1951, p. 187.

7. See Leslie Ingmanson, student paper, University of Wisconsin, 1974.

8. See Sheila Kaye-Smith, *Superstition Corner*, Cassell, 1934, p. 41.

9. Gail Godwin, *The Odd Woman*, Knopf, 1974, p. 267.

10. See *The Dialectic of Sex*, chapter 3.

11. Harper, 1908. Also by John Kendrick Bangs, Elizabeth Jordan, Mary Heaton Vorse, Edith Wyatt, Mary R. Shipman Andrews, Henry Van Dyke, and Mary Stewart Cutting. As "domestic fiction" the genre is ironically reversed, picturing the destructively claustrophobic behavior of a too-extended small-town family in Middle America.

12. May Sarton, *Joanna and Ulysses*, Norton, 1963, pp. 59, 55.

13. Quoted in *The Stereotype of the Single Woman*, p. 175.

14. *Beyond God the Father*, pp. 64–65.

15. Mary Wilkins Freeman, unpublished manuscript quoted in Edward Foster, *Mary Wilkins Freeman*, Hendricks House, 1956, pp. 142–43. Citation from Ann Douglas Wood, "The Literature of Impoverishment: The Local Woman Colorists in America 1865–1914," *Women's Studies* 1, no. 1 (1972), p. 27.

16. Robin Morgan, *Monster*, Random, 1972, p. 81.

17. Sylvia Townsend Warner, *Lolly Willowes, or, the Loving Huntsman*, Grosset and Dunlop, 1926, pp. 18–19.

18. Ibid., pp. 195–96.

19. Ibid., p. 239.

20. See below, pp. 175–76.

21. Elizabeth Goudge, *The White Witch*, Hodder and Stoughton, 1958, pp. 100–101.

22. Lynne Banks, *The L-Shaped Room*, Simon and Schuster, 1961, p. 231.

23. Margaret Drabble, *The Millstone*, Weidenfield and Nicolson, 1965, p. 164. See Nancy Hardin, "Drabble's *The Millstone*: A Fable for Our Times," *Critique* 15, no. 1 (1973), p. 34.

24. *Journal of a Solitude*, p. 33.

25. Epigraph of *Mrs. Stevens*.

26. See Janice Hetzer Struve, student paper, University of Wisconsin, 1974.

27. *Journal of a Solitude*, p. 113.

28. Quoted by August Derleth in *Still Small Voice*, Appleton-Century, 1940, p. 157.

29. *The Woman Within*, p. 166.

30. Vita Sackville-West, *All Passion Spent*, Doubleday Doran, 1931, p. 170.

31. See Annis Pratt, "Sexual Imagery in *To the Lighthouse*: A New Feminist Approach," *Modern Fiction Studies* 18, no. 3 (Autumn 1972), pp. 417–31.

32. Mary Ellen Chase, *The Edge of Darkness*, Norton, 1957, pp. 19–20.
33. *Journal of a Solitude*, p. 40.
34. Ibid., p. 37.

## 8. NOVELS OF REBIRTH AND TRANSFORMATION

1. *Beyond God the Father*, p. 161.
2. Carol P. Christ, "Margaret Atwood: The Surfacing of Women's Spiritual Quest and Vision," *Signs* 2, no. 2 (Winter 1976), p. 317.
3. C. G. Jung, "Concerning Rebirth," *The Archetypes and the Collective Unconscious*, Princeton, 1969, p. 114.
4. *Woman's Mysteries*, pp. 245–46.
5. C. G. Jung, "The Psychological Aspects of the Kore," *The Archetypes and the Collective Unconscious*, p. 187.
6. *The Secular Scripture*, p. 183.
7. Shirley Rose, " 'The Unmoving Center': Consciousness in *Pilgrimage*," *Contemporary Literature* 10, no. 3 (Summer 1969), p. 375.
8. See my "Aunt Jennifer's Tigers: Notes Towards a Pre-Literary History of Women's Archetypes," *Feminist Studies* 4, no. 1 (February 1978), pp. 163–94.
9. See my "Sexual Imagery in *To the Lighthouse*," pp. 422–25.
10. Virginia Woolf, *To the Lighthouse*, Hogarth, 1960, pp. 60–61.
11. Ibid., pp. 61–62.
12. Virginia Woolf, *The Common Reader*, Harcourt, 1963, p. 156.
13. Karen Horney, *Feminine Psychology*, Norton, 1967, p. 64.
14. C. G. Jung, *Symbols of Transformation*, Princeton, 1956, p. 293.
15. *To the Lighthouse*, pp. 100–104.
16. Ibid., p. 244.
17. Ibid., p. 319.
18. *A Room of One's Own*, p. 148.
19. *Myths, Rites, Symbols: A Mircea Eliade Reader*, vol. 2, ed. Wendell C. Beame and William G. Doty, Harper, 1976, pp. 285, 288.
20. *To the Lighthouse*, p. 308.
21. Anaïs Nin, *Seduction of the Minotaur*, volume 5 of *Cities of the Interior*, Swallow, 1974, p. 531.
22. Ibid., p. 540.
23. *Ladders to Fire*, volume 1 of *Cities of the Interior*, p. 58.
24. Ibid., p. 14.
25. Ibid., p. 18.
26. Ibid., p. 59.
27. *Seduction of the Minotaur*, p. 544.
28. "Margaret Atwood: The Surfacing of Women's Spiritual Quest and Vision," p. 330.
29. Margaret Atwood, *Surfacing*, Popular Library, 1972, p. 171.
30. Ibid., p. 191.
31. Ibid., p. 208.
32. *Beyond God the Father*, pp. 65–66.
33. Doris Lessing, *The Four-Gated City*, Knopf, 1969, p. 39.
34. Ibid., p. 59.
35. Carol Christ, "Spiritual Quest and Women's Experience," *Anima* 1, no. 2 (Spring 1975), p. 10. See also Carol Christ, *Diving Deep and Surfacing: Women Writers on Spiritual Quest*, Beacon, 1981.
36. Christ, "Spiritual Quest," p. 14.
37. *A Literature of Their Own*, pp. 215, 297.

38. Jean Pickering, "The Connection Between the 'Politics of the Left' and 'The Politics of Madness' in the Work of Doris Lessing," Doris Lessing Seminar Paper, The Modern Language Association, 1973, pp. 13–14. See also Judith Plaskow, "On Carol Christ on Margaret Atwood: Some Theological Reflections," *Signs* 2, no. 2 (Winter 1976), pp. 331–39, and Francine du Plessix Gray, "Nature vs Nunnery," *New York Times Book Review*, 17 July 1977, pp. 3, 21. For further readings on the power of the mother-daughter quest in literature see Cathy N. Davidson and E. M. Broner, eds., *The Lost Tradition: Mothers and Daughters in Literature*, Ungar, 1980.

39. "The Qualitative Leap Beyond Patriarchal Religion," p. 29. See also *Beyond God the Father*, p. 189.

## 9. ARCHETYPAL PATTERNS IN WOMEN'S FICTION

1. Walter Allen, *The Modern Novel in Britain and the United States*, Dutton, 1965, p. xiii.

2. *Feminine Consciousness in Modern British Fiction*, p. 10. Kaplan cites Shirley Rose, "The Unmoving Center: Consciousness in Dorothy Richardson's *Pilgrimage*," *Contemporary Literature* 10 (Summer 1969), p. 367.

3. *Psychoanalysis and Feminism*, p. 366.

4. *The Dialectic of Sex*, p. 157.

5. "The Psychological Aspects of the Kore," p. 188.

6. From C. G. Jung and C. Kerényi, *Essays on a Science of Mythology: The Myth of the Divine Child and the Mysteries of Eleusis*, trans. R. F. C. Hull, Princeton, 1950, p. 177.

7. Jane Ellen Harrison, *Prolegomena to the Study of Greek Religion*, Meridian, 1966, p. 120.

8. "The Psychological Aspects of the Kore," p. 184.

9. Further documentation can be found in *When God Was a Woman*, chapter 4 ("The Northern Invaders"), pp. 62–102 and in Jean Markale, *Women of the Celts*, trans. Gordon Cremonesi, Cremonesi Publications, 1975.

10. My principal sources are Harrison's *Prolegomena* and C. Kerényi, *Eleusis: Archetypal Images of Mother and Daughter*, trans. Ralph Manheim, Schocken, 1971.

11. *From Ritual to Romance*, pp. 37, 43, 47. Sarah Pomeroy, in *Goddesses, Whores, Wives and Slaves: Women in Classical Antiquity*, also discusses the centricity of the dying-god motif to rites celebrated through Greek and Roman history by and for women.

12. *Women of the Celts*, pp. 197–98.

13. "It also turns out," confirms Emma Jung, "that the hermit is a brother of Perceval's mother and of the rich Fisher's father. In the matriarchal order of society the mother's brother is granted the standing of a godfather." In Wolfram von Eschenbach's grail narrative, she explains, "it is also significant that the guardian of the Grail is Parzival's mother's brother, or else his grandfather or forebear on his mother's side." *The Grail Legend*, pp. 226, 73–74.

14. *Women of the Celts*, chapter 3.

15. *The Grail Legend*, p. 25.

16. Edward Davies, a nineteenth-century scholar of Celtic lore, identifies the sacred vessel with a caer, or magically enclosed place, "and the same caer is described as an island" that the bard Taliesson described as containing nine damsels presiding over a cauldron "in a quadrangular sanctuary, within a sacred island." *The Mythology and Rites of the British Druids,*

Booth, 1809, p. 154. In the first century A.D. Strabo wrote that "in an Island close to Britain, Demeter and Persephone are venerated with rites similar to the orgies of Samothrace." Quoted in *The Witch-Cult in Western Europe*, Oxford, 1971, p. 21.

17. *Women of the Celts*, pp. 170–71.

18. See H. R. Trevor-Roper, *The European Witch-Craze of the Sixteenth and Seventeenth Centuries and Other Essays*, Harper, 1967.

19. "Witchcraft: The Art of Remembering," p. 43, n. 3.

20. Ibid., p. 44. See also Gerald B. Gardner, *Witchcraft Today*, London, 1954, p. 34, and *The European Witch-Craze*, pp. 93, 145, 161.

21. "Witchcraft: The Art of Remembering," p. 44.

22. This is Trevor-Roper's particular thesis: see *The Witch-Craze*, pp. 91–93.

23. Carolyn Heilbrun, *Toward a Recognition of Androgyny*, Knopf, 1973, p. 51.

24. *The Female Imagination*, p. 411.

25. *Beyond God the Father*, pp. 152–53.

26. Christiane Makward, "Interview with Hélène Cixous," trans. Ann Liddle and Beatrice Cameron, in *Sub-stance* no. 13 (1976), pp. 25–26. See also Hélène Cixous, "Le rire de la Méduse," *L'arc* no. 61 (May 1975), p. 42; trans. as "The Laugh of the Medusa," trans. Keith Cohen and Paula Cohen, *Signs* 1 (Summer 1976), pp. 875–93.

27. Elizabeth Zimmerman, *Knitter's Almanac*, Scribner's, 1974, pp. 75–76.

# Bibliography

*The original publication date appears in parentheses at the end of the entry when it differs from the date of the cited edition.*

## NOVELS AND STORIES BY WOMEN

Alcott, Louisa May. *Little Women.* New York: Grosset & Dunlap, 1947 (1869).

Allingham, Margery. *The Fashion in Shrouds.* London: Heinemann, 1965.

Arnold, June. *The Cook and the Carpenter.* Plainfield, Vt.: Daughters, 1974 (1973).

Arnow, Harriet. *The Dollmaker.* New York: Macmillan, 1954.

———. *The Weedkiller's Daughter.* New York: A. A. Knopf, 1970.

Ashton, Winifred [Clemence Dane]. *Legend.* New York: Macmillan, 1920.

———. *Regiment of Women.* New York: Macmillan, 1932 (1917).

Atherton, Gertrude. *American Wives and English Husbands.* New York: Dodd, Mead & Co., 1898.

———. *Ancestors.* New York: Harper & Bros., 1907.

———. *Immortal Marriage.* New York: Boni & Liveright, 1927.

———. *Julia France and Her Times.* New York: Macmillan, 1912.

———. *Patience Sparhawk and Her Times.* Cambridge, Mass.: The University Press, 1900 (1895).

Atwood, Margaret. *The Edible Woman.* Toronto: McClelland & Stewart Ltd., 1969.

———. *Surfacing.* New York: Popular Library, 1972.

Austen, Jane. *Emma.* New York: E. P. Dutton, 1906 (1816).

———. *Northanger Abbey.* London: J. M. Dent, 1910 (1798).

———. *Persuasion.* London: Zodiac Press, 1949 (1818).

———. *Pride and Prejudice.* New York: Macmillan, 1962 (1813).

———. *Sense and Sensibility.* London: R. Bentley, 1833 (1811).

Austin, Mary. *Outland.* New York: Boni & Liveright, 1919.

Baldwin, Faith. *The Faith Baldwin Omnibus.* New York: Grosset & Dunlap, 1930.

Banks, Lynne. *The L-Shaped Room.* New York: Simon & Schuster, 1961.

Banning, Margaret Culkin. *The Dowry.* New York: Harper & Bros., 1954.

———. *Pressure.* New York: A. L. Burt, 1927.

———. *Spellbinders.* New York: G. H. Doran, 1922.

———. *The Will of Magda Townsend.* New York: Harper and Row, 1974 (1973).

———. *You Haven't Changed.* New York: Harper & Bros., 1938.

Barnes, Margaret Ayer. *Edna, His Wife, an American Idyll.* Boston/New York: Houghton Mifflin, 1935.

————. *Within This Present*. Boston/New York: Houghton Mifflin, 1933.

Behn, Aphra. *Oroonoko*. New York: W. W. Norton, 1973 (1688).

Bentley, Phyllis Eleanor. *A Modern Tragedy*. New York: Macmillan, 1934.

Bisno, Beatrice. *Tomorrow's Bread*. Philadelphia: Jewish Publication Society of America, 1938.

Bowen, Elizabeth. *The Death of the Heart*. London: Jonathan Cape, 1948 (1938).

————. *The House in Paris*. London: Jonathan Cape, 1949 (1935).

————. *The Little Girls*. New York: A. A. Knopf, 1964 (1963).

Boyd, Blanche. *Nerves*. Plainfield, Vt.: Daughters, 1973.

Boyle, Kay. *The Underground Woman*. Garden City, N.Y.: Doubleday, 1975.

Bray, Anna Eliza Stothard. *Trials of Domestic Life*. London: H. Colburn, 1848.

Broner, E. M. *Her Mothers*. New York: Holt, Rinehart and Winston, 1975.

Brontë, Anne. *Agnes Grey*. London: Cassell, 1966 (1847).

————. *The Tenant of Wildfell Hall*. London: Allan Wingate, 1949 (1848).

Brontë, Charlotte. *Jane Eyre*. New York: Signet, 1960 (1847).

————. *Shirley*. London: Allan Wingate, 1949 (1849).

————. *Villette*. London: Allan Wingate, 1949 (1853).

Brontë, Emily. *Wuthering Heights*. New York: Random House, 1943 (1847).

Brophy, Brigid. *The Finishing Touch*. London: Secker & Warburg, 1963.

Brown, Alice. *Meadow-Grass; Tales of New England Life*. Boston: Copeland and Day, 1895.

Brown, Alice; Andrews, M. S.; Bangs, J. K.; Cutting, M. S.; Freeman, M. W.; Howells, W. D.; James, H.; Jordan, E.; Phelps, E. S.; Van Dyke, H.; Wyatt, E.; Vorse, M. H. *The Whole Family—A Novel by Twelve Authors*. New York: Harper & Bros., 1908.

Brown, Rita Mae. *Rubyfruit Jungle*. Plainfield, Vt.: Daughters, 1973.

Buchanan, Cynthia. *Maiden*. New York: Morrow, 1972.

Burney, Fanny. See D'Arblay, Frances.

Cather, Willa. *A Lost Lady*. New York: A. A. Knopf, 1923.

————. *Lucy Gayheart*. New York: A. A. Knopf, 1935.

————. *My Ántonia*. Boston: Houghton Mifflin, 1926.

————. *O Pioneers!* Boston: Houghton Mifflin, 1913.

————. *Youth and the Bright Medusa*. New York: A. A. Knopf, 1920.

Chase, Mary Ellen. *The Edge of Darkness*. New York: W. W. Norton, 1957.

Chopin, Kate. *The Awakening*. New York: Capricorn, 1964 (1899).

Compton-Burnett, Ivy. *More Women Than Men*. London: Heinemann, 1933.

Craigie, Pearl Richard [John Oliver Hobbes]. *The Dream and the Business*. London: T. Fisher Unwin, 1906.

Dane, Clemence. See Ashton, Winifred.

D'Arblay, Frances [Fanny Burney]. *The Wanderer, or Female Difficulties*. London: Longman, 1814.

Davis, Rebecca Harding. *John Andross*. New York: Orange Judd & Co., 1874.

————. *Life in the Iron Mills*. New York: Feminist Press, 1972 (1861).

Day, Dorothy. *The Eleventh Virgin*. New York: A. & C. Boni, 1924.

Delafield, E. M. See da la Pasture, Elizabeth M.

Deland, Margaret. *The Awakening of Helena Richie*. New York: Harper & Bros., 1906.

de La Pasture, Elizabeth M. [E. M. Delafield]. *Diary of a Provincial Lady*. New York: Harper & Bros., 1931.

Delmar, Vina. *Women Live Too Long*. New York: Harcourt, Brace and Co., 1932.

Dickens, Dorothy Lee. *Black on the Rainbow*. New York: Pageant Press, 1952.

Didion, Joan. *Play It as It Lays*. New York: Farrar, Straus & Giroux, 1970.

Donisthorpe, G. Sheila. *Loveliest of Friends*. New York: C. Kendall, 1931.

Doolittle, Hilda [H.D.]. *Bid Me to Live*. New York: Grove Press, 1960.

Drabble, Margaret. *The Garrick Year*. New York: Morrow, 1965 (1964).

―――. *The Millstone*. London: Weidenfeld & Nicolson, 1965.

―――. *The Needle's Eye*. London: Weidenfeld & Nicolson, 1972.

―――. *The Realms of Gold*. New York: Alfred Knopf, 1975.

―――. *The Waterfall*. New York: Signet, 1969.

Edgeworth, Maria. *The Absentee*. New York: Dodd, Mead & Co., 1893 (1812).

―――. *Belinda*. New York: Dodd, Mead & Co., 1893 (1801).

―――. *Castle Rackrent*. London: Oxford University Press, 1964 (1800).

―――. *Letters for Literary Ladies*. London, 1799 (1795).

Eliot, George. See Evans, Marian.

Elizabeth, Charlotte. See Tonna, Charlotte Elizabeth.

Evans, Marian [George Eliot]. *Adam Bede*. New York: Harcourt, Brace & World, 1962 (1859).

―――. *Middlemarch*. Baltimore: Penguin Books, 1968 (1871–72).

―――. *The Mill on the Floss*. New York: Harper & Row, 1965 (1860).

Fairbank, Janet Ayer. *Rich Man, Poor Man*. Boston: Houghton Mifflin, 1936.

―――. *The Smiths*. Indianapolis: Bobbs-Merrill, 1925.

Fauset, Jessie Redmon. *Plum Bun*. New York: F. A. Stokes, 1929.

Ferber, Edna. *Come and Get It*. Garden City, N.Y.: Doubleday, Doran & Co., 1935.

―――. *Emma McChesney & Co*. New York: Grosset & Dunlap, 1915.

―――. *Roast Beef Medium*. New York: Grosset & Dunlap, 1913 (1911).

Fern, Fanny. See Parton, Sara Payson.

Fisher, Dorothy Canfield. *The Home-Maker*. New York: Harcourt, Brace & Co., 1924.

―――. *The Squirrel Cage*. New York: Grosset & Dunlap, 1912.

Fisher, Dorothy Canfield, et al. *The Sturdy Oak*. Edited by Elizabeth Jordan. New York: H. Holt, 1917.

Follen, E. L. C. *Sketches of Married Life*. Boston: Crosby and Nichols, 1847 (1838).

Forbes, Esther. *A Mirror for Witches*. Boston/New York: Houghton Mifflin, 1928.

―――. *Miss Marvell*. Boston/New York: Houghton Mifflin, 1935.

Forster, Margaret. *The Bogeyman*. London: Secker & Warburg, 1965.

Foster, Hannah. *The Coquette, or the History of Eliza Wharton*. New York: Columbia University Press, 1939 (1797).

Franken, Rose. *Young Claudia*. New York: Rinehart and Co., 1946.

Freeman, Mary Wilkins. *Jane Field*. New York: Harper & Bros., 1893.

―――. *A New England Nun*. New York: Harper & Bros., 1891.

―――. *The Portion of Labor*. Ridgewood, N.J.: Gregg Press, 1967 (1901).

Gale, Zona. *A Daughter of the Morning*. Indianapolis: Bobbs-Merrill, 1917 (1913).

―――. *Miss Lulu Bett*. New York: Appleton & Co., 1920.

Gaskell, Elizabeth. *Mary Barton: A Tale of Manchester Life*, in *The Works of Mrs. Gaskell*. Harmondsworth: Penguin Books, 1970 (1848).

―――. *Ruth*. London: J. M. Dent, 1967 (1853).

Gilbert, Mercedes. *Aunt Sara's Wooden God*. College Park, Md.: McGrath, 1969 (1938).

Gilman, Charlotte Perkins. *Herland*. New York: Pantheon, 1979 (1915).

———. *What Diantha Did*. New York: Charlton Co., 1910.

———. *The Yellow Wallpaper*. New York: Feminist Press, 1973 (1892).

Glasgow, Ellen. *Barren Ground*. Garden City, N.Y.: Doubleday, Page & Co., 1925.

———. *In This Our Life*. New York: Harcourt, Brace and Co., 1941.

———. *The Sheltered Life*. Garden City, N.Y.: Doubleday, Doran & Co., 1932.

———. *Vein of Iron*. New York: Harcourt, Brace and Co., 1935.

Glass, Joanna. *Reflections on a Summer Mountain*. New York: A. A. Knopf, 1974.

Godwin, Gail. *The Odd Woman*. New York: A. A. Knopf, 1974.

Goudge, Elizabeth. *The Scent of Water*. New York: Coward-McCann, 1963.

———. *The White Witch*. London: Hodder & Stoughton, 1958.

Haggerty, Joan. *Daughters of the Moon*. Indianapolis: Bobbs-Merrill, 1971.

Hall, Radclyffe. *The Well of Loneliness*. New York: Sun Dial Press, 1928.

Hays, Mary Huber. *The Victim of Prejudice*. London: Johnson, 1799.

H.D. See Doolittle, Hilda.

Herbst, Josephine. "Dry Sunday in Connecticut," *American Mercury*, 8 (July 1926), 339–44.

———. *The Executioner Waits*. New York: Harcourt, Brace and Co., 1934.

———. "The Golden Egg." *Scribner's Magazine*, 87 (May 1930), 492–99.

———. "A Man of Steel." *American Mercury*, 31 (Janaury 1934), 32–40.

———. *Money for Love*. New York: Coward-McCann, 1929.

———. *Nothing Is Sacred*. New York: Coward-McCann, 1928.

———. *Pity Is Not Enough*. New York: Harcourt, Brace and Co., 1933.

———. *Rope of Gold*. New York: Harcourt, Brace and Co., 1939.

Hobbes, John Oliver. See Craigie, Pearl Richards.

Holtby, Winifred. *South Riding*. New York: Macmillan, 1936.

———. *Truth Is Not Sober*. London: W. Collins, 1934.

Hunter, Kristin. *God Bless the Child*. New York: Scribner's, 1964.

Hurst, Fannie. *Back Street*. New York: A. L. Burt, 1931.

———. *Imitation of Life*. New York: Collier, 1933.

———. *Lonely Parade*. New York: Harper & Bros., 1942.

Hurston, Zora Neale. *Their Eyes Were Watching God*. New York: Negro Universities Press, 1969 (1937).

Inchbald, Elizabeth. *Nature and Art*. London: G. G. and J. Robinson, 1796.

Isabel, Sharon. *Yesterday's Lessons*. Oakland, Calif.: Woman's Press Collective, 1974.

Jackson, Shirley. *We Have Always Lived in the Castle*. New York: Viking Press, 1962.

James, Norah. *Sleeveless Errand*. Paris: Babau and Co., 1929.

Jameson, M. Storm. *Lady Susan and Life, An Indiscretion*. London: Hurst & Blackett, 192–?

———. *The Lovely Ship*. London: Heinemann, 1927.

———. *The Pot Boils*. London: Constable, 1919.

———. *A Richer Dust*. London: Heinemann, 1931.

———. *The Voyage Home*. London: Heinemann, 1930.

Janeway, Elizabeth. *Daisy Kenyon*. Garden City, N.Y.: Doubleday, Doran & Co., 1945.

Jewett, Sarah Orne. *The Country of the Pointed Firs*. Boston: Houghton, Mifflin & Co., 1896.
———. *Deephaven*. Boston: J. R. Osgood & Co., 1877.
Johnson, Josephine. *Jordanstown*. New York: Simon & Schuster, 1937.
———. *Now in November*. New York: Simon & Schuster, 1935.
Johnson, Pamela Hansford. *An Avenue of Stone*. London: M. Joseph, 1947.
———. *Blessed Above Women*. London: Chapman & Hall, 1936.
———. *Catherine Carter*. New York: A. A. Knopf, 1952.
———. *An Impossible Marriage*. New York: Harcourt, Brace and Co., 1954.
———. *This Bed Thy Centre*. London: Macmillan, 1962 (1935).
Johnston, Mary. *Hagar*. Boston: Houghton Miffllin, 1913.
Jong, Erica. *Fear of Flying*. New York: New American Library, 1973.
Kaufman, Sue. *Diary of a Mad Housewife*. New York: Random House, 1967.
Kaye-Smith, Sheila. *Joanna Godden*. New York: Cassell, 1921.
———. *Mrs. Gailey*. New York: Harper & Bros., 1951.
———. *Superstition Corner*. London: Cassell, 1934.
Kelley, Edith Summers. *Weeds*. Carbondale, Ill.: Southern Illinois University Press, 1972 (1923).
Lawrence, Josephine. *The Sound of Running Feet*. New York: F. A. Stokes, 1937.
Lee, Hannah F. S. *Elinor Fulton*. Boston: Whipple & Damrell, 1837.
Lees, Hannah. *Till the Boys Come Home*. New York: Harper & Bros., 1944.
Le Guin, Ursula. *The Left Hand of Darkness*. New York: Ace, 1969.
———. *Planet of Exile*. New York: Ace, 1966.
Lehmann, Rosamond. *The Ballad and the Source*. New York: Reynall and Hitchcock, 1945.
———. *Dusty Answer*. New York: Reynall & Hitchcock, 1927.
———. *The Echoing Grove*. New York: Harcourt, Brace and Co., 1953.
———. *Invitation to the Waltz*. New York: Reynall and Hitchcock, 1932.
———. *The Weather in the Streets*. New York: Reynall and Hitchcock, 1936.
Lessing, Doris. *Briefing for a Descent into Hell*. New York: A. A. Knopf, 1971.
———. *The Four-Gated City*. (*Children of Violence*, vol. 5). New York: A. A. Knopf, 1971 (1969).
———. *The Golden Notebook*. New York: McGraw-Hill, 1963 (1962).
———. *Landlocked*. (*Children of Violence*, vol. 4). London: MacGibbon & Kee, 1965.
———. *Martha Quest*. (*Children of Violence*, vol. 1). St. Albans: Panther, 1973 (1952).
———. *The Memoirs of a Survivor*. New York: A. A. Knopf, 1975 (1974).
———. *A Proper Marriage*. (*Children of Violence*, vol. 2). London: M. Joseph, 1954.
———. *A Ripple from the Storm*. (*Children of Violence*, vol. 3). London: M. Joseph, 1958.
———. *The Summer Before the Dark*. New York: A. A. Knopf, 1973.
———. *The Temptation of Jack Orkney and Other Stories*. New York: A. A. Knopf, 1972.
Linton, Elizabeth Lynn. *The New Woman: In Haste and At Leisure*. New York: Merriam, 1895.
———. *The True History of Joshua Davidson, Christian and Communist*. Philadelphia: J. F. Lippincott & Co., 1873 (1872).

Macaulay, Rose. *Dangerous Ages.* New York: Boni & Liveright, 1921.

McCaffrey, Anne. *Dragonflight.* New York: Ballantine, 1968.

McCarthy, Mary. *A Charmed Life.* New York: Harcourt, Brace and Co., 1954.

———. *The Company She Keeps.* New York: Harcourt, Brace and Co., 1942.

———. *The Group.* New York: Harcourt, Brace and World, 1963.

———. *The Groves of Academe.* New York: Harcourt, Brace and Co., 1952.

McCullers, Carson. *Clock Without Hands.* Boston/New York: Houghton Mifflin, 1961.

———. *The Heart is a Lonely Hunter.* Boston/New York: Houghton Mifflin, 1940 (1936).

———. *The Member of the Wedding.* Boston/New York: Houghton Mifflin, 1946.

———. *Reflections in a Golden Eye.* Boston/New York: Houghton Mifflin, 1941.

McIntyre, Vonda. *Dream Snake.* New York: Dell, 1978.

———. *The Exile Waiting.* Greenwich, Conn.: Fawcett Crest, 1975.

Manning, Olivia. *The Camperlea Girls.* New York: Coward-McCann, 1969.

———. *The Doves of Venus.* Surrey: Windmill Press, 1955.

Marshall, Paule. *Brown Girl, Brownstones.* New York: Random House, 1959.

Martineau, Harriet. *Forest and Game-Law Tales.* London: E. Moxon, 1845–46.

———. *Illustrations of Political Economy.* Boston: L. C. Bowles, 1832–33.

———. *Illustrations of Taxation.* London: C. Fox, 1834.

Meriwether, Louise. *Daddy Was a Number Runner.* Englewood Cliffs, N.J.: Prentice-Hall, 1970.

Miller, Isabel. See Routsong, Alma.

Mitchison, Naomi. *The Corn King and the Spring Queen.* London; J. Cape, 1949 (1931).

———. *We Have Been Warned.* London: Constable and Co., 1935.

Mitford, Nancy. *The Blessing.* New York: Random House, 1951.

———. *Love in a Cold Climate.* London: H. Hamilton, 1953 (1949).

———. *The Pursuit of Love.* New York: Random House, 1945.

More, Hannah. *Coelebs in Search of a Wife.* London: Cadell and Davies, 1808.

Morrison, Toni. *The Bluest Eye.* New York: Holt, Rinehart and Winston, 1970.

———. *Sula.* New York: A. A. Knopf, 1974 (1973).

Mortimer, Penelope. *The Pumpkin-Eater.* London: Hutchinson, 1962.

Nachman, Elana. *Riverfinger Woman.* Plainfield, Vt.: Daughters, 1974.

Nin, Anaïs. *Cities of the Interior.* Chicago: Swallow Press, 1974. (*Ladders to Fire*, 1946; *The Four Chambered Heart*, 1950; *Children of the Albatross*, 1947; *A Spy in the House of Love*, 1954; and *Seduction of the Minotaur*, 1961).

Oates, Joyce Carol. *Do With Me What You Will.* Greenwich, Conn.: Fawcett Crest, 1973.

———. *Marriages and Infidelities.* Greenwich, Conn.: Fawcett Crest, 1972.

———. *Wonderland.* New York: Vanguard Press, 1971.

O'Brien, Edna. *August is a Wicked Month.* New York: Simon & Schuster, 1965.

Oliphant, Margaret. *Agnes.* 3 vols. London: Hurst and Blackett, 1866.

————. *Lady Car*. New York: Harper & Bros., 1899 (1889).

Olsen, Tillie. *Yonnondio: From the Thirties*. New York: Delacorte Press, 1974.

Opie, Amelia. *Adeline Mowbray, or Mother and Daughter*. Philadelphia: Crissy, 1841 (1804).

Parton, Sara Payson [Fanny Fern]. *Rose Clark*. New York: Mason Brothers, 1856.

————. *Ruth Hall*. London: J. M. Dent, 1967 (1853).

Petry, Ann Lane. *The Street*. Boston/New York: Houghton Mifflin, 1946.

Phelps, Elizabeth Stuart. *The Silent Partner*. Ridgewood, N.J.: Gregg Press, 1967 (1871).

————. *The Story of Avis*. Boston: J. R. Osgood, 1877.

Piercy, Marge. *Small Changes*. Garden City, N.Y.: Doubleday & Co., 1973.

Porter, Katherine Ann. *Pale Horse, Pale Rider*. New York: Harcourt, Brace and Co., 1939.

————. *Ship of Fools*. Boston: Little, Brown, 1962.

Radcliffe, Ann. *The Mysteries of Udolpho*. New York: E. P. Dutton, 1931 (1794).

Rhys, Jean. *After Leaving Mr. Mackenzie*. New York: Random House, Vintage Books, 1974 (1931).

————. *Quartet*. New York: Harper & Row, 1957 (*Postures*, 1928).

————. *Wide Sargasso Sea*. London: Deutsch, 1966.

Richardson, Dorothy M. *Pilgrimage*. New York: A. A. Knopf, 1967 (*Pointed Roofs*, 1915; *Backwater*, 1916; *Honeycomb*, 1917; *The Tunnel*, 1919; *Interim*, 1919; *Deadlock*, 1921; *Revolving Lights*, 1923; *The Trap*, 1925; *Overland*, 1927; *Dawn's Left Hand*, 1931; *Clear Horizon*, 1935; *Dimple Hill*, 1938; and *March Moonlight*, 1967).

Roberts, Dorothy. *A Durable Fire*. New York: Macmillan, 1945.

Roberts, Marta. *Tumbleweeds*. New York: G. P. Putnam's, 1940.

Robinson, Rose. *Eagle in the Air*. New York: Crown, 1969.

Routsong, Alma [Isabel Miller]. *Patience and Sarah*. New York: McGraw-Hill, 1969.

Rowson, Susanna. *Charlotte Temple: A Tale of Truth*. Edited by Clara M. Kirk and Rudolf Kirk. New York: Twayne, 1964 (1790).

Royde-Smith, Naomi. *The Island*. New York: Harper & Bros., 1930.

Rule, Jane. *Against the Season*. New York: McCall, 1971.

————. *The Desert of the Heart*. Toronto: Macmillan, 1964.

————. *This is Not for You*. New York: McCall, 1970.

Russ, Joanna. *The Female Man*. New York: Bantam Books, 1975.

Sackville-West, Vita. *All Passion Spent*. New York: Doubleday, Doran & Co., 1931.

Sarton, May. *As We Are Now*. New York: W. W. Norton, 1973.

————. *Crucial Conversations*. New York: W. W. Norton, 1975.

————. *Joanna and Ulysses*. New York: W. W. Norton, 1963.

————. *Kinds of Love*. New York: W. W. Norton, 1970.

————. *Mrs. Stevens Hears the Mermaids Singing*. New York: W. W. Norton, 1965.

————. *The Single Hound*. Boston/New York: Houghton Mifflin, 1938.

————. *The Small Room*. New York: W. W. Norton, 1961.

Sayers, Dorothy. *Busman's Honeymoon*. London: Gollancz, 1937.

Schaeffer, Susan Fromberg. *Falling*. New York: Macmillan, 1973.

Schreiner, Olive. *The Story of an African Farm*. Greenwich, Conn.: Fawcett Crest, 1968 (1883).

Shea, Margaret. *The Gals They Left Behind*. New York: I. Washburn, 1944.

Sheridan, Frances. *Memoirs of Miss Sidney Bidulph*. London: J. Dodsley, 1770–72 (1761).

Shulman, Alix K. *Memoirs of an Ex-Prom Queen*. New York: A. A. Knopf, 1972.

Sinclair, May. *The Immortal Moment*. New York: Doubleday, Page & Co., 1908.

———. *Mary Olivier*. New York: Macmillan, 1919.

Smedley, Agnes. *Daughter of Earth*. New York: Feminist Press, 1973 (1929).

Smith, Charlotte Turner. *Emmeline, The Orphan of the Castle*. London/ New York: Oxford University Press, 1971 (1788).

Smith, Elizabeth Oakes. *The Newsboy*. New York: J. C. Derby, 1854 (1852).

Spark, Muriel. *The Girls of Slender Means*. London: Macmillan, 1963.

———. *The Mandelbaum Gate*. London: Macmillan, 1965.

———. *The Prime of Miss Jean Brodie*. London: Macmillan, 1961.

———. *Robinson*. London: Macmillan, 1958.

Spencer, Sharon. *The Space Between*. New York: Harper & Row, 1973.

Stafford, Jean. *The Mountain Lion*. New York: Harcourt, Brace and Co., 1947.

Stead, Christina. *The Man Who Loved Children*. New York: Simon & Schuster, 1940.

Stein, Gertrude. *Things As They Are*. Fawlet, Vt.: Banyan Press, 1950 (1903).

Stockbridge, Dorothy. *Angry Dust*. Garden City, N.Y.: Doubleday & Co., 1946.

Stowe, Harriet Beecher. *Oldtown Folks*. Boston: Houghton, Mifflin & Co., 1882 (1869).

———. *Uncle Tom's Cabin*. New York: Collier Books, 1962 (1852).

Strang, Clara. See Weatherwax, Clara.

Suckow, Ruth. *Cora*. New York: Readers League of America, 1929.

———. *Country People*. New York: A. A. Knopf, 1924.

———. *The Folks*. New York: Farrar and Rinehart, 1934.

Taylor, Elizabeth. *At Mrs. Lippincote's*. New York: A. A. Knopf, 1946 (1945).

Thirkell, Angela Mackail. *The Brandons*. New York: A. A. Knopf, 1939.

———. *Growing Up*. London: H. Hamilton, 1950 (1943).

Tindall, Gillian. *Someone Else*. New York: Walker, 1969.

Tonna, Charlotte Elizabeth [Charlotte Elizabeth]. *Helen Fleetwood*, in *The Works of Charlotte Elizabeth*. New York: M. W. Dodd, 1844 (1841).

———. *The Wrongs of Women*. New York: J. S. Taylor & Co., 1843.

Vorse, Mary Heaton. "Affairs of the House," 1919 (courtesy of the Walter Reuther Library of Labor and Urban Affairs, Wayne State University).

———. "Confessions of a College Woman," 1909 (courtesy of the Walter Reuther Library of Labor and Urban Affairs, Wayne State University).

———. "Dog: Story of the Great Game of Marriage," 1912 (courtesy of the Walter Reuther Library of Labor and Urban Affairs, Wayne State University).

———. *Men and Steel*. New York: Boni and Liveright, 1920.

———. *Strike!* New York: H. Liveright, 1930.

Walker, Margaret. *Jubilee!* Boston/New York: Houghton Mifflin, 1966.

Walker, Mildred. *Unless the Wind Turns*. New York: Harcourt, Brace and Co., 1941.

Ward, Mary Augusta. *Delia Blanchflower*. New York: Hearst International Library Co., 1914.

————. *Lady Rose's Daughter*. New York: Harper & Bros., 1903.

————. *Marcella*. New York: Macmillan, 1894.

————. *Marriage a la Mode*. New York: Doubleday, Page & Co., 1909.

————. *Sir George Tressady*. London: C. Arthur Pearson, Ltd., 1896.

Warner, Susan [Elizabeth Wetherell]. *The Wide, Wide World*. Philadelphia: J. B. Lippincott Co., 1885.

Warner, Sylvia Townsend. *Lolly Willowes, or, the Loving Huntsman*. New York: Grosset & Dunlap, 1926.

Watts, Mary Stanbery. *The Rise of Jennie Cushing*. New York: Macmillan, 1914.

Weatherwax, Clara [Clara Strang]. *Marching! Marching!* New York: International Publishers, 1935.

Webb, Mary. *Gone to Earth*. London: Butler and Tanner, 1952 (1917).

Weldon, Fay. *Down Among the Women*. New York: Warner Books, Inc., 1972.

————. *Female Friends*. New York: St. Martin's Press, 1974.

West, Jessamyn. *Cress Delahanty*. New York: Harcourt, Brace and Co., 1953 (1945).

West, Rebecca. *Harriet Hume*. Garden City, N.Y.: Doubleday, Doran & Co., 1929.

Wetherell, Elizabeth. See Warner, Susan.

Wharton, Edith. *The Age of Innocence*. New York: Scribner's, 1968 (1920).

————. *The Children*. New York: Appleton & Co., 1928.

————. *The Collected Short Stories of Edith Wharton*. Edited by R. W. B. Lewis. New York: Scribner's, 1968.

————. *The Custom of the Country*. New York: Scribner's, 1913.

————. *The Fruit of the Tree*. New York: Scribner's, 1907.

————. *The Greater Inclination*. New York: Scribner's, 1899.

————. *The House of Mirth*. New York: Scribner's, 1905.

————. *The Old Maid*. New York: Appleton & Co., 1924.

————. *A Son at the Front*. New York: Scribner's, 1923.

————. *Summer*. New York: Appleton & Co., 1917.

————. *Twilight Sleep*. New York: Appleton & Co., 1927.

Wilhelm, Gale. *We Too Are Drifting*. New York: Arno Press, 1975 (1935).

Williams-Ellis, Amabel. *The Big Firm*. Boston/New York: Houghton Mifflin, 1938 (1934).

Wollstonecraft, Mary. *The Cave of Fancy*. London: 1787.

————. *Maria: or, The Wrongs of Woman*. New York: W. W. Norton, 1975 (1798).

————. *Mary, A Fiction*. London, 1788.

Woolf, Virginia. *Between the Acts*. New York: Harcourt, Brace and Co., 1951 (1941).

————. *Mrs. Dalloway*. London: Hogarth, 1925.

————. *Night and Day*. New York: Harcourt, Brace and Co., 1948 (1919).

————. *Orlando*. New York: Harcourt, Brace and Co., 1928.

————. *To the Lighthouse*. New York: Harcourt, Brace and Co., 1927.

————. *The Voyage Out*. New York: Harcourt, Brace and Co., 1948 (1915).

————. *The Years*. New York: Harcourt, Brace and World, 1965 (1937).

————. *The Waves*. New York: Harcourt, Brace and Co., 1937 (1931).

Wright, Sarah E. *This Child's Gonna Live*. New York: Delacorte Press, 1969.

Yonge, Charlotte. *The Daisy Chain; or, Aspirations, a Family Chronicle*. London: J. W. Parker, 1856.

NONFICTION BY WOMEN

Alcott, Louisa May. *Louisa May Alcott, Her Life, Letters and Journals.* Edited by Ednah D. Cheney. Reprint. Boston: Little, Brown & Co., 1910 (1889).

Atherton, Gertrude. *Adventures of a Novelist.* New York: Liveright, 1932.

Browne, Martha Griffith [Mattie Griffiths]. *Autobiography of a Female Slave.* Reprint. Miami: Mnemosyne Publishing Co., 1969 (1857).

Cross, J. W. *George Eliot's Life as Related in Her Letters and Journals.* New York: Harper & Bros., 1885.

Ellis, Sarah. *The Daughters of England, Their Position in Society, Character, and Responsibilities.* Reprint. New York: Walker, 1848 (1842).

———. *Family Secrets.* London: Fisher, Son & Co., 1841.

Ferber, Edna. *A Kind of Magic.* Garden City, N.Y.: Doubleday, 1963.

———. *A Peculiar Treasure.* Garden City, N.Y.: Doubleday, 1960.

Flynn, Elizabeth Gurley. *Rebel Girl: An Autobiography.* 1955. Revised edition. New York: International Publishers, 1973.

Glasgow, Ellen. *The Woman Within.* New York: Harcourt, Brace and Co., 1954.

Griffiths, Mattie. See Browne, Martha Griffith.

Holtby, Winifred. *Women and a Changing Civilisation.* London: John Lane, 1934.

Lessing, Doris. *In Pursuit of the English.* London: MacGibbon & Kee, 1960.

———. *A Small Personal Voice.* Edited by Paul Schlueter, New York: Knopf, 1974.

Porter, Katherine Anne. *The Collected Essays and Occasional Writings of Katherine Anne Porter.* Reprint. New York: Dell Publishing Co., Delta Books, 1973 (1923).

Sarton, May. *Journal of a Solitude.* New York: W. W. Norton, 1973.

———. *Plant Dreaming Deep.* New York: W. W. Norton, 1968.

Smith, Elizabeth Oakes. *The Autobiography of Elizabeth Oakes Smith.* Edited by Mary Alice Wyman. Lewiston, Maine: Lewiston Journal Co., 1924.

Stowe, Harriet Beecher. *The Chimney-Corner.* Boston: James R. Osgood and Co., 1877.

Suckow, Ruth. "Literary Soubrettes." *The Bookman*, 63 (July 1926), 517–21.

Wharton, Edith. *French Ways and Their Meanings.* New York: Appleton and Co., 1919.

Woodhull, Victoria, and Claflin, Tennessee. *Woodhull and Claflin's Weekly: The Lives and Writings of the Notorious Victoria Woodhull, and Her Sister, Tennessee Claflin.* Edited by Arlene Kisner. Washington, N.J.: Times Change Press, 1972.

Woolf, Virginia. *A Room of One's Own.* London: Hogarth Press, 1929.

———. *Three Guineas.* New York: Harcourt, Brace and World, 1963 (1938).

FEMINIST THEORY AND ITEMS OF USE TO

FEMINIST THEORETICIANS

*Books*

Adams, Henry. *Mont-Saint-Michel and Chartres.* Reprint. Garden City, N.Y.: Doubleday, 1959 (1904).

Ariès, Philippe. *Centuries of Childhood.* Translated by Robert Baldick. Reprint. New York: Random House, Vintage Books, 1965 (1962).

Atkinson, Ti-Grace. *Amazon Odyssey.* New York: Link Books, 1974.

Barber, C. L. *Shakespeare's Festive Comedy.* Cleveland: World Publishing Co., Meridian Books, 1963.

Beauvoir, Simone de. *The Second Sex.* New York: Knopf, 1953.

Bodkin, Maud. *Archetypal Patterns in Poetry.* Reprint. London: Oxford University Press, 1963 (1958).

Briffault, Robert. *The Mothers: A Study of the Origins of Sentiments and Institutions.* 3 vols. Reprint. New York: Macmillan, 1952 (1927).

Christ, Carol P. *Diving Deep and Surfacing: Women Writers on Spiritual Quest.* Boston: Beacon Press, 1980.

Daly, Mary. *Beyond God the Father, Toward a Philosophy of Women's Liberation.* Boston: Beacon Press, 1973.

Deegan, Dorothy Yost. *The Stereotype of the Single Woman in American Novels.* New York: King's Crown Press, 1951.

Donovan, Josephine. *Feminist Literary Criticism.* Lexington, Ky.: University Press of Kentucky, 1975.

Ellman, Mary. *Thinking About Women.* New York: Harcourt, Brace and World, 1968.

Firestone, Shulamith. *The Dialectic of Sex.* New York: Bantam Books, 1970.

Flexner, Eleanor. *Century of Struggle: The Woman's Rights Movement in the United States.* Cambridge, Mass.: Harvard University Press, Belknap Press, 1959.

Fuller, Margaret Ossoli. *Woman in the Nineteenth Century.* Reprint. New York: Norton, 1971 (1855).

Gilman, Charlotte Perkins. *The Man-Made World, or Our Androcentric Culture.* New York: Charlton, 1911.

————. *Women and Economics.* Edited by Carl N. Degler. New York: Harper & Row, 1966 (1898).

Goldenberg, Naomi R. *The Changing of the Gods: Feminism and the End of Traditional Religion.* Boston: Beacon Press, 1979.

Goldman, Emma. *The Traffic in Women and Other Essays on Feminism.* New York: Times Change Press, 1970.                    :

Greer, Germaine. *The Female Eunuch.* New York: Bantam Books, 1971.

Harding, M. Esther. *Woman's Mysteries Ancient and Modern.* New York: Bantam Books, 1971.

Harrison, Jane Ellen. *Prolegomena to the Study of Greek Religion.* Cambridge: Cambridge University Press, 1922.

Heilbrun, Carolyn. *Toward a Recognition of Androgyny.* New York: A. A. Knopf, 1973.

Houghton, Walter E. *The Victorian Frame of Mind, 1830–1870.* New Haven, Conn.: Yale University Press, 1957.

Janeway, Elizabeth. *Man's World, Woman's Place: A Study in Social Mythology.* New York: Dell Publishing Co., Delta Books, 1971.

Johnston, Jill. *Lesbian Nation.* New York: Simon and Schuster, 1973.

Kelso, Ruth. *Doctrine for the Lady of the Renaissance.* Urbana, Ill.: University of Illinois Press, 1956.

Kendrick, William [pseud.]. *The Whole Duty of Woman.* Walpole, N.H.: David Carlisle, 1797.

Kraditor, Aileen. *The Ideas of the Woman Suffrage Movement 1890–1920.* Reprint. Garden City, N.Y.: Doubleday, 1971 (1965).

McAlexander, Patricia Jewell. "Sexual Morality in the Fiction of Charles Brockden Brown: Index to a Personal and Cultural Debate Regarding

Passion and Reason." Ph.D. dissertation, University of Wisconsin–Madison, 1973.

Martin, Del, and Lyon, Phyllis. *Lesbian/Woman*. San Francisco: Glide Publications, 1972.

Millett, Kate. *Sexual Politics*. Garden City, N.Y.: Doubleday, 1970.

Mitchell, Juliet. *Psychoanalysis and Feminism*. 1974. Reprint. New York: Random House, Vintage Books, 1975 (1974).

Morgan, Elaine. *The Descent of Woman*. New York: Bantam Books, 1972.

Murray, Margaret Alice. *The God of the Witches*. Castle Haddington, Essex: The Daimon Press, 1962.

———. *The Witch Cult in Western Europe*. Oxford: Oxford University Press, 1921.

O'Neill, William. *Everyone Was Brave*. Chicago: Quadrangle Books, 1969.

Reed, Evelyn. *Woman's Evolution*. New York: Pathfinder Press, 1975.

Rideout, Walter. *The Radical Novel in the United States, 1900–1954*. 5th ed. American Century Series. New York: Hill and Wang, 1966 (1956).

Rigney, Barbara Hill. *Madness and Sexual Politics in the Feminist Novel*. Madison, Wis.: University of Wisconsin Press, 1978.

Roberts, Joan, ed. *Beyond Intellectual Sexism: A New Woman, a New Reality*. New York: David McKay, 1976.

Rowbotham, Sheila. *Women, Resistance, and Revolution*. New York: Random House, Vintage Books, 1972.

Sanger, Margaret. *Woman and the New Race*. New York: Brentano's, 1920.

Sejourné, Philippe. *Aspects généraux du roman féminin en Angleterre de 1740–1800*. Aix-en-Provence: Editions Ophrys, 1966.

Stone, Merlin. *When God Was A Woman*. New York: Dial Press, 1976.

Weston, Jessie L. *From Ritual to Romance*. Garden City, N.Y.: Doubleday, Anchor Books, 1957.

Wolff, Charlotte. *Love Between Women*. New York: St. Martin's Press, 1971.

Wollstonecraft, Mary. *A Vindication of the Rights of Woman*. New York: E. P. Dutton & Co., 1929 (1792).

Wysor, Bettie. *The Lesbian Myth: Insights and Conversations*. New York: Random House, 1974.

### Articles

Bowson, Bernard; Marx, Leo; and Rose, Arnold. "Literature and Covert Culture." *American Quarterly*, 9 (Winter 1957), 377–86.

Brown, Rita Mae. "It's All Dixie Cups to Me." *Quest*, 1, no. 3 (Winter 1975), 44–50.

Christ, Carol P. "Margaret Atwood: The Surfacing of Women's Spiritual Quest and Vision." *Signs*, 2, no. 2 (Winter 1976), 316–30.

Cixous, Hélène. "Le rire de la Méduse." *L'arc*, no. 61 (May 1975), 39–54.

Cixous, Hélène, and Makward, Christiane. "Interview with Hélène Cixous." Trans. Ann Liddle and Beatrice Cameron. *Sub-stance*, no. 13 (1976), 25–26.

Conway, Jill. "Stereotypes of Femininity in a Theory of Sexual Evolution." *Victorian Studies*, 14, no. 1 (September 1970), 47–62.

Daly, Mary. "The Qualitative Leap Beyond Patriarchal Religion." *Quest*, 1, no. 4 (Spring 1975), 20–40.

McAlexander, Patricia Jewell. "The Creation of the American Eve: The Cultural Dialogue on the Nature and Role of Women in Late-Eighteenth-Century America." *Early American Literature*, 9, no. 3 (Winter 1975), 255–66.

McFarland, Morgan. "Witchcraft: The Art of Remembering." *Quest*, 1, no. 4 (Spring 1975), 41–48.

Maglin, Nan Bauer. "Women in Three Sinclair Lewis Novels." *Massachusetts Review*, 14, no. 4 (Autumn 1973), 783–801.

Mitchison, Naomi. "The Reluctant Feminists." *Left Review*, 1, no. 3 (December 1934), 93–94.

Rennie, Susan, and Grimstad, Kirsten. "Spiritual Explorations Cross-Country." *Quest*, 1, no. 4 (Spring 1975), 49–51.

Riddle, Dorothy. "New Visions of Spiritual Power." *Quest*, 1, no. 4 (Spring 1975), 7–16.

Roberts, Helen E. "Marriage, Redundancy or Sin." *Suffer and Be Still: Women in the Victorian Age*. Edited by Martha Vicinus. Bloomington, Ind.: Indiana University Press, 1972.

Robinson, Lillian. "Dwelling in Decencies: Radical Criticism and the Feminist Perspective." *College English*, 32, no. 8 (May 1971), 879–89.

Secor, Cynthia. "Androgyny: An Early Reappraisal." *Women's Studies*, 2, no. 2 (1974), 161–69.

Welter, Barbara. "The Cult of True Womanhood: 1820–1860." *American Quarterly*, 18, no. 2 (Summer 1966), 151–74.

## WORKS ON WOMEN AUTHORS

### Books and Dissertations

Austin, Allan E. *Elizabeth Bowen*. New York: Twayne, 1971.

Bell, Quentin. *Virginia Woolf: A Biography*. New York: Harcourt, Brace, Jovanovich, 1972.

Bentley, Phyllis E. *The Brontës*. London: Allan Wingate, 1949.

Bittner, James Warren. "Approaches to the Fiction of Ursula K. Le Guin." Ph.D. dissertation, University of Wisconsin—Madison, 1979.

Blake, Casear R. *Dorothy Richardson*. Ann Arbor, Mich.: University of Michigan Press, 1960.

Calder, Jenni. *Women and Marriage in Victorian Fiction*. New York: Oxford University Press, 1976.

Colby, Vineta. *The Singular Anomaly: Woman Novelists of the Nineteenth Century*. New York: New York University Press, 1970.

Colby, Vineta and Colby, Robert. *The Equivocal Virtue: Mrs. Oliphant and the Victorian Literary Market Place*. Hamden, Conn.: Archon Books, 1966.

Dalziel, Margaret. *Popular Fiction 100 Years Ago: An Unexplored Tract of Literary History*. London: Cohen and West, 1957.

Derleth, August. *Still Small Voice*. New York: Appleton-Century, 1940.

Ewbank, Inga-Stina. *Their Proper Sphere: A Study of the Brontë Sisters as Early-Victorian Female Novelists*. Cambridge, Mass.: Harvard University Press, 1966.

Fletcher, Marie. "The Southern Heroine in the Fiction of Representative Southern Women Writers, 1850–1960." Ph.D. dissertation, Louisiana State University, 1963.

Foster, Jeanette H. *Sex Variant Women in Literature*. New York: Vantage Press, 1956.

George, Margaret. *One Woman's "Situation": A Study of Mary Wollstonecraft*. Urbana, Ill.: University of Illinois Press, 1970.

Godwin, William. *Memoirs of Mary Wollstonecraft*. Edited by W. Clark Durant. Reprint. New York: Haskell House, 1969 (1927).

Grumbach, Doris. *The Company She Kept*. New York: Coward-McCann, 1967.

Hardy, Barbara. *The Novels of George Eliot*. London: University of London, Athlone Press, 1959.

Hilbish, Florence. "Charlotte Smith, Poet and Novelist, 1749–1806." Ph.D. dissertation, University of Pennsylvania, 1941.

Hinkley, Laura L. *Ladies of Literature*. New York: Hastings House, 1946.

Howe, Irving, ed. *Edith Wharton*. Englewood Cliffs, N.J.: Prentice-Hall, 1962.

Kaplan, Sydney Janet. *Feminine Consciousness in the Modern British Novel*. Chicago: University of Illinois Press, 1975.

Kempthorne, Dion Quentin. "Josephine Herbst: A Critical Introduction." Ph.D. dissertation, University of Wisconsin—Madison, 1973.

Krouse, Agate. "The Feminism of Doris Lessing." Ph.D. dissertation, University of Wisconsin—Madison, 1972.

Kuda, Marie, ed. *Women Loving Women: A Select and Annotated Bibliography of Women Loving Women in Literature*. Chicago: Lavender, 1974.

Lawrence, Margaret. *The School of Femininity*. New York: F. A. Stokes, 1936.

MacCarthy, B. G. *The Female Pen: Women Writers, Their Contribution to the English Novel, 1621–1744*. Oxford: Blackwell Ltd., 1946.

Mews, Hazel. *Frail Vessels: Woman's Role in Woman's Novels from Fanny Burney to George Eliot*. London: Athlone Press, 1969.

Moers, Ellen. *Literary Women*. Garden City, N.Y.: Doubleday, 1976.

Overton, Grant. *The Women Who Make Our Novels*. Reprint. Freeport, N.Y.: Books for Libraries Press, 1967 (1928).

Papashvily, Helen Waite. *All the Happy Endings*. Port Washington, N.Y.: Kennikat Press, 1972.

Pendry, E. D. *The New Feminism of English Fiction: A Study in Contemporary Women-Novelists*. Tokyo: Kenkyusha, 1956.

Pratt, Annis, and Dembo, L. S. *Doris Lessing: Critical Studies*. Madison, Wis.: University of Wisconsin Press, 1973.

Rolt-Wheeler, Ethel. *Famous Blue-Stockings*. London: Methuen, 1910.

Rubenius, Aina. *The Woman Question in Mrs. Gaskell's Life and Works*. Cambridge, Mass.: Harvard University Press, 1950.

Seyersted, Per. *Kate Chopin: A Critical Biography*. Baton Rouge, La.: Louisiana State University Press, 1969.

Showalter, Elaine. *A Literature of Their Own*. Princeton, N.J.: Princeton University Press, 1977.

Sinclair, May. *The Three Brontës*. Reprint. Port Washington, N.Y.: Kennikat Press, 1967 (1939).

Spacks, Patricia Meyer. *The Female Imagination*. New York: A. A. Knopf, 1975.

Sprague, Rosemary. *George Eliot*. Philadelphia: Chilton, 1968.

Sprigge, Elizabeth. *The Life of Ivy Compton-Burnett*. New York: Braziller, 1973.

Vadeboncoeur, Paula Marion. "The Novels of Elizabeth Taylor." Ph.D. dissertation, University of Wisconsin—Madison, 1976.

White, Barbara A. *American Women Writers: An Annotated Bibliography of Criticism*. New York: Garland, 1977.

———. "Growing Up Female: Adolescent Girlhood in American Literature." Ph.D. dissertation, University of Wisconsin—Madison, 1974.

Wilson, Mona. *Jane Austen and Some Contemporaries.* London: Cresset Press, 1938.


Articles

Beards, Virginia K. "Margaret Drabble, Novels of a Cautious Feminist." *Critique,* 15, no. 1 (1973), 35–47.

Beck, Evelyn. "Sexism, Racism and Class Bias in German Utopias of the Twentieth Century." *Soundings,* 58, no. 1 (Spring 1975), 112–29.

Brown, Lloyd W. "The Comic Conclusion in Jane Austen's Novels." *PMLA,* 84, no. 6 (October 1969), 1582–87.

Christ, Carol P. "Spiritual Quest and Women's Experience." *Anima,* 1, no. 2 (Spring 1975), 4–14.

Cominus, Peter. "Innocent Femina Sensualis in Unconscious Conflict." *Suffer And Be Still: Women in the Victorian Age.* Edited by Martha Vicinus. Bloomington, Ind.: Indiana University Press, 1972.

Gindin, James. "Rosamond Lehmann: A Revaluation." *Contemporary Literature,* 15, no. 2 (Spring 1974), 203–11.

Gorsky, Susan. "The Gentle Doubters: Images of Women in Englishwomen's Novel's, 1840–1920." *Images of Women in Fiction.* Edited by Susan Koppelman Cornillon. Bowling Green, Ohio: Bowling Green University Press, 1972.

————. "Old Maids and New Women, Alternatives to Marriage in Englishwomen's Novels, 1847–1915." *Journal of Popular Culture,* 7, no. 1 (Summer 1973), 68–85.

Hardin, Nancy. "An Interview with Margaret Drabble." *Contemporary Literature,* 14, no. 3 (Summer 1973), 273–95.

Harvey, B. W. J. "Criticism of the Novel." *Middlemarch: Critical Approaches to the Novel.* Edited by Barbara Hardy. New York: Oxford University Press, 1967.

Katz, Claire. "Flannery O'Connor's Rage of Vision." *American Literature,* 46, no. 1 (March 1974), 54–67.

Kovacevic, Ivanka, and Kanner, S. Barbara. "Blue Book Into Novel: The Forgotten Industrial Fiction of Charlotte Elizabeth Tonna." *Nineteenth Century,* 25, no. 2 (September 1970), 152–73.

Libby, Marion Vlastos. "Fate and Feminism in the Novels of Margaret Drabble." *Contemporary Literature,* 16, no. 2 (Spring 1975), 175–92.

McCarthy, Mary. "The Inventions of Ivy Compton-Burnett." *The Writing on the Wall and Other Literary Essays.* Edited by Mary McCarthy. New York: Harcourt, Brace & World, 1970.

McDowell, Margaret. "Viewing the Custom of Her Country: Edith Wharton's Feminism." *Contemporary Literature,* 15, no. 4 (Autumn 1974), 521–38.

Maglin, Nan Bauer. "Fictional Feminists in *The Bostonians* and *The Odd Women.*" *Images of Women in Fiction.* Edited by Susan Koppelman Cornillon. Bowling Green, Ohio: Bowling Green University Press, 1972.

Moers, Ellen. "Money, the Job, and Little Women." *Commentary,* 55, no. 1 (January 1973), 57–65.

Ohmann, Carol. "Emily Bronte in the Hands of Male Critics." *College English,* 32, no. 8 (May 1971), 906–13.

Pratt, Annis. "Archetypal Approaches to the New Feminist Criticism." *Bucknell Review,* 21, no. 1 (Spring 1973), 3–14.

————. "The Contrary Structure of Doris Lessing's *The Golden Notebook.*" *World Literature Written in English,* 12, no. 2 (November 1973), 150–60.

————. "The New Feminist Criticism." *College English*, 32, no. 8 (May 1971), 872–78.

————. "Sexual Imagery in *To the Lighthouse*: A New Feminist Approach." *Modern Fiction Studies*, 18, no. 3 (Autumn 1972), 417–32.

————. "Women and Nature in Modern Fiction." *Contemporary Literature*, 13, no. 4 (Autumn 1972), 476–90.

Rose, Shirley. "The Unmoving Center: Consciousness in Dorothy Richardson's *Pilgrimage*." *Contemporary Literature*, 10, no. 3 (Summer 1969), 366–82.

Russ, Joanna. "The Image of Women in Science Fiction." *Vortex*, 1, no. 6 (February 1974), 53–57.

Schmidt, Dolores Barracano. "The Great American Bitch." *College English*, 32, no. 8 (May 1971), 900–905.

Scott-James, Marie. "Our Book Page." *Labour Woman*, 24, no. 5 (May 1936), 70.

Snitow, Ann. "The Family in the Novels of Ivy Compton-Burnett." *Aphra*, 1, no. 4 (Autumn 1970), 7–18.

————. "The Front Line: Notes on Novels by Women, 1969–1979." *Signs*, 5, no. 4 (Summer 1980), 702–18.

Stansell, Charlotte. "Elizabeth Stuart Phelps: A Study in Female Rebellion." *Woman: An Issue*. Edited by Lee Edwards, Mary Heath, and Lisa Baskin. Boston: Little, Brown, 1972.

Wilson, Edmund. "Justice to Edith Wharton." *Edith Wharton*. Edited by Irving Howe. Englewood Cliffs, N.J.: Prentice-Hall, 1962.

Wood, Ann Douglas. "The Literature of Impoverishment: The Women Local Colorists in America 1865–1914." *Women's Studies*, 1, no. 1 (1972), 3–45.

————. "The 'Scribbling Women' and Fanny Fern: Why Women Wrote." *American Quarterly*, 23, no. 1 (Spring 1971), 3–24.

OTHER GENERAL SOURCES

Brown, Herbert Ross. *The Sentimental Novel in America, 1789–1860*. Durham, N.C.: Duke University Press, 1940.

Campbell, Joseph. *Hero With a Thousand Faces*. Princeton, N.J.: Princeton University Press, 1949.

————. *The Masks of God: Creative Mythology*. New York: Viking Press, 1968.

————. *The Masks of God: Occidental Mythology*. New York: Viking Press, 1964.

Eliade, Mircea. *Myths, Rite, Symbols: A Mircea Eliade Reader*. Edited by Wendell Beame and William G. Doty. New York: Harper, 1976.

Fielder, Leslie. *Love and Death in the American Novel*. Revised edition. New York: Dell Publishing Co., Laurel Edition, 1969 (1960).

Ford, Ford Madox. *The English Novel*. London: Constable, 1930.

Frye, Northrop. *Anatomy of Criticism*. Princeton, N.J.: Princeton University Press, 1957.

————. *The Secular Scripture*. Cambridge, Mass.: Harvard University Press, 1976.

Gardner, Gerald B. *Witchcraft Today*. London: Rider & Co., 1954.

Gayle, Addison, Jr. "Perhaps Not So Soon One Morning." *Black Expression*. Edited by Addison Gayle, Jr. New York: Weybright and Talley, 1969.

Godwin, William. *An Enquiry Concerning Political Justice and its Influence on Virtue and Happiness*. 2 vols. London: G. G. J. and J. Robinson, 1793.

Jung, C. G. *Archetypes and the Collective Unconscious*. Princeton, N. J.: Bolligen 1969.
————. *The Basic Writings of C. G. Jung*. Edited by Violet Staub de Laszlo. New York: Modern Library, 1959.
————. *The Development of Personality*. Translated by R. F. C. Hull. New York: Pantheon Books, 1954.
————. *Psyche and Symbol*. Edited by Violet Staub de Laszlo. Garden City, N.Y.: Doubleday, Anchor Books, 1958.
————. *Psychological Reflections*. Edited by Jolande Jacobi. New York: Pantheon Books, 1953.
Jung, Emma, and Von Franz, Marie-Louise. *The Grail Legend*. Translated by Andrea Dykes. New York: G. P. Putnam's, 1970.
Kampf, Louis, and Lauter, Paul, eds. *The Politics of Literature: Dissenting Essays on the Teaching of English*. New York: Random House, Vintage Press, 1973.
Keryéni, C. *Eleusis: Archetypal Image of Mother and Daughter*. Translated by Ralph Manheim. New York: Schocken Books, 1977.
Keryéni, C., and Jung, C. G. *Essays on a Science of Mythology: The Myth of the Divine Child and the Mysteries of Eleusis*. Translated by R. F. C. Hull. Princeton, N.J.: Bollingen, 1950.
Laing, R. D. *The Divided Self*. Reprint. Middlesex, England: Penguin Books, 1971 (1960).
Lippert, Julius. *The Evolution of Culture*. Translated and edited by George P. Murdock. New York: Macmillan, 1931.
Lukács, George. *Realism in Our Time*. Translated by John and Necke Mander. New York: Harper and Row, 1964.
Markale, Jean. *Women of the Celts*. Translated by Gordon Cremonesi. London: Cremonesi Publications, 1975.
Pomeroy, Sarah B. *Goddesses, Whores, Wives, and Slaves: Women in Classical Antiquity*. New York: Schocken Books, 1975.
Pratt, Annis. *Dylan Thomas' Early Prose: A Study in Creative Mythology*. Pittsburgh: University of Pittsburgh Press, 1970.
Rougemont, Denis de. *Love in the Western World*. Translated by Montgomery Belgion. 1940. Revised edition. Greenwich, Conn.: Fawcett Crest, 1969.
Trevor-Roper, H. R. *The European Witch-Craze of the Sixteenth and Seventeenth Centuries and Other Essays*. New York: Harper, 1967.
Tuttleton, James W. *The Novel of Manners in America*. Chapel Hill, N.C.: University of North Carolina Press, 1972.
Watt, Ian. *The Rise of the Novel: Studies in Defoe, Richardson, and Fielding*. Berkeley, Calif.: University of California Press, 1957.
Wilson, Edmund. *Patriotic Gore*. New York: Oxford University Press, 1962.

# Index